THE FACULTY FACTOR

Series on Engaged Learning and Teaching
Series Editors: Jessie L. Moore and Peter Felten

THE FACULTY FACTOR

Developing Faculty Engagement With Living–Learning Communities

Edited by Jennifer E. Eidum and Lara L. Lomicka

Foreword by Karen Kurotsuchi Inkelas

Series Foreword by Jessie L. Moore and Peter Felten

Series on Engaged Learning and Teaching

Copublished in association with

STERLING, VIRGINIA

Published by Stylus Publishing, LLC.
22883 Quicksilver Drive
Sterling, Virginia 20166-2019

Library of Congress Cataloging-in-Publication-Data

Names: Eidum, Jennifer E., editor. | Lomicka, Lara, editor.
Title: The faculty factor : developing faculty engagement with living-learning
    communities / edited by Jennifer E. Eidum and Lara L. Lomicka ; foreword by
    Karen Kurotsuchi Inkelas ; series foreword by Jessie L. Moore and Peter Felten ;
    series on Engaged Learning and Teaching.
Description: First Edition. | Sterling, Virginia : Stylus Publishing, LLC, [2023] |
    Series: Series on engaged learning and teaching | "Copublished in association
    with Elon University | Center for Engaged Learning." | Includes bibliographical
    references and index. | Summary: "This practical resource examines how
    colleges and universities foster sustainable faculty involvement in living learning
    communities (LLCs). This book demonstrates that faculty are key to creating
    equitable, engaging, and sustainable LLCs in diverse higher education settings"--
    Provided by publisher.
Identifiers: LCCN 2022056360 (print) | LCCN 2022056361 (ebook) | ISBN
    9781642672527 (Cloth : acid-free paper) | ISBN 9781642672534 (Paperback :
    acid-free paper) | ISBN 9781642672541 (library networkable e-edition) | ISBN
    9781642672558 (consumer e-edition)
Subjects: LCSH: Student learning communities. | Universities and colleges--Faculty.
    | Teachers and community. | Group work in education. | Mentoring in education.
    | Resident assistants (Dormitories)
Classification: LCC LB1032 .F33 2023 (print) | LCC LB1032 (ebook) | DDC
    378.1/2--dc23/eng/20230104
LC record available at https://lccn.loc.gov/2022056360
LC ebook record available at https://lccn.loc.gov/2022056361

13-digit ISBN: 978-1-64267-252-7 (cloth)
13-digit ISBN: 978-1-64267-253-4 (paperback)
13-digit ISBN: 978-1-64267-254-1 (library networkable e-edition)
13-digit ISBN: 978-1-64267-255-8 (consumer e-edition)

Printed in the United States of America

All first editions printed on acid free paper that meets the American National
Standards Institute Z39-48 Standard.

Bulk Purchases

Quantity discounts are available for use in workshops and for staff development.

Call 1-800-232-0223

First Edition, 2023

CONTENTS

SERIES FOREWORD

*T*he *Faculty Factor: Developing Faculty Engagement With Living–Learning Communities* is part of the Series on Engaged Learning and Teaching, published by Stylus in partnership with the Center for Engaged Learning at Elon University. The series is designed for a multi-disciplinary audience of higher-education faculty, staff, graduate students, educational developers, administrators, and policymakers interested in research-informed engaged learning practices. Although individual books in the series might most appeal to those interested in a specific topic, each volume concisely synthesizes research for nonexperts and addresses the broader implications of this particular work for higher education, including effective practices for teaching, curriculum design, and educational policies. All books in the series are supplemented by open-access resources hosted on the Center for Engaged Learning's website.

The Faculty Factor: Developing Faculty Engagement With Living–Learning Communities embraces our goals for this book series. The edited collection features new research on living–learning communities (LLCs) and concrete strategies for magnifying the essential—and too often unrecognized—contributions faculty make in these spaces. This book demonstrates that faculty are key to creating equitable, engaging, and sustainable LLCs in diverse higher-education settings. Chapters delve into both the micro-level experiences of individual faculty—and their families, as in the vignettes at the beginning of each chapter—and the macro-level campus-wide planning that positions LLCs as a meaningful learning experience for students. Supplemental resources for *The Faculty Factor: Developing Faculty Engagement With Living–Learning Communities*—including additional examples, discussion questions for reading groups, video interviews with leading scholars, and more—are available at https://www.centerforengagedlearning.org/books/faculty-factor/.

We extend our thanks to Jennifer E. Eidum, Lara L. Lomicka, and their contributing authors for writing this significant text for the series. Their research and practical strategies will positively inform LLCs across the United States and beyond, foster faculty–staff partnerships in support of these significant learning opportunities, and shape students' relationship-rich college experiences on many campuses.

To learn more about the Series on Engaged Learning and Teaching, including how to propose a book, please visit https://www.centerforengagedlearning.org/publications/.

Series Editors, Jessie L. Moore and Peter Felten
Center for Engaged Learning
Elon University

FOREWORD

W hen I was appointed as the sixth principal of Hereford Residential College at the University of Virginia, I had already been studying living–learning communities (LLCs) for nearly 2 decades. I was also a professor of higher education who studied the impact of college on students and who had taught "The College Student Experience" and "Introduction to Student Affairs" for her master's graduate program several times. Of all people, I surmised, surely I should be better equipped than other faculty members to know what the role of principal of a residential college entailed. My naïveté—or perhaps my arrogance—was soon dispelled.

As an aside, although I think of my experience as principal as wholly unique, I learned through Grabsch, Eidum, Penven, and Post's chapter (chapter 10) that—other than my racial/ethnic background—I am the archetype of a faculty-in-residence (FIR): I am female, age 45–54, married, a parent, a pet owner, have a PhD, have taught at the collegiate level for over 15 years, and have lived in-residence for 2 to 5 years. So much for being an original.

Returning to my naïveté . . . not soon after I had finalized the details of my contract to become Hereford's next principal, I drove to the college and walked into its primary common space, affectionately called the Hub. It was summertime at that point, so the students were gone and the Hub was empty—or so I thought. This was really the first time the gravity was beginning to sink in on what I had just signed up to do. What was I (or wasn't I) thinking? I had to uproot my family to this new house on a college campus. I was to go from seeing students outside of class sporadically to living right next to them and residing directly above their primary social space. I was now in charge of overseeing 200 lives. What had I done? Thinking I was alone, I walked slowly through the Hub, looking through the various spaces with new eyes. What I didn't know was that one of the student leaders, who was staying on grounds for the summer and whom I had met previously when interviewing for the position, was napping on one of the sofas in the Hub. When he awoke and saw me, he jumped up from the sofa, blurted out "Welcome to Hereford!" and gave me a warm hug. The fears melted away in his embrace.

But the reality of working with the residential college remained. The first few weeks and months as principal were often bewildering. Although my research focused on LLCs, and I have been asked to serve on external reviews of residential colleges at universities in the United States and abroad, it is not the same as getting to know and understand intimately one particular residential college and its personality, idiosyncrasies, and nooks and crannies. And unlike the impersonal and often-methodical world of research, a residential college is dynamic, unpredictable, and messy. There are myriad new things one must learn in order to lead a residential college, from administrative aspects like budgets, communication channels, and personnel supervision to beloved traditions like annual events, preferred caterers, and the dispositions of the different floors and halls. One of my first memories as principal was purchasing 200 small succulent plants for move-in weekend on my own credit card (because we had not yet hired a program coordinator and I had no way of charging the university for the plants at the time). I was simply told that Hereford had given away the plants during move-in in the past and, with no prior knowledge to the contrary, I shrugged and stood in line at the Lowe's garden center with 200 succulents on my flatbed cart while I tried to figure out how I was going to get them all back to Hereford and where I was going to store them.

There is no primer that can prepare you for a succulent-filled trip to Lowe's, but despite my own scholarship base in LLCs, I really could have used this book as a transition resource for the principal role. It is a valuable foundation for any faculty member thinking about joining or already participating in an LLC, or any higher education institution working to engage their faculty with LLCs. Whether you consider yourself an LLC novice or a seasoned pro, there is much to be learned through this edited book. For example, for those seeking to help internal or external stakeholders understand why encouraging students to engage with faculty is important in the first place, several of the chapters introduce and review the current literature on faculty–student interactions at large. Many of the chapters and their accompanying vignettes make the connection to faculty–student interaction outside of the classroom or traditional office hours. This type of extra-classroom interaction includes the kind of engagement faculty would participate in as part of an LLC.

In an LLC best practices model introduced in *Living–Learning Communities That Work: A Research-Based Model for Design, Delivery, and Assessment* (2018), Jody Jessup-Anger, Mimi Benjamin, Matt Wawrzynski, and I include a section of the model that depicts faculty involvement in LLCs in two primary domains: teaching courses and serving as academic advisors.

While we acknowledged that faculty members may take on other roles in an LLC, the traditional functions of teaching and advising were the most popular and utilitarian due to the fact that most LLCs catered to first-year students who may see and rely on faculty in conventional roles and may not be developmentally ready for more mature, mentoring types of relationships. However, we have received feedback from LLC practitioners on the best practices model, and they have asserted that faculty members can be stakeholders in many other components of the best practices model, including shaping the LLC's goals and objectives, creating and maintaining student affairs and academic affairs partnerships, garnering needed LLC resources, organizing and participating in cocurricular activities, and conducting assessments. Moreover, as we were reminded, faculty can participate in LLCs in other ways not specified in the best practices model, including giving guest lectures; offering workshops; dining with students; exploring the campus's surrounds through field trips, community service, and cultural events; and simply "hanging out" with students by watching television, playing frisbee, and so on, together. Indeed, in their introduction "Vignette: Faculty Matter—Becoming a Faculty-in-Residence," Lomicka and Eidum identify nine roles that faculty can play in LLCs. Then, of course, there are faculty-in-residence (FIR), who take their LLC involvement one step further by living on site in the residential community.

This book delves deeply into the roles of faculty in LLCs, far further and more comprehensively than our own treatment in *Living–Learning Communities That Work* (Inkelas et al., 2018). It also provides readers with a compilation of the various empirical studies that have examined faculty–student interaction in LLCs over the past 20 years. Included in the chapters are summaries of early studies that tended to focus on the ways in which faculty members may become engaged with LLCs. For example, Golde and Pribbenow (2000) characterized faculty involvement in two phases, initial and continued participation, and further described each phase. Cox and Orehovec (2007) created a typology of the nature of faculty–student interaction, which they articulated as (a) disengagement, (b) incidental contact, (c) functional interaction, (d) personal interaction, and (e) mentoring. Nearly a decade later, Sriram and McLevain (2016) published what might be the first survey instrument devised specifically to measure faculty–student interaction and student outcomes in FIR programs. Finally, subsequent empirical studies expanded upon earlier work, such as Mara and Mara's (2011) extension of Cox and Orehovec's typology.

Yet, what makes this book even more noteworthy is that it moves scholarship forward by focusing less on the *what* of faculty–student interaction (which is what much of the previous research examined) and instead focusing more on the *how* of faculty–student interaction. In other words, instead of listing the ways in which faculty members and students may interact within LLCs and their relationship to students' outcomes, this book emphasizes how LLCs can effectively work to foster constructive faculty–student interaction. Examples of the *how* in this book include:

- Lundeen and Penven (chapter 3) describing how institutions can create supports for recruiting, retaining, and supporting faculty engagement in LLCs
- Krieger (chapter 6) asserting how institutions can identify "good fits" among their faculty who might be ideal candidates to work with LLCs
- Manz, Ward, and Gundlach (chapter 8) outlining how LLCs can create more successful coursework through aligning the courses' learning outcomes with the objectives of the LLC, using integrative assignments, and utilizing various campus resources when beneficial
- Jessup-Anger and Benjamin (chapter 9) explaining how faculty members can interact with other LLC staff (e.g., residence hall staff, LLC staff, student affairs staff) as well as LLC students (e.g., resident advisors, peer mentors, and student residence hall leaders)
- Sriram (chapter 11) underscoring how not only FIRs, but the FIRs' families, can enhance the richness of the residential model
- Kennedy (chapter 12) providing keys to how FIRs can integrate work and life, for "balance" may be a misnomer

The *how* of LLC faculty–student interaction remains of critical importance because the greater the level of engagement that faculty members and students have with one another in an LLC, the more beneficial it is for both the students and the faculty. For LLC students, greater interactions with faculty are associated with their (a) intellectual growth and development (e.g., critical thinking, integrative thinking, and analysis of information), (b) academic achievement, (c) diversity appreciation, (d) clarification of personal values, (e) perceived support from their community, and (f) thriving in academic determination and diverse citizenship (Eidum et al., 2020; Hurtado et al., 2020; Inkelas et al., 2018). For faculty, engaging with LLCs enables them to (a) interact with bright and motivated students who share their scholarly and/or personal interests; (b) work with colleagues in an interdisciplinary and innovative educational environment; (c) experiment with new and creative teaching pedagogies; (d) share their research interests with students and other faculty; and (e) less altruistically gain access to various perks like course releases, meal vouchers, and parking spaces (Golde & Pribbenow, 2000; Haynes & Janosik, 2012).

Yet, despite the empirically established importance of faculty–student interaction in LLCs, it is not a given that all LLCs incorporate faculty involvement into their programming. Although the data are over a decade old, the National Study of Living–Learning Programs, which included information from over 600 LLCs across the United States, showed that nearly 25% of LLCs had no faculty involvement, and 64% had only one to three faculty members involved (Inkelas et al., 2018). Thus, the need for this book is pressing: As LLCs look to augment their efforts in faculty–student interaction, it is crucial to have a resource that outlines the best practices in how this relationship should be cultivated.

Moreover, not only does this book serve as a valuable resource of extant information, it breaks new ground and pushes our knowledge forward by providing theory- and practice-driven models and frameworks for LLC faculty engagement. There are primarily two types of new models introduced in the book. The first type pertains to institutional components that influence faculty–student engagement. In chapter 3, Lundeen and Penven propose a residential learning community faculty engagement model of factors that can affect the degree and scope of a faculty member's involvement with an LLC. Their model, which actually incorporates both institutional and personal domains, includes four distinct spheres: (a) institutional contexts, such as the mission and type of the institution; (b) organizational structure, or the student life and academic affairs relationship, and the financial and human resources; (c) professional motivations, or one's extrinsic professional values such as expectations, goals, and rewards systems; and (d) personal motivations, or one's intrinsic motivations, including the faculty member's personal goals, values, and commitments. In a subsequent chapter (chapter 7), Post extends the previous second sphere of organizational structure into a partnership continuum created at Texas A&M University. The partnership continuum conceives of academic collaborations in increasingly engaged steps, from (a) support, or transactional services between two units; to (b) exchange, or a partnership resulting in a mutually beneficial exchange that is not long term; to (3) cooperation, or a coordinated relationship that is shared in a long-term recurring relationship; to (d) collaboration, or two units sharing full responsibility in an integrated, sustained, and mutually beneficial partnership.

The second new type of model promulgated in the book pertains to issues related to faculty development as agents of student interaction in an LLC. For example, in chapter 9, Jessup-Anger and Benjamin provide an overall framework for faculty–student interaction, building upon Cox and Orehovec's (2007) typology. In their model, the authors articulate some pre-involvement characteristics of faculty and students that are desirable for optimal interaction. They then argue that effective faculty–student interaction should take place in an LLC with an academically and socially supportive climate. They go on to identify the physical and intangible components of a healthy climate, from office space to support from academic departments and senior administrators for their roles in the communities to an atmosphere that encourages exploration and "deeper life interactions" (Sriram et al., 2020).

In chapter 6, Krieger offers guidance for professional staff in recruiting and selecting potential faculty partners. He begins with the identification of faculty candidates through other student support arenas on the campus, such as cocurricular program advising, campus-wide banquets, student-focused committees, and faculty who are nominated for teaching awards. He then transitions to the faculty selection process, in which he outlines issues that faculty members should address when merging LLC involvement with the traditional academic professional triumvirate of teaching, research, and service. In addition, he notes which key LLC stakeholders should be involved with making the ultimate decision on whom to hire. The final step is the onboarding of the faculty member, in which Krieger outlines five steps: (a) conveying role expectations, (b) providing a tour of the community, (c) providing administrative and policy training, (d) introducing faculty to new colleagues, and (e) providing orientation to the community's culture. Sriram, in chapter 11, illustrates how FIR families can enhance the sense of community in an LLC through the four "P" model: people, policies, programs, and places. Finally, Kennedy (chapter 12) provides a visual model depicting FIR work–life balance. In the model, she argues that, instead of thinking of work–life balance as a scale, it should be reimagined as two equally sized triangles that overlap, where work consists of teaching, research, and service and life is composed of the self, family, and community.

These groundbreaking models of factors associated with LLC faculty–student interaction not only contribute to the LLC literature but they also provide the foundation for the articulation of the *how*, or how faculty–student interaction can and should occur to optimize LLC effectiveness. They bring together—in one resource—decades of empirical, theoretical, and practitioner-based knowledge that was once a black box for faculty to discover and figure out on their own. Together, with the LLC best practices model, these new frameworks help practitioners advance their work in creating and sustaining high-quality LLCs that will fulfill their "high impact practice" (Kuh, 2008) moniker of facilitating student achievement, growth, and development. Indeed, although it was a major contribution to the college impact literature to identify the institutional practices associated with positive student outcomes, one of my misgivings about the high-impact practice phenomenon is that too much attention was given to *what* the practices were, and whether or not an institution had them, and not on *how* they should be conducted in order to influence students' outcomes. Once again, it is the *how* of LLC faculty–student interaction that this book addresses that makes it a must-read for all institutions and practitioners seriously invested in their LLCs' success.

I conclude this foreword the way I started it: with an anecdote. At the University of Virginia there are several different housing options for students who wish to live on-grounds. Residential colleges are only one of several possibilities. Thus, it is sometimes difficult for students and their parents to grasp the residential college concept, or at least what makes residential colleges distinct from the other options. It can be particularly confusing because our name, Hereford College, has the word "college" in it, implying to some that it is an entity separate from the University of Virginia. During those conversations, I often use an analogy from Harry Potter. I explain that the University of Virginia is akin to Hogwarts. It's the school in its entirety. Hereford, on the other hand, is like Gryffindor. It is one house within the larger school or, in our case, one college within the larger university. While all students attend Hogwarts, they also belong to a specific house that is not just a place to sleep, but a community with its own history, where students live and learn together and experience a fellowship unique to their house and the people who inhabit it. Almost every time, the students and parents immediately grasp the residential college concept through this example.

However, the more I have thought about this analogy, the more I realize that there is one place where it falls short: While we all know that certain professors at Hogwarts are associated with a certain house (Professor McGonagall is the faculty head of Gryffindor House, Severus Snape is the head of Slytherin, etc.), one shortcoming of the plot is that it does not straightforwardly depict how the heads interact with the students in the respective houses. Sure, Professor McGongall secured Harry a spot on the Gryffindor quidditch team, but she is rarely seen interacting with the Gryffindor students in their common room, or holding teas for the students in her salon, or bringing in guest speakers from the Ministry of Magic to talk about potential future careers. In fact, come to think of it, where does Professor McGonagall even live? Is she a FIR, or does she have a home somewhere else in the British countryside? Just as the faculty–student interaction in the houses of Hogwarts is somewhat of a mystery, so was that same interaction in real life LLCs and residential colleges. Until now.

Karen Kurotsuchi Inkelas
University of Virginia

References

Cox, B. E., & Orehovec, E. (2007). Faculty–student interaction outside the classroom: A typology from a residential college. *The Review of Higher Education, 30,* 343–362. https://psycnet.apa.org/doi/10.1353/rhe.2007.0033

Eidum, J., Lomicka, L., Chiang, W., Endick, G., & Stratton, J. (2020). Thriving in residential learning communities. *Learning Communities Research and Practice, 8*(1), Article 7.

Golde, C. M., & Pribbenow, D. A. (2000). Understanding faculty involvement in residential learning communities. *Journal of College Student Development, 41*(1), 27–40.

Haynes, C., & Janosik, S. M. (2012). Faculty and staff member benefits from involvement in living–learning programs. *Journal of College & University Student Housing, 38/39*(2/1), 32–45.

Hurtado, S. S., Gonyea, R. M., Graham, P. A., & Fosnacht, K. (2020). The relationship between residential learning communities and student engagement. *Learning Communities Research and Practice, 8*(1), Article 5.

Inkelas, K. K., Jessup-Anger, J., Benjamin, M., & Wawrzynski, M. R. (2018). *Living–learning communities that work: A research-based model for design, delivery, and assessment.* Stylus.

Kuh, G. D. (2008). *High-impact educational practices: What they are, who has access to them, and why they matter.* Association of American Colleges and Universities.

Mara, M., & Mara, A. (2011). Finding an analytic frame for faculty–student interaction within faculty-in-residence programs. *Innovative Higher Education, 36,* 71–82. https://doi.org/10.1007/s10755-010-9162-8

Sriram, R., Haynes, C., Weintraub, S. D., Cheatle, J., Marquart, C. P., & Murray, J. L. (2020). Student demographics and experiences of deeper life interactions within residential learning communities. *Learning Communities Research and Practice, 8*(1), Article 8.

Sriram, R., & McLevain, M. (2016). Developing an instrument to examine student–faculty interaction in faculty-in-residence programs. *Journal of College Student Development, 57*(5), 604–609. http://doi.org/10.1353/csd.2016.0065

ACKNOWLEDGMENTS

The idea for this project arose during conversations at the 2017–2019 Research Seminar on Residential Learning Communities as a High-Impact Practice, a multi-institutional research initiative hosted by Elon University's Center for Engaged Learning (www.CenterForEngaged Learning.org). Our heartfelt thanks go out to our seminar leaders (Mimi Benjamin, Jody Jessup-Anger, Cara Lucia, and Shannon Lundeen) and our research group (Warren Chiang, Ghada Endick, Jill Stratton). We are also indebted to the support of the Series on Engaged Learning and Teaching book series editors (Jessie L. Moore and Peter Felten) and the Center for Engaged Learning's managing editor (Jennie Goforth) for their encouragement, support, and feedback.

As faculty-in-residence balancing our professional and personal lives, we thank our home departments, our residence life colleagues, and our families (Jennifer's husband, Daniel, and children Nikita and Shiloh, Lara's husband, Andy, and children Maleah and Ashlyn) for their ongoing support of this project.

VIGNETTE

Faculty Matter—Becoming a Faculty-in-Residence

Lara L. Lomicka

In December 2015, as I was about to begin a semester-long sabbatical, I read a job description for a faculty-in-residence position at my institution. Three colleagues had nudged me to apply for the position, but in my head I had trouble reconciling how I could uproot my family (husband and two children) from our quiet home near campus and move all of us into a residential space. How would my husband adapt? Where would my children play? Would the environment compromise our safety or well-being? As a professor, I was (intellectually) ready to embrace a different type of challenge and open a new avenue for research. I had taught and worked alongside undergraduate students for the entirety of my career, but I still wondered, did I really know them? Did I know their struggles? Their worries? Their challenges? I was eager to find out more.

One of my roles on campus prior to learning of this job opening was serving as a faculty associate for my institution's residential college. My family participated in activities and dined with students. Enjoying meals with students opened opportunities to get to know each other on a deeper level. We have fond memories of our shared meals: My oldest daughter lost her first tooth in the dining hall, and my youngest daughter gave out artwork to students as a conversation starter. At the end of the day, however, we packed up our kids and returned to the comforts of our home in a nearby neighborhood.

I had never been in the private space of the residence (only the public lobby and classroom areas). I wondered what it would be like for me and my family to live with students 24/7. How would I (and the rest of my family) adjust to not having a backyard, privacy of a home, and a certain amount of independence? After many late-night talks with my husband, I decided to apply for the position and was extended an offer as the faculty principal of Preston Residential College. The rest is history. In the summer of 2016, we moved into the faculty apartment. My husband mentored and established some important friendships with some of the male students. My daughters (ages 8 and 10 at the time) were befriended by students, rode scooters in the halls on rainy days, delivered cookies to each room, helped cook dinners, and hosted slime-making pop-up events—we lived life with and alongside the residents. We became a visible and active family-in-residence, who frequently opened our apartment to students and their families.

Having served as a faculty associate, I understand the importance of cultivating relationships with students. As Felten and Lambert (2020) advocated, "Relationships are the beating heart of the undergraduate experience" (p. 1), which we wholeheartedly embrace as a family. In the last 5 years, we have come to realize how important it is to build and sustain those relationships with students and campus partners in order to have a thriving community. As a faculty member, much of what I had to learn was new to me. I did not know much about student affairs professionals, their role at the university, or how vital they are to making campus a successful place. I learned to cultivate and nurture relationships with campus partners—from dining to landscaping to undergraduate research. I didn't know that each residence had a curriculum to follow and was part of assessments each year. After 5 years in the residential space, I realize that all of the partners must work together to create a rich residential experience for students.

I have also learned that faculty matter to students—not just in the classroom but perhaps just as significantly outside of the classroom. In Preston Residential College, I wanted to be approachable as well as an advocate and a mentor, where the students refer to me as "Doc Lo," which I tell them is short for Dr. Lomicka. Students fill my office each Wednesday evening for "student hours," where I offer them friendly conversation, the occasional debate, plenty of food, and stress relief toys. We talk about life, academics, family, and what is going on in the world. We make time for each other and walk through life together. Faculty–student interaction "need not be formal or academic to hold value" (Cox & Orehovec, 2007, p. 360); simply building relationships and community by being present and being among students can be life changing.

INTRODUCTION TO FACULTY ENGAGEMENT IN LIVING–LEARNING COMMUNITIES

Jennifer E. Eidum and Lara L. Lomicka

Faculty play an important role in living–learning communities (LLCs): Three-quarters of LLCs have some level of faculty involvement, and those with significant faculty involvement show more positive student outcomes (Inkelas et al., 2018). Faculty–student interaction can lead to increased GPAs (Anaya & Cole, 2001); persistence (Mayhew et al., 2016); self reports of learning (Lundberg & Schreiner, 2004); sense of community and belonging (Spanierman et al., 2013); positive campus climate (Cress, 2008); career attitudes and intention to innovate (Mayhew et al., 2018); and critical thinking, cognitive complexity, and appreciation of liberal learning (Inkelas et al., 2008). Faculty–student interaction is especially important for first-generation students' thriving at college (Eidum et al., 2020) and for students of color (Vetter et al., 2019). Faculty involvement and, more important, the quality of student–faculty interaction, may be critical to successful LLCs. In fact, more focused interaction can lead to a higher impact on knowledge acquisition and skill development (Kuh & Hu, 2001).

Although they are best known as LLCs, learning communities with a residential component are also known as *residential learning communities* (RLCs), *living–learning programs* (LLPs), and *residential colleges* (RCs; Inkelas et al., 2008). Although specific researchers and programs may prefer one term over another for their specific purposes (see, e.g., chapter 3), for the purposes of this book we use the term *LLC* unless otherwise noted.

Because LLCs are prominent spaces for faculty–student engagement, this volume brings faculty to the forefront by providing research-based, theoretical, and practical evidence that helps to promote the roles that faculty can play in LLCs. Eidum et al. (2020) found that faculty interaction with students in LLCs may be more impactful than only having faculty teach residentially linked courses. Although we know that faculty can make a difference in LLCs, more research—both theoretical and practical—is needed to situate the roles, practices, and engagement of faculty with students in residential spaces. This edited book attempts to fill that gap by supporting faculty in their LLC work while also assisting student affairs professionals in understanding faculty and how to best collaborate with them.

This book examines how colleges and universities might foster sustainable faculty involvement in LLCs. More specifically, the chapter authors contemplate one fundamental question: Why do faculty in LLCs matter, now and in the future? We argue that faculty are an essential component of LLC success. This volume delivers evidence-based research as well as practical examples and voices from the field, to guide and support faculty serving in different capacities in LLCs, to serve as a resource for student affairs practitioners collaborating with faculty in residential environments, and to offer guidance to administrators developing new or revising existing LLC programs.

Why LLCs?

In their recent book *Living–Learning Communities That Work*, Inkelas et al. (2018) defined LLCs as "cohorts of students intentionally grouped together in a residence hall who have a shared academic experience along with co-curricular learning activities for engagement with their peers" (p. 5). There are over 600 LLCs on U.S. campuses, ranging from 2-year colleges to research-extensive universities (Inkelas et al., 2008). A more recent count of the Association of College and University Housing Officers–International database indicates that over 125 colleges and universities have multiple LLCs on their campuses (Kinzie, 2018). Although there is currently no registry of LLCs, news reports indicate that universities are expanding the number and type of LLCs being offered at universities across the United States (Kern, 2019; Mendez, 2017; Peterkin, 2013; Spencer, 2019). In addition, universities in Australia, Germany, Singapore, and other countries are beginning to adopt this higher-education practice.

Why is the presence of LLCs growing worldwide? LLCs provide a home away from home for many students in residential spaces on campus; they offer support through a smaller community within the context of the institution. Pascarella et al. (1994) noted that an "integration of the student's living environment with his or her academic or learning environment" (p. 32) is central to LLC practices. Often thematically linked, LLCs can provide a more intimate environment and can seamlessly blend the academic and living experiences, creating opportunities for faculty and peer interaction (Inkelas & Weisman, 2003), as well as social experiences and experiential learning. LLCs have many documented benefits, which make them an attractive addition to campus life. These benefits include heightened capacities for critical thinking (Inkelas et al., 2006), improvements to a student's overall academic performance (Inkelas & Soldner, 2011), a sense of being part of a community (Inkelas et al., 2018), and more opportunities to interact with faculty (Garrett & Zabriskie, 2004; Inkelas & Soldner, 2011). One of the most compelling reasons to justify the academic component of LLCs is the presence of faculty.

The Role(s) of Faculty in LLCs

When thinking about the question "Why should faculty have a role in LLCs?" it is perhaps more engaging to ask "Why not?" Although teaching and research are widely recognized as the crucial tasks of a faculty member, faculty also serve as mentors, coaches, counselors, recommenders, readers, directors of theses and study abroad, advisors of organizations, and much more. Gonzáles (2017) pointed out that as times change, today's faculty play a greater role in delivering a positive student experience: "There is more faculty–student engagement in and outside the classroom. Many faculty are aware that High-Impact-Practices (HIP)—like service learning/internships, undergraduate research, learning communities, and so on—are important toward attaining student success" (para. 12). Perhaps more important, faculty can connect students with a network or web of overlapping relationships that will help them to be successful in life beyond the university (Felten & Lambert, 2020; St. Amor, 2020).

Why Faculty Presence Is Important in LLCs

Aside more traditional roles that faculty play in academia, their early contributions to residential colleges, such as Oxford and Cambridge as long as 800 years ago, should not be overlooked. In the United States, as early as 1933 faculty were living in residential spaces such as the Harvard house system (Ryan, 1993). It is now common to find faculty in a variety of residential roles, such as serving as a faculty advisor to an LLC, teaching a class connected with a residence hall, or being a guest speaker at a hall event. Table I.1 details nine common faculty roles in LLCs, ordered alphabetically.

It is important to note that an individual faculty member can participate in an LLC in multiple ways; for example, a professor teaching a course

TABLE I.1
Faculty Roles in Living–Learning Communities (LLCs)

Faculty role	Description
Academic advisor	Formally advise students in the LLC with academic planning.
Academic leader	Collaborate with other faculty and staff; provide direction to the LLC students.
Curriculum designer	Develop or codevelop LLC curricula; advise faculty teaching in the LLC.
Experiential learning guide	Lead students in the LLC in study abroad, service-learning, or other experiential learning experiences.
Guest speaker	Present information to students in the LLC (e.g., research presentation, film discussion).
Mentor	Mentor students in the LLC in academic, social, or experiential spheres; serve as a role model.
Participant	Attend LLC events, interacting with students in the LLC.
Representative	Serve on an LLC advisory board.
Teacher	Teach or coteach a class affiliated with an LLC.

affiliated with an LLC would be a "teacher," but they might also serve as a "mentor" outside of class for students in the LLC, they may headline an event as a "guest speaker," and they may also attend other LLC events as a "participant." Moreover, it is important to recognize that faculty participation can accumulate over time: One semester a faculty member might teach a class affiliated with an LLC, and the next semester they might be invited back as an "experiential learning guide" to lead a service-learning experience for LLC students, all the while mentoring a group of students from the LLC in a research project and occasionally participating in LLC events. These layered and ongoing faculty affiliations are important for students and for the LLC culture over time (Fullam & Hughes, 2020).

Finally, the most intensive of faculty roles, faculty-in-residence (FIR), are defined by Healea et al. (2014) as roles where "faculty members have contracted with colleges or universities to live alongside students in campus residence halls (p. 475). The specific goals of FIR differ across institutions, but they largely offer social, intellectual, personal, and even preprofessional development to students in a manner that augments the work of their allies in the student affairs ranks. Regardless of the role faculty play in LLCs, they often collaborate with student affairs professionals in residence halls to conduct their work and they are, at the same time, often supervised by a combination of academic affairs and student affairs professionals.

How Faculty Engage in LLCs

Faculty and student interaction in LLCs is characterized as a "dynamic process," providing both breadth and depth to the campus experience (Davenport & Pasque, 2014, p. 59). Interactions between students and faculty outside the classroom setting contribute substantially to student success and positively correlate with student learning, personal development, cognitive thinking, problem solving, student satisfaction, and academic achievement (see Astin, 1993; Frazier & Eighmy, 2012; Kuh et al., 2005; and Kuh & Hu, 2001 for examples). Specific to LLCs, faculty participation is most often characterized as engagement in (a) academic programming, (b) social programming, and/or (c) experiential programming, with faculty often playing a key role in the planning and implementation of these programs. Faculty can connect students with a wealth of resources at the institution, inspire curiosity, intellectual development, rigor, and skills for lifelong learning, and introduce them to experiential learning.

First, in terms of academic programming within the LLC, faculty are key players in deciding which academic courses to offer (which may be taught by them or other colleagues) and/or what linked courses or clusters to include in the LLC for residents. One common type of academic programming in the LLC that encourages students to learn together are *linked courses* or *learning clusters*, defined as two or more courses, often interdisciplinary, in which students co-enroll (Tinto, 1987). These courses can offer purposeful connections among academic, residential, and social components of the university experience. In addition to teaching and/or coordinating courses, faculty can advise students (formally and informally) and serve as a faculty mentor, offering an academic component to some of the social programming in the LLC. A study by Shushok and Sriram (2010) suggested that students in an LLC were 7.4 times more likely than non-LLC students to meet informally or socially with a faculty member outside of class or faculty office hours, emphasizing the need for faculty affiliated with LLCs. In a study by Arensdoft and Naylor-Tincknell (2016), the results suggested that students who had more access to faculty played a role in the success of their overall college experience: "These connections not only provided academic and non-academic opportunities and comfort about approaching faculty but also fostered relationships that were more caring, mentor-like, and friendlier than those of typical college students in the non-LLC group" (p. 10). In the same study, non-LLC students reported limited interaction (office hours, class, advising) with faculty members. Whether faculty are involved with course teaching and/or advising/mentoring, the academic presence that they bring to the LLC is critical to the richness of the student experience.

Next, in terms of social programming, LLCs can serve as a means of social support to help students meet others and to network with campus partners (Spanierman et al., 2013). Consistent faculty participation can enhance student learning outcomes and cultivate a more holistic student development. Crucial to successful social support is the development of a sense of belonging. If students feel like they belong to a space, they are more inclined to participate, engage, and communicate with peers with whom they are living. Student support can range from informal interaction and engagement (social outings, shared dining experiences, making friends, off-campus experiences) to connections with faculty (community office hours, organized events, dining). The simple presence of and participation by faculty members in the LLC (Eidum et al., 2020; Inkelas et al., 2018) is a key element to success. Eidum et al.'s (2020) study indicated the impact faculty have on students in the LLC may be independent of whether faculty are teaching courses to students. They further suggested that

> focusing resources on a variety of pathways for faculty involvement—such as creating live-in faculty homes, developing faculty affiliate programs for [RLCs], and promoting faculty attendance at RLC social and academic events—may have more impact than focusing only on courses and requiring co-curricular participation. (p. 16)

Faculty should be encouraged to participate in a variety of ways in the LLCs beyond merely academic roles. As suggested by Eidum et al. (2020), these events could include both informal and formal conversations between faculty and students about major, career, and life questions, as well as involvement in dinners, advising, workshops, and social gatherings.

Finally, the role of faculty in experiential programming in LLCs (e.g., study abroad, service-learning) can encourage learning beyond the four walls of the traditional classroom. Experiential learning can be thought of as an active process of engaging the learner in the academic content through guided reflection and intellectual development (Kolb, 1984). Led by a faculty member, an LLC could provide experiential programming that provides students with the opportunity to focus on interdisciplinary and interprofessional collaboration across disciplines, promote intellectual development, and foster community learning. This programming might come in the form of internships, service work in the community, volunteer opportunities, or even short-term faculty-led study abroad experiences. Experiential learning can encourage the in-depth exploration of academic disciplines and/or special interests. At the University of South Carolina, the FIR at Preston Residential College developed a short-term residential study abroad opportunity that takes community members to Morocco. While in Africa, students are immersed in a culture quite different than their own as they discover and learn more about culture through guided talks, cuisine, and family stays with locals (Kelly & Lomicka, 2018). Experiential learning can provide ways for affiliated LLC faculty to extend learning outside of the LLC and the classroom.

In each of these programming spheres—academic, social, and experiential—faculty can play an important role in creating programming with and for new majority students. As Dahl, Youngerman, Stipeck, and Mayhew describe in chapter 1, new majority students are those who are non-White, first generation, transfer, veteran, or older than 22. New majority students at college can be challenged not only financially but also with emotional support, connections, engagement, and intentional mentoring. Faculty, especially those working in residential settings, can provide support and mentoring to these students to help them thrive in college. Moreover, LLC faculty leaders who themselves are a part of these underrepresented groups can serve as role models for new majority students.

Whether academic, social, or experiential, the presence of faculty in LLCs is fundamental to their success. While there are many and varied roles faculty can play within the residential community, the engagement and interaction of faculty with residents can lead to stronger relationships, a sense of belonging, and intellectual development. If faculty can emphasize intentionality at all levels, they can develop stronger programs and create an academic–social environment where student learning and development can thrive.

Purpose of This Book

The underlying theme of this book is that faculty matter: Their presence is vital to the mission and vision of a campus, from sharing their knowledge and passions in the classroom to engaging students in learning and serving through LLCs. Umbach and Wawrzynski (2005) explored the relationship between faculty practices and student engagement, finding that faculty play an important role in fostering overall student engagement and learning. In fact, they stated that "Institutions where faculty create an environment that emphasizes effective educational practices have students who are active participants in their learning and perceive greater gains from their undergraduate experience" (p. 173). They claim that the impact of faculty members on the student experience is present both within and beyond the classroom. Moreover, the relationships that faculty build and foster with students also matter (Felten & Lambert, 2020). Using data from over 400 interviews with students, faculty, and staff at 29 institutions of higher education in the United States, Felten and Lambert (2020) advocated that "Individual relationships can be educationally powerful, but a network of overlapping relationships is more likely to meet a student's evolving needs than any single mentor can" (p. 15).

While we've just made the case for why faculty presence is important and why faculty matter in the residential community, it is also important to point out that collaboration is crucial to their success. Faculty must cultivate relationships with colleagues in student affairs, in dining, in experiential learning, with academic affairs partners, and with other campus partners in order to build a successful community. The importance of this collaboration is inextricably linked to how the three parts of this book are structured: Part One details the campus conditions that foster successful faculty engagement in LLCs. Part Two focuses on the partnerships and logistics that enable faculty to be successful in LLCs. And finally, Part Three focuses on the deepest form of faculty engagement with LLCs, the FIR, and the particular needs this group of faculty has.

Each chapter is similarly structured, with an opening vignette from a practitioner in the field, offering lived examples that help illustrate theory and research in practice; a review of existing literature on the topic; and then a move to practice where authors utilize their own experiences, as well as academic research, to make suggestions for faculty, staff, and administrators working with LLCs. Each chapter is accompanied by materials hosted online at the Center for Engaged Learning's website, including reflection questions to guide program development at the readers' individual institutions (see https://www.centerforengagedlearning.org/books/faculty-factor).

The aim of this book is that it can be read as a whole by faculty, staff, and administrators involved with living–learning programs to guide their thinking as they initiate new LLCs or revise existing LLCs. We also envision that each chapter can be read on its own for professional development workshops, training sessions, and personal interest. We challenge readers to continue dialogue about the role of faculty and important themes that emerge across the chapters:

1. **Engagement:** What types of engagement are common to LLCs—and are some better than others? How might LLC curricula support this engagement?

2. **Equity and Inclusion:** How can LLCs support new majority students? How can institutions create equitable opportunities for minoritized faculty?

3. **Support and Incentives:** How can institutions support faculty work in LLCs effectively and efficiently? How can faculty engagement be assessed and improved?

In the chapters to follow, it is our hope that you will be challenged, enlightened, and nourished as you learn more about the role of faculty in residential spaces, their relationships with campus partners, their collaboration with student affairs professionals, and their role in the residential curriculum.

Finally, it is important to note that the majority of this book was written during the early days of the COVID-19 pandemic. With the impact of COVID and physical distancing affecting the day-to-day operations of campus life for all of us, we noticed that the pandemic highlighted a widespread desire for relationship-rich education. LLCs can play an important role in meeting that need. During the pandemic, students experienced a loss of human connections and an overdose of screen time, as well as consistent uncertainty and disruption. Faculty and staff in residence have found creative ways to keep their communities safe while continuing to foster connections with students. In an article about Baylor's FIR, Garrett summed up the importance of connection nicely: "It's really important to us is to be able to offer to students an experience that shows how faculty care for their students' wellbeing and that Baylor faculty are willing to live life out on a daily basis with their residents" (Harris, 2020, para. 10).

References

Anaya, G., & Cole, D. G. (2001). Latina/o student achievement: Exploring the influence of student–faculty interactions on college grades. *Journal of College Student Development, 42*(1), 3–14.

Arensdoft, J., & Naylor-Tincknell, J. (2016). Beyond traditional retention data: A qualitative study of the social benefits of living learning communities. *Learning Communities Research and Practice, 4*(1), Article 4.

Astin, A. W. (1993). *What matters in college: Four critical years revisited.* Jossey-Bass.

Cox, B. E., & Orehovec, E. (2007). Faculty–student interaction outside the classroom: A typology from a residential college. *The Review of Higher Education, 30*(4), 343–362.

Cress, C. M. (2008). Creating inclusive learning communities: The role of student–faculty relationships in mitigating negative campus climate. *Learning Inquiry, 2*(2), 95–111. http:doi.org/10.1007/s11519-008-0028-2

Davenport, A. M., & Pasque, P. A. (2014). Adding breadth and depth to college and university residential communities: A phenomenological study of faculty-in-residence. *The Journal of College and University Student Housing, 40*(2), 46–66.

Eidum, J. E., Lomicka, L., Chiang, W., Endick, G., & Stratton, J. (2020, May). An investigation of thriving in residential learning communities. *Learning Communities Research and Practice, 8*(1), Article 7.

Felten, P., & Lambert, L. M. (2020). *Relationships-rich education: How human connections drive success in college.* Johns Hopkins University Press.

Frazier, W., & Eighmy, M. (2012). Themed residential learning communities: The importance of purposeful faculty and staff involvement and student engagement. *The Journal of College and University Student Housing, 18*(2), 23.

Fullam, J. P., & Hughes, A. J. (2020). "Bridging the gap": Relationships and learning beyond the classroom in a faculty-in-residence program. *Journal of College and University Student Housing, 47*(1), 44–61.

Garrett, M. D., & Zabriskie, M. S. (2004). The influence of living-learning program participation on student-faculty interaction. *Journal of College & University Student Housing, 33*, 38.

Gonzáles, G. (2017, October 19). Changing with times: Faculty's role in delivering a great student experience. *The EvoLLLution.* https://evolllution.com/programming/teaching-and-learning/changing-with-the-times-facultys-role-in-delivering-a-great-student-experience/

Harris, M. (2020, May 15). Even with COVID-19, faculty in residence choose to live on campus. *Baylor Lariat.* https://baylorlariat.com/2020/10/15/even-with-covid-19-faculty-in-residence-choose-to-live-on-campus/

Healea, C. D., Scott, J. H., & Shilla, S. (2014). The work of faculty-in-residence: An introduction and literature review. *Work, 52*(3), 472–480. https://doi.org/10.3233/WOR-152189

Inkelas, K. K., Jessup-Anger, J. E., Benjamin, M., & Wawrzynski, M. R. (2018). *Living learning communities that work: A research-based model for design, delivery, and assessment.* Stylus.

Inkelas, K. K., Johnson, D., Lee, Z., Daver, Z., Longerbeam, S., Vogt, K., & Leonard, J. B. (2006). The role of living-learning programs in students' perceptions of intellectual growth at three large universities. *NASPA Journal, 43*(1), 115–143.

Inkelas, K. K., & Soldner, M. (2011). Undergraduate living-learning programs and student outcomes. In J. C. Smart & M. B. Paulsen (Eds.), *Higher education: Handbook of theory and research* (Vol. 26, pp. 1–55).

Inkelas, K. K., Soldner, M., Longerbeam, S. D., & Brown Leonard, J. (2008). Differences in student outcomes by types of living-learning programs: The development of an empirical typology. *Research in Higher Education, 49*(6), 495–512.

Inkelas, K. K., & Weisman, J. L. (2003). Different by design: An examination of student outcomes among participants in three types of living-learning programs. *Journal of College Student Development, 48*(5), 525–542.

Kelly, S., & Lomicka, L. (2018, November 1–3). *Residential adventures: Pathways to global learning* [Poster presentation]. Fifth Annual Residential College Symposium, Waco, TX.

Kern, J. (2019, August 20). Living–learning communities expand at UC. *UC News*. https://www.uc.edu/news/articles/2019/08/n20849800.html

Kinzie, J. (2018). Foreword. In K. Inkelas, J. Jessup-Anger, M. Benjamin, & M. Wawrzynski (Eds.), *Living-learning communities that work a research-based model for design, delivery, and assessment*. Stylus.

Kolb, D. A. (1984). *Experiential learning: Experience as the source of learning and development*. Prentice Hall.

Kuh, G. D., & Hu, S. (2001). The effects of student–faculty interaction in the 1990's. *Review of Higher Education, 24*(3), 309–332.

Kuh, G. D., Kinzie, J., Schuh, J. H., & Whitt, E. J. (2005). *Assessing conditions to enhance educational effectiveness: Inventory for student engagement and success*. Jossey-Bass.

Lundberg, C. A., & Schreiner, L. A. (2004). Quality and frequency of faculty–student interaction as predictors of learning: An analysis by student race/ethnicity. *Journal of College Student Development, 45*(5), 549–565. https://doi.org/10.1353/csd.2004.0061

Mayhew, M., Dahl, L., Hooten, Z., Duran, A., Stipeck, C., & Youngerman, E. (2018). *2018 assessment of collegiate residential environments & outcomes*. https://www.acreosurvey.org/

Mayhew, M., Rockenbach, A., Bowman, N., Seifert, T., Wolniak, G., Pascarella, E., & Terenzini, P. (2016). *How college affects students: 21st century evidence that higher education works*. Wiley.

Mendez, M. (2017, July 24). UT housing introduces first-year students to new living learning communities. *The Daily Texan*. https://www.dailytexanonline.com/2017/07/24/ut-housing-introduces-first-year-students-to-new-living-learning-communities

Pascarella, E., Bohr, L., Nora, A., Desler, M., et al. (1994). Impacts of on-campus and off-campus work on first year cognitive outcomes. *Journal of College Student Development, 35*(5), 364–370.

Peterkin, C. (2013, January 21). Colleges design new housing to engage and retain students. *The Chronicle of Higher Education*. https://www.chronicle.com/article/Colleges-Design-New-Housing-as/136713/

Ryan, M. B. (1993). Residential colleges: A historical context. In T. S. Smith (Ed.), *Gateways: Residential colleges and the freshman year experience* (Monograph No. 14). The University of South Carolina, National Resource Center for The First-Year Experience and Students in Transition.

Shushok, F., & Sriram, R. (2010). Exploring the effect of a residential academic affairs–student affairs partnership: The first year of an engineering and computer science living–learning center. *Journal of College and University Student Housing, 36*(2), 68–81.

Spanierman, L. B., Soble, J. R., Mayfield, J. B., Neville, H. A., Aber, M., Khuri, L., & Rosa, D. L. (2013). Living learning communities and students' sense of community and belonging. *Journal of Student Affairs Research and Practice, 50*(3), 308–325. http://doi.org/10.1515/jsarp-2013-0022

Spencer, C. (2019, February 24). Three new Fulbright college living learning communities launch. *The Fulbright Review.* https://fulbrightreview.uark.edu/four-new-fulbright-college-living-learning-communities-launch/

St. Amor, M. (2020). As times and students change, can faculty change, too? *Inside Higher Education.* https://www.insidehighered.com/news/2020/04/03/faculty-face-uphill-battle-adapting-needs-todays-students

Tinto, V. (1987). *Leaving college: Rethinking the causes and cures for student attrition.* University of Chicago Press.

Umbach, P. D., & Wawrzynski, M. R. (2005). Faculty do matter: The role of college faculty in student learning and engagement. *Research in Higher Education, 46,* 153–184. https://doi.org/10.1007/s11162-004-1598-1

Vetter, M., Schreiner, L., & Jaworski, B. (2019). Faculty attitudes and behaviors that contribute to thriving in first-year students of color. *Journal of the First-Year Experience & Students in Transition, 31*(1), 9–28.

PART ONE

CREATING THE CONDITIONS FOR SUCCESSFUL FACULTY ENGAGEMENT IN LIVING–LEARNING COMMUNITIES

Jennifer E. Eidum and Lara L. Lomicka

This section focuses on the ways campuses can foster faculty engagement in living–learning communities (LLCs), as this engagement proves to be a key factor in student success in higher education. More specifically, the chapters in this section envision a future of faculty–student engagement that meets the needs of new majority students and faculty through intentional planning and forward-looking models of faculty engagement. Campus culture and administrator involvement play important roles in creating residential spaces where equity and inclusion are prioritized among students and faculty.

Looking at the new directions of faculty–student engagement initiatives, Dahl, Youngerman, Stipeck, and Mayhew (chapter 1) focus on defining the new majority and the success of faculty engagement at various institutions. In the next chapter, Shushok and Bohannon (chapter 2) channel their perspectives as a senior administrator and a live-in faculty member to frame how campus partners can attract and sustain faculty leadership in LLCs. In chapter 3, Lundeen and Penven introduce a conceptual model of faculty engagement to help faculty, student affairs practitioners, and university leaders who are interested in increasing the quantity of faculty and the quality of their engagement in LLCs. Finally, Book and Stein (chapter 4) present an intentional approach to mapping a residential campus at a mid-sized institution. In offering a map of their approach, the authors hope to assist other campuses in planning their own residential campus.

VIGNETTE

I'll Meet You Where You Are

Darleny Cepin

I have dedicated most of my professional life to serving students on elite college campuses, placing a particular emphasis on the importance of diversity, inclusion, and wellness. I am drawn to this field: I know from personal experience the transformative benefits of living and learning among a truly engaged community. As the director of student life (DSL) of a residential college at Princeton University and a Dominican-born first-generation student myself, I have become adept at serving all students, regardless of their status or demographics. To be truthful, I see a little bit of myself in every type of student with whom I engage.

It has been my experience, however, that at a school like Princeton, institutional cultures, spaces, and policies need to play catch-up to authentically fulfill their declared commitments to openness and inclusivity. By way of background, in Princeton's undergraduate class of 2023 49.5% are American students of color, 24% are eligible for federal Pell Grants for low-income students, and 16% are first-generation college students (Princeton University Undergraduate Admissions, 2020). They are supported by one of the most generous financial aid programs in the country (Princeton University Undergraduate Admissions, 2021). Programs such as the Freshman Scholars Institute and the Scholars Institute Fellows Program provide first-generation and low-income students with a community and peer/faculty support. Princeton's residential colleges have a professor as head of college and a three-person professional advising staff, and each incoming first-year student has a faculty advisor attached to their residential college.

Despite such structures, a cadre of the "new majority" students regularly voice that they sense an undercurrent of alienation and isolation throughout their undergraduate experience. Some students report derogatory remarks referencing affirmative action or painful assumptions from professors. Furthermore, as students adjust to living away from home, the road can be bumpy. Early in the school year, students sometimes feel discomfort with their assigned roommates or hall-mates. Such lived experiences matter, and I use them to guide my student life programming.

As my residential college's DSL, I have the opportunity to stay connected, to make a larger institution feel smaller. This is especially important for those students experiencing "imposter syndrome," an insidious self-doubt that they do not belong in the Ivy League. In the summer of 2018, when I was the dedicated DSL for the Freshman Scholars Institute, I placed special emphasis on using my positionality to tamp down students' instinct to demonstrate a veneer of effortless perfection, encouraging them instead to avail themselves of a wide spectrum of resources and supports, including faculty.

I am particularly proud of one signature residential college program, the "zee group." *Zee* is a term of endearment for advisee: a first-year student. There are 12 zee groups in my residential college, and the college staff make sure that each group is diverse in gender, race, religion, home geography, socioeconomic background, and interests. Zee groups form a strong and enviable bond through programs (e.g., study breaks, discussion groups, dinners, and group activities). By the spring semester, students absolutely value and appreciate their zee group diversity.

During the semester, I reach out to students at specific times when I feel they might need to hear targeted messages. Through the "Live Well Be Well" program, I engage students on social–emotional learning: loneliness and homesickness during the first month of school or at Thanksgiving; managing stress during midterms; coping with rejection in the spring if they do not get an internship, social club invitation, or some other achievement.

Although I have a robust outreach strategy, I do not wait for students to come see me. I enjoy regularly attending their performances and athletic events. If they are sick or in crisis, I visit them in the hospital. Sometimes, we relax during a study break together or enjoy a one-on-one or small-group meal in the dining hall. My physical presence among students can be subtle or significant, but it is frequent. My approach is nuanced: Different students have different needs, barriers, and concerns.

ELEVATING EQUITY IN LIVING–LEARNING COMMUNITIES

Faculty Strategies for Engaging "New Majority" Students

Laura S. Dahl, Ethan Youngerman, Christopher J. Stipeck, and Matthew J. Mayhew

I t was a perfectly conceived program: a chance for students to have a casual conversation about the usefulness of office hours with two faculty members who lived in New York University (NYU) residence halls. The faculty members (one of whom is a coauthor of this chapter) knew where to get the best falafel in town, they created eye-catching posters, and they even came up with a funny yet serious title for the program: "Office Hours Are Literally for You." They also had both literature and personal experience that told them the need for this event was real: All over campus, students were not showing up to faculty office hours much, and first-generation students (those whose parents do not hold a 4-year baccalaureate degree) reported that they almost never attended—it wasn't something with which students whose families had never been to college were familiar. So, the faculty created this program because they knew they needed to decode this hidden part of the curriculum that can be valuable to student learning, career outcomes, and so much more.

The only problem? Despite being open to thousands of students who lived on campus, no one attended the very event meant to combat the problem of people not showing up to office hours. These faculty, cognizant of the insidious ways that institutions can perpetuate systemic inequalities, had created an event that would particularly benefit first-generation and other "new traditional students" (Knox & Henderson, 2010), but unlike Darleny Cepin, the author of our chapter's opening vignette, they hadn't figured out a way to reach these students so that they would actually take advantage of that benefit. Faced with piles of flashy handouts, the faculty members ate a lot of pita sandwiches and a lot of humble pie.

Interactions with faculty are crucial for several student outcomes, including critical thinking, leadership, personal development, and wellness (Mayhew et al., 2016). However, it is also crucial for faculty to understand the significant student demographic shifts of the past couple of decades. Institutions nationwide have made incomplete but genuine gains in increasing equitable access to higher education (Mayhew et al., 2016): White, male, 18- to 22-year-old students are no longer the majority populations on campuses. *New majority* and *new traditional* are both terms used to help convey (and, indeed, normalize) these demographic shifts (Eagan et al., 2016). We specifically define *new majority* as non-White, first-generation, transfer, veteran, or older than 22. If these populations are indeed the "new majority," it is important for faculty and staff to understand what works and what does not when engaging them in residential programs. This knowledge will not only help faculty engage with the actual students they encounter but will also help individual faculty in living–learning communities (LLCs) contribute to tackling systemic inequalities in higher education, a worthy goal that LLCs are particularly well-positioned to achieve.

In this chapter, we outline new directions for faculty–student engagement initiatives in LLCs that support non-White, first-generation, transfer, veteran, and older-than-22 students. We begin by defining who new majority students are and how demographics have changed. We then discuss how faculty are engaging with these students at different institutions and what works (and what does not). We use data from the Assessment of Collegiate Residential Environments and Outcomes (ACREO), a multi-institutional study of residential experiences and programs (Mayhew et al., 2019), to illustrate how these efforts have played out practically at three universities. We close the chapter with recommendations for faculty and staff.

The Changing Demographics of Higher Education

Higher education in the United States has seen both dramatic growth and tremendous demographic shifts since the mid-20th century (Eagan et al., 2016). Campuses are not as homogeneous as they once were, with fewer proportions of students who identify as White, male, Christian, and affluent; more than 50% of college students are non-White, first generation, transfer, veteran, or are older than 22. These populations constitute the new majority. In 1971, 90.1% of first-time, full-time, first-year students identified as White, a number that by 2015 had decreased to 57.6% (Eagan et al., 2016). In that time, the proportion of Asian (0.5%–10.0%), Black (7.0%–8.5%), Latino (0.4%–9.7%), and multiracial/ethnic (1.3%–12.9%) students increased, with most of the significant changes occurring since 2005. Students are also relying less on their families' financial resources to support their college attendance. The Cooperative Institutional Research Program (CIRP) Freshman Survey noted that 81.1% of students in 2015 indicated dependence on their families to pay for the first year of college, compared with 89.3% in 2001 (Eagan et al., 2016). This drop is even more significant for first-generation students (Higher Education Act of 1965 as amended through 2016, Pub. L. 111-39); in 2001, 80.3% of first-gen students relied on family financial support, compared with 65.5% in 2015.

Additionally, traditional-aged (i.e., age 18 years) first-time, full-time, new students are no longer the norm on campuses around the United States (MacDonald, 2018). It is increasingly common that students delay postsecondary enrollment, are financially independent, attend classes part time, work full time, have served in the armed forces, have dependents, have earned a nontraditional high school diploma, or have reentered a college program (National Center for Education Statistics, 2015, 2016). Finally, 65% of Black and 63% of American Indian/Alaska Native collegians are older than 22, and most older students are women (Cruse et al., 2018). In short, the "traditional" student is not the typical one anymore.

These shifting demographics have pushed campus administrators and postsecondary scholars to redefine a new majority of college students and to reconsider practices to ensure their success (Ross, 2016). Students from historically marginalized populations, for instance, continue to face hostile campus climates and microaggressions as they navigate collegiate life (Harper & Hurtado, 2007), which can contribute to lower retention and persistence rates (Johnson et al., 2014). First-generation students—many of whom experience these harsh environments—also tend to lack the cultural capital to navigate collegiate environments (Stipeck, 2019) and graduate at rates lower than their continuing-generation peers (DeAngelo et al., 2012). Financial barriers compound this outcome: Only 11% of low-income first-generation students earn a bachelor's degree within 6 years of enrollment (Pell Institute, 2011). In addition to these barriers, many new majority students must balance jobs, family, and school obligations (MacDonald, 2018). More than two thirds of new traditional students work in addition to attending classes, with 57% working at least 20 hours a week and 31% working full time (Institute for Women's Policy Research [IWPR], 2016). These extended hours can increase the time to degree completion, which decreases the probability that these students will graduate at all (Kuh et al., 2007). IWPR (2016) also noted that about one third of students with dependent children complete their degree program within 6 years of enrollment. All of this considered, traditional faculty and administrator efforts to engage students beyond the classroom (e.g., office hours, LLCs, student organizations) may not appeal to new majority students who have such limited time, familial obligations, and experience social barriers.

So, what role can faculty play in supporting the new majority and combating systemic inequities? Relatively little research has focused on the effects of student–faculty interactions for new majority students (Mayhew et al., 2016; Stipeck, 2019). Most of the extant scholarship focuses on classroom and instructional practices that assist students' transition into and through postsecondary education. Older students are less likely to live on campus compared with their peers (Choy, 2001), and they are more likely to attend a 2-year institution, where residential programs with faculty are less prevalent (Choy, 2001; Inkelas et al., 2008). However, contact with faculty in a residential learning community has shown to have a positive effect on student thriving (Eidum et al., 2020). More specifically, faculty interactions positively influence academic outcomes and persistence for new majority students (Kim & Sax, 2009), as long as the faculty consider the distinctive needs and experiences of this group of students.

Research on faculty engagement with students has examined interactions both within and beyond the classroom. Kim and Sax (2009), for example, found that course-related interaction with faculty was positively associated with cognitive development for Latinx students, Asian Americans, students of lower socioeconomic status, and first-generation students, with effect sizes around 0.11 SD for each of these groups (Mayhew et al., 2016).[1] However, engaging in activities outside the classroom has shown mixed effects depending on the outcome considered. Black students, for instance, experienced the most gains in self-development from working on faculty research projects compared with students in other racial or ethnic groups, whereas interacting with faculty at social events benefited the Latinx students' self-development more than other groups (Einarson & Clarkberg, 2010). Last, working on research and discussing career plans with faculty was more beneficial to self-reported intellectual gains for White and Asian American students compared to their Black or Latinx peers (Einarson & Clarkberg, 2010). Although it appears that different subgroups of college students benefit differently from their instructors, the cohesive theme shows that faculty interactions matter to student outcomes.

Turning to first-generation students more specifically, several studies (Kim & Sax, 2009; Longwell-Grice & Longwell-Grice, 2008; Padgett et al.,

2012) have noted that many first-generation students were more intimidated and less satisfied with their interactions with faculty than were continuing generation students. These feelings can negatively affect outcomes such as psychosocial well-being and need for cognition (i.e., "a student's desire to seek and engage in purposeful cognitive activities" as well as retention and persistence; Padgett et al., 2012, p. 249). In response to these issues of intimidation and challenges around asking for help, MacDonald (2018) outlined four strategies faculty should consider when working with new traditional students: early intervention, flexibility, differentiated instruction, and instructor support.

Flexibility is especially important, as are clear expectations for coursework, considering that new majority students are more likely to juggle personal, professional, and academic lives (Kuh et al., 2008). In addition, because older students enter classrooms with more life experiences and interest in the practical applications of academic material compared with younger students, faculty are advised to incorporate hands-on learning practices that emphasize future use (Vandenberg, 2012). For students who live on campus, Eidum et al. (2020) found that residential learning communities fostered increased levels of thriving for first-generation students.

Current Data From the Assessment of Collegiate Residential Environments and Outcomes

The ACREO project has collected data about students' experiences in residential programs every spring semester since 2015.[2] In 5 years of data collection, more than 133,000 students at 19 institutions across the United States participated in the survey, which measures campus experiences (including faculty interaction and level of support in the residential environment) and outcomes (e.g., academic confidence, intent to persist, and sense of belonging; see Mayhew et al., 2019). Results from the combined 2017, 2018, and 2019 administrations, which included responses from more than 15,500 students at 11 universities (see Mayhew et al., 2019, for data on respondent demographics), suggest that faculty interaction was beneficial for several academic and social outcomes for students, including career outcome expectations, integrative learning, campus engagement, and a sense of belonging. However, students from various racial and ethnic backgrounds were not homogenous in their responses to many of these items. White students reported higher average scores for academic confidence, academic major persistence intention, career outcome expectations, and integrative learning. In comparison, Asian American students reported consistently lower average scores on these outcomes than their peers. Black students, however, indicated the highest average scores on their academic confidence. In addition, first-generation students reported lower academic confidence and a sense of campus belonging than their continuing-generation peers, and transfer students indicated a lower sense of belonging than nontransfer students (Mayhew et al., 2019). These findings should not be surprising given the barriers that many first-generation and transfer students face as they navigate collegiate environments not necessarily designed for them (see Duran et al., 2020).

With this information in mind, we revisited the ACREO data set and conducted new analyses to better understand how new majority students engaged with faculty-in-residence. When asked if faculty live in their current residence hall, 43% of all survey respondents from the past 3 years indicated yes, 24% said no, and 33% said they did not know. We then asked students about the types of programs in which faculty affiliated with their residence halls planned, whether live-in or not. The results indicated that 41% of students with faculty-in-residence said that the faculty planned academic programs, 37% said they taught classes, and 67% said they planned social events. Of the 57% of students who did not have faculty-in-residence (or were not sure), 16% said affiliated faculty planned academic programs, 10% said affiliated faculty taught classes, and 25% said affiliated faculty planned social events.

The ACREO survey also asked students about the types and frequency of their interactions with faculty affiliated with their residence hall. Of all students in the sample, 51% said they discussed career plans and ambitions, 42% said they discussed personal problems or concerns, 41% said they visited informally about nonacademic issues, 39% said they discussed an assignment or reviewed content from class, and 35% said they either met for extra assistance regarding in-class content or attended office hours at least once during the academic year. These values, however, shift by demographic (see Table 1.1). For instance, Black students met more frequently with faculty-in-residence compared with their White peers. First-generation students also met with residential faculty more frequently than continuing-generation students; very similar results were found for Pell-eligible students, which is unsurprising given that 66% of the first-generation students in this sample also received financial aid in the form of federal grants.

The implications of the ACREO findings are profound for institutions that wish to support new majority students. As previous studies have noted (Eidum et al., 2020; Inkelas et al., 2018), affiliating faculty with residence halls benefits all students, and our data suggest it particularly benefits Black students and first-generation students, who met more often with affiliated faculty than White students and continuing-generation students. A crucial

TABLE 1.1
**Percentages of Students Who Interacted With Faculty Affiliated
With Their Residence Hall on a Weekly or Daily Basis**

Reason for visit	Black students	White students	First-generation students	Continuing-generation students	Pell-eligible students	Non-Pell-eligible students
Discussed career plans and ambitions at least once during the academic year	22%	11%	15%	11%	14%	11%
Discussed personal problems or concerns	18%	10%	13%	10%	12%	9%
Visited informally about nonacademic issues	16%	10%	12%	10%	11%	9%
Discussed an assignment or reviewed content from class	17%	10%	13%	9%	12%	10%
Met for extra assistance regarding in-class content	14%	7%	11%	8%	10%	8%
Attended office hours	12%	6%	9%	7%	9%	7%

takeaway from these results is that faculty need not live in the residence halls or teach connected courses (Eidum et al., 2020) to make an impact. It appears that one way to support new majority students in particular—on everything from career planning and classwork to personal issues—is simply to have faculty available and engaged with residence hall communities.

Move to Practice

In this section, we examine models for faculty engagement in residence life from three institutions that participated in ACREO: NYU, The Ohio State University (OSU), and Clemson University. Some institutions create communities where themes are explicitly tied to salient identities, such as race or transfer student status. Other initiatives demonstrate the influence on new majority students of LLCs, which, although heavily structured and faculty driven, are not designed specifically for any one group of students. Finally, several models suggest the role of faculty in creating mission-driven learning communities that explicitly connect college to careers for new majority students.

Research from the ACREO study has revealed that students in such programs had higher levels of non-course–related faculty interactions with nonresident faculty (Mayhew et al., 2017, 2019). Similar programs were also associated with students reporting more welcoming campus climates for all studied minoritized identities (race, worldview, gender, sexuality, and international students).

NYU has two main avenues for faculty participation in the residential environments: faculty affiliates and faculty fellows in residence (FFIRs). Faculty affiliates live off campus but are connected to a themed living–learning program known as Explorations. These communities' themes are not typically connected to courses but instead run the gamut of student interests, from comedy to social justice. Faculty members are either recruited on the basis of their area of expertise or university involvement (many of the recruits have expressed interest in collaborating with Residential Life and Housing Services), or are recommended by a student. Students apply for these communities and, if selected, live on the same floor. On the basis of the needs and interests of those on the floor, the staff, resident assistants, and faculty collaborate to plan monthly educational experiences and social outings related to the theme, but they have no other formal academic disciplinary relationship. Given the acculturation challenges that first-generation students face in transitioning to college, having faculty engagement in the residential setting that isn't predicated on the role as a professor of a particular class can reduce barriers for students to participate.

Similarly, at least one FFIR lives in every NYU residence hall on campus; again, there is no formal relationship between this role and the classroom. In many ways, FFIRs at NYU are encouraged to perform the role of a faculty member in general, as opposed to the discipline-specific role they play in their department; FFIRs are encouraged to program events that reveal varied interests other than their scholarly expertise. Again, this can lower barriers, especially for new majority students, who may find academic specialization, or even faculty in general, intimidating (Longwell-Grice & Longwell-Grice, 2008). Given the findings from ACREO we have noted, these faculty programs would appear to benefit new majority students even though they are open and geared to all students.

That said, there are several practices at NYU that specifically address new majority students. NYU has three Explorations floors whose theme is first-generation students (two are for first-year students, and the third is for upper-class students). Faculty members create programming for these communities meant to decode the academy. Giving first-generation students the opportunity to meet other students with similar backgrounds under the occasional guidance of a faculty member appears to be a successful practice (Whitley et al., 2018). NYU also runs an Explorations community primarily for international students; although the programs are slightly different, the emphasis on creating connections for new majority students both to peers and to support networks across the university is consistent.

NYU's Residential College is the most faculty-driven residential environment on NYU's campus; all students are connected to one of the faculty-led themed communities throughout their time in the "res college." Between the many faculty affiliate and FFIR events, students have a wide variety of options from community service to theater viewings. It is interesting that, in order to pass the no-credit course associated with living in the Residential College, students are required to attend a certain number of faculty-led programs, fostering extracurricular engagement. Although this strategy of required participation may feel at odds with long-held notions of extracurricular choice, it is a way to ensure that events reach all students, including new majority students, equitably. For instance, the "Office Hours Are Literally for You" program we described at the outset of this chapter was intended to encourage students to engage with other faculty. If that event had been required for, say, all first-year students, it might have encouraged new majority students to attend office hours at rates similar to other students.

OSU's Scholars Program offers different though equally compelling practices for engaging new majority students. Students in the Scholars Program select a residence from themed LLCs, most of which directly tie to OSU schools and majors (e.g., business scholars, engineering scholars, biological sciences scholars). Students in these LLCs enroll together in scholars seminars (somewhat akin to college 101 courses), and many have linked "clustered courses" (traditional academic classes either exclusively for program students or with sections reserved specifically for those students). Each LLC also has faculty-involved programming related to the academic theme. In short, participation in the OSU Scholars Program is highly structured, bridging curricular, cocurricular, and extracurricular experiences. The ACREO research suggests that students in similar programs have more positive experiences and outcomes, such as cocurricular engagement, academic confidence, discussing learning with peers, academic major persistence intention, and career attitudes, than nonparticipants (Mayhew et al., 2019). Although the literature shows that college environments are not always created to equitably benefit new majority students (Harper & Quaye, 2014), the ACREO research reveals that some programs can successfully influence new majority students at rates similar to those of other students even without being explicitly directed to new majority groups.

Clemson University runs LLCs specific to new majority student groups, including an LLC for first-year students of color, another for transfer students, and two for Reserve Officers' Training Corps (ROTC) students (in the Air Force and Army). The ACREO research suggests this emphasis is effective, perhaps because of the engagement it fosters. Students in similar programs who identified as other than White or other than cisgender men reported more inclusive campus climates in terms of race and gender at a statistically significant level (Mayhew et al., 2019). Perhaps relatedly, Clemson LLC students appear to have many opportunities to engage with faculty, both those in residence and otherwise: Although Clemson has eight faculty in residence, not all LLCs have a dedicated residential faculty member, but all have at least one academic campus partner.

Perhaps the most striking practice that has emerged from Clemson is the Call Me MiSTER program (Jones et al., 2019), which began in 2000 and has now expanded to more than 30 institutions. "MiSTER" stands for "mentors instructing students toward effective role models." The program recruits and trains Black male students to become teachers through a program that includes a living–learning component as a part of the model. As such, the program suggests the power of combining academic coursework, career training, cohorts for minoritized student groups, and residential education. Alongside the ROTC LLCs, Call Me MiSTER exemplifies the role faculty can play in mission-driven community building. Simply put, the ways faculty can engage with new majority students can be holistically woven into the academic community's raison d'être.

Implications

New majority students need extra support from colleges because their status as majority is new; historically underrepresented and minoritized student populations cannot be expected to thrive in institutions that have, for so long, been designed and run without them in mind. That said, faculty have many different avenues for creating meaningful, equitable communities and outcomes for all students, from designing LLCs for particular populations to foregrounding personal, professional, or academic interests. Wielded thoughtfully, these avenues can be part of how faculty can work within the LLC structure to counter systemic inequalities in higher education.

Faculty can help design and run LLCs for new majority student populations. If student outcomes are inequitable, an LLC could be seen as a kind of intervention. For example, Clemson's School of Education had concerns about potential barriers to success for their Black male population, so an LLC was developed and a program built around empowerment and not deficit. Finally, of course, faculty can take into consideration their own identities and interests. Roy Jones, the founder of Call Me MiSTER, is both a Black man and an expert in teacher education. We hasten to add that our research does not examine faculty identity or characteristics. Although such future research would be valuable, we believe that all professors who are invested in helping students connect their academic and campus lives are a boon to the student experience.

Indeed, the NYU models suggest that faculty engagement with new majority students can be centered on student—faculty shared interests as much as faculty members' professional expertise. The FFIR programs that target whole buildings suggest that even student interests need not be the binding force for a community to benefit from faculty involvement. The faculty integration into multiple aspects of the residential experience ultimately amplifies the value behind building student—faculty relationships. The increased faculty presence creates a culture that shows faculty are, in fact, approachable and invested in the student experience. Perceived barriers to and intimidation by faculty could be subsequently dismantled. In addition, the ACREO results suggest that some of these finer distinctions about how faculty-run programs are organized may fade away in the bigger picture: Faculty affiliation with a residence hall, in some form or other, will benefit all students and new majority students in particular.

That said, faculty engagement fostered by LLCs attached to specific academic courses and majors does appear to be beneficial. Simply put, faculty interactions that are attached to curricular and even career-related programs can powerfully address new majority students. An LLC that is designed to address a systemic inequity can give a larger, societal purpose to the individual, holistic goals of student support.

Next Steps

Faculty and staff who have LLCs on their campuses should investigate how they might wield these powerful tools to support new majority students in particular. A first step is surely a targeted assessment plan. Although all of the present authors are involved with a quantitative project (ACREO), we encourage varied assessment methods. Focus groups, in particular those that include students who are not participating in existing LLCs, offer a valuable way to learn about student experiences. Similarly, purposeful collaboration with new majority-facing campus groups can yield striking insights; for example, the Black Student Union at NYU recently articulated a need for themed housing for Black students. Faculty and staff may also focus on faculty partner recruitment (see the recommendations in chapter 2, this volume).

Conclusion

The semester after the unsuccessful office hours event, one of the FFIRs organized a similar event in their residence hall, open to only their hall's residents (instead of to all on-campus students). It was additionally targeted to students who were beginning their first year at college in the spring semester. In other words, the event was tailored to a particular new majority student population, within a particular community, with particular needs. The faculty involved were nervous about a repeat (non-) performance; however, more than 40 students filled a basement lounge on a winter Sunday, eager to talk through how to take advantage of office hours.

The shifts in campus demographics that have resulted in a new majority mandate similar shifts in how faculty engage with students outside the classroom. Research from ACREO suggests that a simple commitment to having faculty affiliated with residence halls creates a more supportive environment for all students, and for Black and first-generation students in particular. However, faculty can commit to even more unique communities that speak to even more specific needs. In fact, using Call Me MiSTER as a model, faculty may want to look at systemic inequities in their fields of expertise and then imagine communities whose mission is to tackle those inequities. Institutions currently benefit old majority students more than new majority students, but faculty who connect with students outside the classroom provide a powerful corrective. Equity and inclusion can often sound like abstract and daunting goals; the fight for a just higher education landscape can feel long. However, achieving these goals for new majority students can start with a very concrete, very simple step: engaging faculty in the fight.

Notes

1. Effect sizes measure the practical difference found between two groups by attempting to quantify the magnitude of such difference using standard deviation (*SD*) as the unit of measurement. Cohen (1988) suggested that effect size measures greater than 0.8 be classified as large, values between 0.5 and 0.8 as medium, values between 0.2 and 0.5 as small, and values less than 0.2 as trivial.

2. From 2015 to 2017, ACREO was administered as the Study of Integrated Living Learning Programs. This project is a continuation of the National Study of Living Learning Programs, which was administered under the direction of Karen Inkelas and Aaron Brower in 2004 and 2007 (see Inkelas et al., 2008).

References

Choy, S. P. (2001). *Students whose parents did not go to college: Postsecondary access, persistence, and attainments* (NCES 2001-126). National Center for Education Statistics, U.S. Department of Education.

Cohen, J. (1988). *Statistical power analysis for the behavioral sciences* (2nd ed.). Erlbaum.

Cruse, L. R., Eckerson, E., & Gault, B. (2018, February). *Understanding the new college majority: The demographic and financial characteristics of independent students and their postsecondary outcomes.* Institute for Women's Policy Research. https://iwpr.org/wp-content/uploads/2020/10/C462_Understanding-the-New-College-Majority_final.pdf

DeAngelo, L., Franke, R., Hurtado, S., Pryor, J. H., & Tran, S. (2012). *Completing college: Assessing graduation rates at four-year institutions.* Higher Education Research Institute, University of California, Los Angeles.

Duran, A. A., Dahl, L. S., Stipeck, C., & Mayhew, M. J. (2020). Critical perspectives on students' sense of belonging: A quantitative analysis of race, generation status, and collegiate environments. *Journal of College Student Development, 61*(2), 133–153. https://doi.org/10.1353/csd.2020.0014

Eagan, M. K., Stolzenberg, E. B., Ramirez, J. J., Aragon, M. C., Suchard, M. R., & Rios-Aguilar, C. (2016). *The American freshman: Fifty-year trends, 1966–2015.* Higher Education Research Institute, University of California, Los Angeles. https://www.heri.ucla.edu/monographs/50YearTrendsMonograph2016.pdf

Eidum, J., Lomicka, L., Chiang, W., Endick, G., & Stratton, J. (2020). Thriving in residential learning communities. *Learning Communities Research and Practice, 8*(1), Article 7. https://washingtoncenter.evergreen.edu/lcrpjournal/vol8/iss1/7

Einarson, M. K., & Clarkberg, M. E. (2010). Race differences in the impact of students' out-of-class interactions with faculty. *Journal of the Professoriate, 3*(2), 101–136.

Harper, S. R., & Hurtado, S. (2007). Nine themes in campus racial climates and implications for institutional transformation. In S. R. Harper & L. D. Patton (Eds.), *Responding to the Realities of Race on Campus* (New Directions for Student Services, no. 120, pp. 7–24). Wiley.

Harper, S. R., & Quaye, S. J. (Eds.). (2014). Making engagement equitable for students in U.S. higher education. In *Student engagement in higher education: Theoretical perspectives and practical approaches for diverse populations* (2nd ed., pp. 1–14). Taylor & Francis.

Higher Education Act of 1965, Part 1: General Higher Education Programs (as amended through P.L. 111-39, enacted December 23, 2016).

Inkelas, K. K., Jessup-Anger, J. E., Benjamin, M., & Wawrzynski, M. R. (2018). *Living learning communities that work: A research-based model for design, delivery, and assessment.* Stylus.

Inkelas, K. K., Szelényi, K., Soldner, M., Brower, A. M., Survey Sciences Group LLC, & 2006–2008 Graduate Assistants at the University of Maryland. (2008). *National study of living–learning programs: 2007 report of findings.* https://drum .lib.umd.edu/bitstream/handle/1903/8392/2007%20NSLLP%20Final%20 Report.pdf?sequence=1&isAllowed=y

Institute for Women's Policy Research. (2016). Institute for Women's Policy Research (IWPR) analysis of data from the U.S. Department of Education, National Center for Education Statistics, *2011–12 National Postsecondary Student Aid Study* (NPSAS:12).

Johnson, D. R., Wasserman, T. H., Yildirim, N., & Yonai, B. A. (2014). Examining the effects of stress and campus climate on the persistence of students of color and white students: An application of Bean and Eaton's psychological model of retention. *Research in Higher Education, 55*(1), 75–110. https://doi.org/10.1007/ s11162-013-9304-9

Jones, R., Holton, W., & Joseph, M. (2019). Call Me MiSTER: A Black male grow your own program. *Teacher Education Quarterly, 46*(1), 55–68. https://www .jstor.org/stable/10.2307/26558182

Kim, Y. K., & Sax, L. J. (2009). Student–faculty interaction in research universities: Differences by student gender, race, social class, and first-generation status. *Research in Higher Education, 50*(5), 437–459. https://doi.org/10.1007/s11162- 009-9127-x

Knox, M. J., & Henderson, B. D. (2010). Nontraditional is the new traditional: Understanding today's college student. In J. A. Ward-Roof (Ed.), *Designing successful transitions: A guide for orienting students to college* (Monograph No. 13, 3rd ed., pp. 11–28). National Resource Center for the First-Year Experience and Students in Transition, University of South Carolina.

Kuh, G. D., Cruce, T. M., Shoup, R., Kinzie, J., & Gonyea, R. M. (2008). Unmasking the effects of student engagement on first-year college grades and persistence. *The Journal of Higher Education, 79*(5), 540–563. https://doi.org/10 .1080/00221546.2008.11772116

Kuh, G. D., Kinzie, J., Cruce, T., Shoup, R., & Gonyea, R. M. (2007). *Connecting the dots: Multi-faceted analyses of the relationships between student engagement results from the NSSE, and the institutional practices and conditions that foster student success.* Center for Postsecondary Research, Indiana University. https://hdl.handle .net/2022/23684

Longwell-Grice, R., & Longwell-Grice, H. (2008). Testing Tinto: How do retention theories work for first-generation, working-class students? *Journal of College Student Retention, 9*(4), 407–420. https://doi.org/10.2190/CS.9.4.a

MacDonald, K. (2018). A review of the literature: The needs of nontraditional students in postsecondary education. *Strategic Enrollment Management Quarterly, 5*(4), 159–164. https://doi.org/10.1002/sem3.20115

Mayhew, M. J., Dahl, L. S., & Hooten, Z. (2019). *2019 annual report: Assessment of collegiate residential environments & outcomes.* https://www.acreosurvey.org/s/2019-ACREO-Report.pdf

Mayhew, M. J., Dahl, L. S., Hooten, Z. J., Duran, A. A., Stipeck, C., & Youngerman, E. (2017). *2017 annual report: Assessment of collegiate residential environments and outcomes annual report.* https://acreosurvey.org/s/2017-SILLP-Annual-Report.pdf

Mayhew, M. J., Rockenbach, A. N., Bowman, N. A., Seifert, T. A., & Wolniak, G. C. (2016). *How college affects students: 21st century evidence that higher education works.* Jossey-Bass.

National Center for Education Statistics. (2015, September). *Demographic and enrollment characteristics of nontraditional undergraduates: 2011–12.* U.S. Department of Education.

National Center for Education Statistics. (2016). Postsecondary education. In *Digest of education statistics: 2014.* U.S. Department of Education. https://nces.ed.gov/programs/digest/d14/ch_3.asp

Padgett, R. D., Johnson, M. P., & Pascarella, E. T. (2012). First-generation undergraduate students and the impacts of the first year of college: Additional evidence. *Journal of College Student Development, 53*(2), 243–266. https://doi.org/10.1353/csd.2012.0032

Pell Institute. (2011). *6-year degree attainment rates for students enrolled in a postsecondary institution.* http://www.pellinstitute.org/downloads/fact_sheets-6-Year_DAR_for_Students_Post-Secondary_Institution_121411.pdf

Princeton University Undergraduate Admissions. (2020). *Admission statistics.* https://admission.princeton.edu/how-apply/admission-statistics

Princeton University Undergraduate Admissions. (2021). *Cost & aid.* https://admission.princeton.edu/cost-aid

Ross, K. A. (2016). *Breakthrough strategies: Classroom-based practices to support new majority college students.* Harvard Education Press.

Stipeck, C. J. (2019). *Influences of living–learning programs on persistence and engagement of first-year, first-generation students* [Unpublished doctoral dissertation]. New York University.

Vandenberg, L. (2012, May). *Facilitating adult learning: How to teach so people learn.* Michigan State University. https://www.canr.msu.edu/od/uploads/files/PD/Facilitating_Adult_Learning.pdf

Whitley, S., Benson, G., & Wesaw, A. (2018). *First-generation student success: A landscape of analysis of programs and services at four-year institutions.* NASPA—Student Affairs Administrators in Higher Education. https://firstgen.naspa.org/2018-Landscape-Analysis

VIGNETTE

Saying "Yes"

Timothy D. Baird

Years before I applied to lead the new creativity and innovation district living–learning community (LLC), Virginia Tech's fourth residential college, several aspects of the university's culture and infrastructure supported my intrinsic motivation to teach well and understand student learning. Not only did the decision to lead the community represent a return to a culture and environment that affected me in a tremendously positive way in my own education, but also the design and goals of the program aligned with my personal interests to better serve students and their learning—and practice my own work with a greater emphasis on compassion, flexibility, and creativity.

My journey to LLC leadership began my first semester as an assistant professor. Through a well-staffed, comprehensive course design workshop, I gained confidence and learned strategies to be creative and take chances in my early classes. Then, formal and informal encounters with colleagues in the university's School of Education nudged me to collect and analyze data on a radical assignment I created to promote intrinsic motivation. Publishing this work moved me further down a path of greater curiosity about students' lives and learning.

My efforts were recognized by the university's communications team, and they wrote stories about my work with students that drew the interest and support of others, including deans, assistant vice presidents, institute directors, and teachers. This recognition boosted my confidence and nudged me further. I learned that although it can be easy to think that you either have the desire to engage students, or that you do not, this skill can be cultivated through practice, time, and support.

From these early experiences, I was given new opportunities to participate in education grant proposals and campus-wide general education reform. These opportunities allowed me to gather with diverse, committed faculty from across campus for sustained, engaging discussions about what matters to students. I was also invigorated by the university's investments in SCALE-UP classrooms (student-centered active learning environment with upside-down pedagogies), which gave my colleagues and me new tools to engage students spatially and otherwise.

My experiences grew out of a university culture that nurtures interdisciplinarity, increases path crossing, and facilitates creative collisions. A culture of professional mentorship helped channel these collisions toward meaningful outcomes. In this spirit, an early and wise mentor of mine contradicted the advice new faculty commonly receive, saying, "You need to learn how to say 'yes'!"

The decision to say "yes" to being the faculty principal for an LLC is among the most exciting decisions I have made in my academic career. I want to practice communicating more widely and with greater empathy in my life and career, and the foundational and cherished memories of my liberal arts education, and the faculty who engaged me in and out of the classroom, compel me. Also, my wife and I have young children and feel that this rare experience will be radiant for them. In fact, I have observed this through warm engagements with other residential college families. In the end, we signed up because we thought we'd have an adventure—one like no other.

2

CAMPUS CULTURES THAT ATTRACT AND SUSTAIN FACULTY LEADERSHIP IN LIVING–LEARNING COMMUNITIES

Frank Shuskok Jr. and C.L. Bohannon

The vignette for this chapter illustrates how an institutional commitment to teaching and experiential learning, when combined with residential environments that are framed in a visionary manner, can entice those faculty committed to student praxis and learning to engage with students in a new, holistic manner. There are many faculty members who, like Tim, ask questions such as How can I help students understand why I'm so passionate about my discipline? How do I find ways for students to apply the material they are learning in class? How can I connect with students in a more holistic manner? For many faculty, there is no greater incentive for engagement than seeing practical ways to accomplish these things. In turn, it is crucial for institutions to provide ample and effective incentivization to promote continued engagement and a sustainable growth outcome for living–learning communities (LLCs) over time.

The Vision of This Chapter

In this chapter, Frank Shushok, a senior administrator who has championed faculty engagement, will reflect on the culture-changing processes at two different universities that have embraced living–learning programs. C.L. Bohannon, an associate professor of landscape architecture and faculty principal in the Leadership and Social Change Residential College at Virginia

Tech, offers personal reflections on and practical insights into fostering an institutional culture that prioritizes the educational potential of living–learning programs and incentivizes faculty to explore and embrace this new venue for teaching and learning. Together, the stories will help frame how campus partners can attract and sustain faculty leadership in LLCs.

With a focus on solution-based thinking and practicality, we argue that engaging faculty in this effort requires institutions to: (a) identify connections between academic programs and faculty interests with programmatic opportunities in the residential environment, (b) broaden reward systems to bolster faculty and academic program participation, (c) celebrate and recognize faculty for teaching in an experiential and integrated format, and (d) build and sustain structures that strengthen a sense of community among student affairs and faculty colleagues committed to academic and student life integration.

Literature Review

For LLCs to find success, sustainability, and acceptance in the university landscape, institutions must embrace a holistic learning mindset that positions the residential experience as an important educational environment (Shushok et al., 2011). Literature has suggested that although faculty and student affairs administrators may in fact have a common goal surrounding LLCs, it is crucial from an administrative perspective to approach faculty as partners in a community's development, curricular enhancement, and programming (Jessup-Anger et al., 2011). Although substantive faculty engagement in LLCs is encouraging, institutional practices often prohibit faculty leadership in this sphere; therefore, institutional leaders who champion LLCs need to understand traditional faculty roles and rewards, along with faculty needs, pressures, time constraints, and quality of life, to best identify challenges to and opportunities for engaging faculty to support the potential success of growing and sustaining LLCs.

Traditional Faculty Roles and Rewards

As colleges and universities have responded to a changing and complex higher education landscape, pressures on faculty have increased monumentally, with the literature showing an evolution from the model of teaching to encompass research, scholarship, service to the community within the university, and upholding of ideals within all three areas (Boyer, 1990). Although administrators may easily see the positive benefits students receive from living and learning in an LLC, we must ask how faculty can remain engaged, appropriately incentivized, and nurtured by the community. Tenure and other traditional faculty reward systems heavily value research and teaching, and tenure committees, departments, and faculty may not perceive involvement in LLC programming as a scholarly pursuit compared with these other factors. This discerned lack of incentives from a faculty perspective is especially true if they feel continuously called on for acts of service with lesser perceived advantages (Golde & Pribbenow, 2000; Inkelas et al., 2018). As Inkelas et al. (2018) cautioned, "Conducting research and teaching are fundamental and time-consuming aspects of [faculty] work" (p. 34). In a study of first-year faculty involved in a residential college, participants reported the tension of being pulled in many directions (Jessup-Anger et al., 2011) as well as balancing the strain of expectations on multiple levels.

Challenges to Incentivizing Faculty

In addition to competing priorities, faculty involved with LLCs may feel underresourced when there is a lack of collaboration between student life administration and faculty. In some instances, this lack of discourse may lead to a poor understanding about how student affairs leaders can assist in alleviating these pressures (Jessup-Anger et al., 2011). As Magolda (2005) argued, the collaboration between faculty and student affairs may be seen as a "managerial" partnership—focusing on roles and structures—rather than a moral one, which is built on questions such as "'Will the creation of this partnership be good for students and partners[?]' and 'How does collaboration fit with the partners' teaching and learning beliefs?'" (p. 17). If faculty and student affairs administrators do not ask themselves, and each other, these kinds of questions and reach an understanding, rifts may form and undermine collaboration.

Magolda (2005) emphasized the differences in philosophy toward students and learning between student affairs administrators and faculty as follows:

> Faculty generally coalesce around core values such as the generation and dissemination of knowledge; autonomy rooted in academic freedom; and collegiality. Student Affairs professionals generally coalesce around core values such as tending to students' multiple needs, respecting differences, developing citizen-leaders, and increasing students' self-awareness and self-direction. (p. 20)

This difference in praxis can certainly be more of a hindrance than a catalyst to developing holistic LLC programming.

Similarly, Inkelas et al. (2018) argued that many student affairs professionals are called to support students, foster community, and facilitate their personal growth beyond the traditional convention of the classroom, but those concepts may not necessarily align with the needs and philosophies of academic departments and faculty affairs. This difference in philosophy can cause tension, as the authors noted: "Because faculty may not be rewarded for their work in an LLC in the same way student affairs professionals are, it can be enticing for student affairs professionals to 'go it alone'" (p. 35). Partners must recognize that the values they bring to the work may be different, but no less important, and are unequivocally equal in value to creating a successful outcome.

Ways to Reward and Incentivize Faculty in LLCs

Regardless of the differences between faculty and student affairs, not all faculty perceive unconventional interactions—beyond the three chief constructs of research, teaching, and university commitments (fellowships, grants, organizations, etc.)—as something that requires outside incentives. One study found that faculty who seek relationships with students beyond common convention do so not because of university-given compensation but because of an intrinsic desire to make a meaningful difference (Einarson & Clarkberg, 2004). Golde and Pribbenow (2000) discovered that many faculty involved in LLC programs benefited from stronger connections with students and a deeper understanding of the pressures and anonymity surrounding student life at large-scale universities. This insight influenced their classroom teaching and involvement in an interdisciplinary network of committed colleagues, and it helped faculty feel more connected to the institution's broader mission.

Similarly, the faculty-in-residence development model created by Sriram et al. (2011) showed that, by being immersed in the life of students from a residential perspective, faculty were able to renew their commitment to learning, refresh their teaching philosophy, and find meaningful relationships beyond the context of the classroom. They also found personal benefits, including improvements to their family life and parenting. If LLCs can be structured in such a way as to foster positive relationships in addition to providing meaningful incentives to faculty, a symbiotic relationship among the university, the faculty, and the students can be achieved.

Incentivizing Faculty Engagement: Personal Reflections and Practical Strategies

As we began discussing what we have learned about incentivizing faculty to engage in LLCs, we could not help but first reflect on how our own residential experiences as undergraduates have influenced our commitment to building LLCs on our campus. Recognizing challenges that traditional faculty roles and rewards present to faculty engagement in LLCs, we offer an alternative vision of university campus culture—a culture that attracts and sustains faculty engagement. In the next section, we offer personal reflections that come from our own experiences engaging with LLCs. Moreover, we offer contrasting perspectives, with Frank describing his experiences as a student, faculty member, and administrator, and C.L. describing his leadership as a faculty principal to an LLC.

Frank had an uninspiring residential experience—one that almost derailed his educational journey. Resident advisors' roles emphasized policy enforcement, educational integration was nonexistent, and facilities were utilitarian at best. Like other first-year students, he spent the vast majority of his time in his residence hall—but the "university experience" was nowhere to be found. That was something students were expected to go out and find. Some students had the agency to do so, but he was not yet one of them. He felt isolated and disconnected from the campus enterprise.

C.L. recalls his undergraduate experience as positive and life changing, and his time at the University of Arkansas at Fayetteville set him on his current career path as a landscape architect. Reflecting back on this time allows him to see what he did not know he was missing. For the first 2 years of his undergraduate experience, his academic studies were disconnected from his life in his residence hall. He and his fellow students had hall hangouts and get-to-know-you activities, but there was little programming that sought to bridge or contextualize what he was learning as a student in landscape architecture to the cocurricular events in the residence halls.

These memories and missed opportunities motivated each of us professionally. Together, we have learned that many faculty members share our enthusiasm for the transformational potential of living–learning programs, in spite of the common retort Frank heard from colleagues in 2001 when he first began to explore faculty leadership in Baylor: "Good luck getting faculty to be involved in that."

Our personal experiences reflect how individual and institutional mindsets, or existing systems of belief regarding residential life, are either among the greatest motivators or are the biggest barriers to "what can be" when it comes to faculty leadership in LLCs. In the "Tale of Three Campuses," Shushok et al. (2011) highlighted three predominant mindsets that quietly conspire to shape a campus culture. These include a *sleep and eat model*, in which students' academic and residential experiences are viewed as distinctly separate; a *market model*, in which residential facilities are designed to entice students with amenities; and a *learning model*, in which the residential experience is viewed as a key part of students' holistic education. Shushok et al. (2011) argued that

> residence halls are powerful vehicles for facilitating student learning, but our theories about residential life—both personally and institutionally—have a dramatic influence on what facilities we build, who we assign to live there, and how we enact day-to-day operations. (p. 14)

For institutions with leaders operating from "sleep and eat" or "market model" mindsets, it is important to present research and evidence that demonstrates ways that living–learning programs enhance institutional learning objectives while also looking for opportunities to form faculty–student affairs partnerships and therefore create a tangible exemplar of a holistic learning approach.

When Frank arrived at Baylor in the early 2000s, the university was able to successfully shift the vision from a sleep-and-eat mindset to a live-and-learn one while resisting the emerging market model that champions amenities above all else. The progress began simply with an invitation to reimagine traditional dorms as integrated LLCs with the potential to become powerful vehicles for delivering cherished educational aims. The initial discernible shift happened in partnership with the dean for the School of Engineering and Computer Science, with whom Frank and his colleagues worked hand in hand to design, launch, and study the outcomes of Baylor's first living–learning program. Along the way, they decided to test the idea of a live-in faculty leader to serve as the intellectual inspiration for the community. While skeptics asked "What faculty would live in a residence hall?," the first person selected was a distinguished professor and associate dean. By finding committed partners, working collaboratively on designing the experience, and embracing a collective new vision to shape the residential experience, they were able to set in motion the beginning of a progressive paradigm for residence life. Because of the experiment's undeniable success, other academic units and faculty members became interested in championing additional LLCs. Other faculty were inspired by the example of their colleague living among students, integrating academic and student life, remaining a committed scholar, and having fun during the experience. By 2009, just 8 years later, a dozen tenured faculty members were interviewed for every new faculty-in-residence position. By the time Baylor's 10-year strategic plan concluded in 2012, there were 10 thriving living–learning programs, two residential colleges, 10 faculty-in residence and 60 faculty partners involved regularly in the daily activities of residential life (Hankins & Schmeltekopf, 2007).

Frank left Baylor in 2009 when he was offered a position at Virginia Tech, a quintessential land-grant university. He wondered whether a large, public research university housing 10,000 students could be transformed by LLCs, residential colleges, and faculty-in-residence programs. He quickly realized that the faculty at Virginia Tech, just like those at Baylor, are deeply committed to students and their learning but were confined by a traditional model of residential life. In addition, student affairs staff had not yet vigorously extended the invitation to faculty to view residence halls as tools for delivering curricular aims or academic life.

Now, a decade later, there are 10 flourishing LLCs, four faculty-in-residence, and three residential colleges. The recent university strategic plan includes a goal of having two-thirds of all residential spaces occupied by students participating in living–learning programs. Academic–student life integration in the residence halls represents an institutional value and prioritized delivery system for facilitating the kind of education Virginia Tech values. Virginia Tech has plans to open a new creativity-and-innovation LLC to facilitate student and faculty collaboration at the intersection of design, technology, and the visual and performing arts. Faculty from across the university have been intimately involved in the design of the community, further incentivizing leadership and engagement. Like Baylor, Virginia Tech needed to offer an invitation to view residence halls differently, secure an early adopter as a partner for creating an exemplar, and undertake a commitment to measure the effectiveness of these efforts.

Based on our experiences, we offer several best practice strategies: determining pragmatic links between faculty interests and LLC programing, increasing participation through reward systems, designing tangible incentive programs, offering evaluation, incorporating LLC service as an integral part of the tenure process, celebrating experiential learning, and creating sustainable community structure. With thoughtful integration and prudent planning, these strategies can be implemented and designed to enhance the experience of students and staff in many different types of institutions.

Identify Connections Between Academic Programs and/or Faculty Interests

A frequent misstep in well-intended efforts to integrate academic units in cocurricular campus life is the promotion of activities that create an "in addition to" pattern of work for faculty. Although the goodwill of faculty may solicit an initial yes, these efforts are rarely sustainable and can become a disincentive for future engagement. Disincentives include inviting faculty to speak on subjects about which they are not passionate, or soliciting faculty to partner in efforts that are outside the scope of their teaching domain, intellectual interests, or research agenda.

As a practical example, a residence life program may believe that faculty engagement with students in residence hall environments is important—as is teaching time-management skills as part of the transition from high school to college. In response, residence life administrators may encourage resident assistants to invite faculty to come speak to students about this subject. A student-centered faculty member may accept such an assignment, and invest time developing a presentation about a topic in which they may have little interest or expertise and from which they gain little energy. This assignment comes "in addition to" all of the other faculty member's duties. If the activity is not motivating to the faculty member, the decision to decline a next invitation is likely.

In contrast, asking faculty to come to the residential space and share their research with students, or information about careers students might pursue when studying in their department, enables faculty to talk about their life's work or passion as well as potentially recruit students to take classes or pursue a major or minor in their academic unit. The opportunity to share ideas and passion may spark a new idea for the faculty member, asking: "Could we develop a living–learning program that could be beneficial for students, for my department, and for the common good?"

By gaining clarity about individual goals of faculty and the academic units in which they operate, the designers of LLCs connect programmatic efforts with the energy and reward systems in which partners operate. In collaboration with living–learning efforts, faculty are more likely to advance and strengthen efforts that are already important for success rather than divert energy toward something "in addition to" a previously existing motivation.

C.L. was introduced and drawn to LLCs this way. In 2016, he was invited to give a presentation about his research as part of a faculty lecture series. Participating in this lecture series was an opportunity for him to experience how curricular and cocurricular goals could come together in the LLC environment. The space was specifically and intentionally designed for students and faculty to share ideas and envision new ways of working together. The students represented majors from across campus, and they were curious and engaged in a way that was different from his typical settings and fieldwork experiences with students. The following semester he received an email that announced the start of a new residential college that would focus on leadership and social change, and he immediately knew that he wanted to apply for the position.

Since his first faculty appointment at Florida A&M 10 years earlier, C.L. had ruminated on questions centered around working with communities on social justice issues, including food security and access to green space. When he began a new position at Virginia Tech in 2014 as an assistant professor in the landscape architecture program, one of the agreements of his appointment within the department centered on establishing community-engaged design pedagogy in the program. When he learned about Virginia Tech's commitment to experiential learning and the role of living–learning programs, signing on as a faculty principal was a natural extension of his own academic interests and his department's strategic goals and thus an excellent example of designing LLCs to fulfill not only the needs, but also the passions, of faculty.

His enthusiasm for the opportunity was based on three key motivators. First, he wanted to work with students from across the university to cultivate their understanding of the interconnectedness of societal problems and create programming with students that empowered them to be inclusive, equitable, and sustainable leaders for social change. Second, he sought to develop programming in congruence with his beliefs about innovative and interdisciplinary education, weaving community engagement into a model that builds leadership skills and promotes social change through action. Third, this programming fits well into his existing research that develops holistic approaches that intervene on contemporary social, environmental, and spatial inequalities. Teaching and research that bring together everyday practices of justice and social change are not only about identifying injustices but are also intentionally designed to prepare students with the necessary tools to deal with complex issues at multiple scales and across disciplines.

By facilitating roles and positions for faculty within their area of expertise, their specific focus, and their personal interests, institutions will be better able to serve the needs of faculty while allowing for growth, development, and an enhancement of disciplinary experience for both students and staff.

Broaden Reward Systems to Bolster Faculty and Academic Program Participation

Even when LLCs advance strategic initiatives of faculty, the structures and policies of the institution must be adapted to recognize and reward these efforts. For example, teaching, and the way faculty are acknowledged for doing it, is conceived around credit hours, grades, and the physical classroom environment. Leaders on our campus ask an important question as a result: Can traditional conceptions of teaching be expanded to include designing and leading a cocurricular environment such as a living–learning program? An affirmative answer requires policies and structures that allow these environments to count as teaching. If there is no structure that endorses this alternative format, the incentive for leading one is negated.

Offer Course-Load Reductions and Annual Stipends for Faculty and Departments

At Virginia Tech, we have invested heavily in the creation of faculty-led residential colleges. Selected tenured and tenure-track faculty champion robust interdisciplinary learning environments that facilitate intellectual discourse, student exploration, faculty–student engagement, and hands-on learning. Designing and stewarding these environments is a time-consuming but incredibly important commitment. As part of the selection process, the supporting college and department also make a commitment to the LLC by agreeing to substitute the assignment for an annual course-load reduction. In addition to the faculty member receiving housing and an annual administrative stipend, the host department receives an annual stipend that can be used to backfill the faculty member's teaching assignment. In some cases, selected faculty do not want to reduce their course load and may instead opt to use the departmental stipend to hire a graduate student to help with teaching or research projects.

Provide Faculty Evaluations for Teaching in an LLC

In traditional classroom environments, faculty are evaluated for their teaching, and a similar process had to be developed to assess faculty success in teaching in the alternative format of a living–learning program. A carefully conceived process was developed that includes student feedback, evaluation of learning outcomes, and pedagogical practices; all findings are reported to the department chair, college dean, and provost's office. Faculty also document their work in a residential college or LLC as part of their "faculty activity report," which allows for their work with students outside of their tenure/home department to be evaluated for promotion purposes.

Understanding LLC Participation as "Teaching" in Addition to "Service" in the Tenure Process

While participation in LLC activities was originally understood as "service" in the tenure and promotion process, the campus community is adapting to acknowledge this work as not only service, but also as teaching. Since our first faculty member in residence was selected in the College of Liberal Arts and

Human Sciences, the program has grown to include scholars in the College of Engineering, the College of Agriculture and Life Sciences, the College of Natural Resources and Environment, and the College of Architecture and Urban Studies. Over a decade, awareness and commitment to these alternative forms of teaching have become more valued, understood, and embraced as part of the academic culture.

C.L. became the faculty principal of the leadership and social change LLC when he was still an assistant professor. Although his role in the community was naturally connected to his existing work as a scholar, it was paramount for him to be creative and clear in the ways his role resonated with his existing research, teaching, and service agendas. The integration of his teaching, research, and faculty principal role was particularly important as he was coming up for tenure because of the time commitment it takes to be an effective leader of a living–learning program. As a way to attract more faculty into in-residence roles, it is critical for institutions to acknowledge and value faculty work in LLCs that contributes to their teaching and research portfolios.

Recognize and Celebrate Faculty for "Teaching" in an Experiential and Integrated Format

For many faculty members, a powerful incentive for engagement in cocurricular life is evidence that their contributions are impactful on students and their learning. Sharing stories and recognizing faculty for their work through multiple communication platforms (university news releases, social media, videos, and public appearances) serves multiple purposes. Sharing and recognition reinforces a culture of what faculty leadership in residential environments looks like, validates for faculty that their contributions are seen and noticed, and, most important, offers evidence for the ways living–learning programs are advancing the espoused mission of the university.

Not only do we tell stories about faculty, but we also ask faculty to share their own stories. In doing so, other faculty begin to envision themselves pursuing the same kinds of engagement as their colleagues. For example, each time we select a faculty member for a live-in role as principal, we create a news release with university relations to highlight the faculty member, their family, their passions, and the residential college. We also recognize faculty at semester receptions and annual awards events. Senior administration, departmental leadership, and faculty colleagues are invited to be part of the celebrations. At these events, students share how they have been influenced by these faculty, and faculty share how their pedagogy has been transformed by their work in LLCs. The president, provost, and other leaders highlight how the mission of the university is advancing because of the collaboration between faculty and administrators in student affairs. All of these efforts—media coverage, press releases, and the awards ceremonies—signal to the campus community that this type of engagement has value in our institutional culture.

Of course, changing the culture of an institution, especially around faculty leadership in cocurricular life, requires patience. What it means to be a faculty member (and what it looks like in practice) represents a cumulative process over decades. Without meaningful examples of leadership that differ from what has been the usual experience, transformation is unlikely, yet with sustained efforts at storytelling, the culture begins to shift. At Virginia Tech, interest in the first living–learning and faculty-in-residence programs was muted at first. Many of our faculty were acculturated at other land-grant institutions where they had seen few examples of these efforts. Our first selection process, in 2011, yielded just two applicants, both of whom had attended universities as undergraduates that had a fully developed ethos for academic–student life integration. However, more than a decade into our efforts at Virginia Tech, the momentum has shifted. Our most recent search for our fourth faculty-in-residence position resulted in a dozen tenured, highly qualified, diverse, and motivated faculty members. In fact, our faculty-in-residence roles have become prized and coveted positions.

Build And Sustain Structures That Strengthen Community Among Student Affairs and Faculty Colleagues

Faculty are often drawn to serving in an LLC because of the unique opportunity it presents to develop as educators. This development can be spurred, in large part, through their partnership with student affairs administrators, who bring expertise in student development and the use of reflection as a tool for developing a reciprocal learning environment with students (Sriram et al., 2011). At our institution, faculty principals in residential colleges partner with live-in residence life professionals, and they cocreate programming that is based on a shared philosophy and learning outcomes and supports students through academic and nonacademic successes and challenges. In addition, although support for life challenges is often seen as the purview of student affairs staff, faculty in LLCs often recognize that developing those skills and relationships with students enhances their own experience as educators.

C.L. found that this kind of holistic connection is by far one of the most rewarding aspects of his role as faculty principal, but it does not come easily. Just like establishing relationships with communities as a landscape architect, building trust with students takes time, but it can offer rewarding outcomes. More than one student has written to him, for example, and confided that they had considered dropping out of college and that connecting with him encouraged them to press on. The time that he shares with students, in one-on-one meetings, at events, and through community engagement projects, allows him to understand their interests, personal goals, and how they see themselves in the world. Moreover, it allows him to recognize when a student's experience is not optimized, and he can encourage them, connect them with resources on campus that they may not know about, or bring them into leadership positions in the community with the knowledge that such opportunities could be transformational.

In addition to collaboration with partners in student affairs, one of the least discussed but most powerful incentives for faculty leadership in LLCs is the opportunity to find and sustain community with other faculty who are deeply committed to the integration of academic and student life (Golde & Pribbenow, 2000; Kennedy, 2011). Even at universities with less student engagement (especially outside the traditional classroom), faculty may be interested but too dispersed to find this type of holistic fellowship, often because individuals are isolated in departments. LLCs provide the opportunity to convene communities of practice from across the university where similarly dispositioned faculty can collaborate, support, and become energized by one another in their mutual commitment to student engagement. Expanding the faculty network can take place informally, by inviting faculty into the community, and formally, through faculty fellow programs.

At our institution, faculty principals (faculty-in-residence) and LLC directors gather regularly to share ideas, successes, and failures. They also collaborate on interdisciplinary partnerships that lead to research and writing projects and abiding friendships (Golde & Pribbenow, 2000). Part of the role of faculty principals at our institution is to gather a cadre of faculty fellows to support each residential college or LLC. These connected leaders build communities of faculty who support each other in ways that are life giving, meaningful, and sustaining. In one of our residential colleges, one faculty principal hosts "Writing Wednesdays," when faculty engaged in her residential college gather for 2 hours to support each other's research and writing goals. At a research university, departments can feel competitive and isolating. When they convene regularly, LLC faculty find a community that offers support, inspiration, and scholarly collaborations.

Conclusion

Creating sustainable incentives for faculty in living–learning communities is a complex and nuanced process. Meaningful faculty engagement and leadership in LLCs is an essential ingredient for creating conditions that integrate academic and student life and, most important, encourage holistic learning. Although LLCs with substantive faculty engagement are widely acknowledged for facilitating prized student outcomes, institutional practices often prohibit faculty leadership in this sphere.

In reflecting on our careers building LLCs, residential colleges, and faculty engagement programs, we realize that the most profound barrier has been mindsets about who faculty are, what they will and will not do, and what they value. Changing mindsets requires understanding belief systems already in play, a bold articulation of a new narrative to replace the old one, early adopters in the administration and faculty, and a relentless determination to avoid retrenching to the historical narrative. Associated with the sleep-and-eat mindset is a belief that successful faculty teach in classrooms and write research articles. At the most fundamental level, therefore, campus leaders have to unearth the narratives deeply embedded in the campus culture, hold them up for observation, and challenge them in order to build an ethos that will attract and sustain faculty leadership in residential environments. In order to shape a new paradigm, leaders must first understand the systems of belief, often unconscious, that undergird and support the culture already in place.

References

Boyer, E. L. (1990). *Scholarship reconsidered: Priorities of the professoriate.* Carnegie Foundation for the Advancement of Teaching.

Einarson, M. K., & Clarkberg, M. E. (2004, November 3–6). *Understanding faculty out-of-class interaction with undergraduate students at a research university* [Paper]. 18th Annual Conference of the Association for the Study of Higher Education, Kansas City, MO.

Golde, C. M., & Pribbenow, D. A. (2000). Understanding faculty involvement in residential learning communities. *Journal of College Student Development, 41*(1), 27–40.

Hankins, B., & Schmeltekopf, D. (Eds.). (2007). *The Baylor project: Taking Christian higher education to the next level.* St. Martin's Press.

Inkelas, K. K., Jessup-Anger, J. E., Benjamin, M., & Wawrzynski, M. R. (2018). *Living–learning communities that work: A research-based model for design, delivery, and assessment.* Stylus.

Jessup-Anger, J., Wawrzynski, M. R., & Yao, C. W. (2011). Enhancing undergraduate education: Examining faculty experiences during their first year in a residential college and exploring the implications for student affairs professionals. *Journal of College and University Student Housing, 38*(1), 56–69.

Kennedy, K. (2011). Understanding faculty's motivation to interact with students outside of class. *Journal of College and University Housing, 38*(1), 10–24.

Magolda, P. M. (2005). Proceed with caution: Uncommon wisdom about academic and student affairs partnerships. *About Campus*, *9*(6), 16–21. https://doi.org/10.1002/abc.113

Shushok, F., Scales, L., Sriram, R., & Kidd, V. (2011). A tale of three campuses: Unearthing theories of residential life that shape the student learning experience. *About Campus*, *16*(3), 13–21. https://doi.org/10.1002/abc.20063

Sriram, R., Shushok, F., Perkins, J., & Scales, L. (2011). Students as teachers: What faculty learn by living on campus. *Journal of College & University Student Housing*, *38*(1), 40–55.

VIGNETTE

Engaging With Students as Our Whole Selves

Kevin Leander

M y body isn't meant to just "carry my brain from the library to the classroom," as the joke goes. Residential faculty work is not about "heads of faculty" residing on a campus. It is about residing itself—learning to become present with our whole, embodied selves in the midst of other whole selves.

For several years I served as faculty head of Memorial House at Vanderbilt University. The live-on roles available to faculty at Vanderbilt are clearly valued by the institution, and getting departmental support for such work is not difficult if one has tenure. As a recently tenured professor, I was motivated to engage with students in their residential environment because I wanted a new challenge not offered by the ongoing work of research, teaching, and writing. I was drawn to the community-building aspect of the live-on role and to the challenge of relating to students as whole people outside of the classroom. I wanted to stretch. What I didn't imagine very well at the outset was how much I would learn about my own "whole self" in the process and how that would continue to motivate me and inform my work as an educator.

About 2 years into my role as residential faculty, I went through a very difficult and protracted divorce proceeding that caused an enormous amount of pain and trauma. It was challenging and heart-wrenching at times to have to wrestle with the pain in my private life while showing up and being present for students in the house. Some might wonder why I didn't move out and step away from my live-on role at that time. But, continuing to serve as faculty head was a gift of growth I gave myself and, by extension, was able to offer to students. I could show up as a curious, ordinary, vulnerable person who was learning about life as it came to me. I learned that faculty engaged in students' residential communities can have embodied and affectively intense experiences that remarkably mirror the kinds of experiences our students go through, living out much of their private lives in the public spaces of a college campus. I continued to be motivated to do this work because it cultivated in me a holistic appreciation and understanding of my students that made me a better teacher and a better mentor.

Although I am no longer living on campus, my residential faculty role continues to offer intangible professional rewards because it has fundamentally altered the way in which I show up as an educator. All of our ideas about becoming educated that focus too much on concepts and abstractions and formulae are half-baked at best. Because, for knowledge to reside in the body, the body has to first show up. As faculty head, I learned the value of offering my whole self while engaging with students and asking them to offer the same.

3

A MODEL FOR FACULTY ENGAGEMENT IN RESIDENTIAL LEARNING COMMUNITIES

Shannon B. Lundeen and James C. Penven

W e have worked at the intersection of academic affairs and student life for 2 decades. Organizationally, we have been positioned in two different divisions: academic affairs (Shannon B. Lundeen) and student life (James C. Penven). Yet, we share the evidence-based understanding that the collaborative work we do across academic and student affairs to foster student learning and mentoring outside of the classroom has positive outcomes for our students, faculty, and institutions. For the purposes of this chapter, our discussion of such cross-divisional work will focus on residential learning communities that involve faculty. Throughout this chapter we use "residential learning community" (RLC) as an umbrella term to describe a range of residentially based undergraduate learning communities. Some forms of RLCs include living–learning communities, living–learning programs, residential colleges, college houses, and first-year interest groups. There is ample evidence in the literature that demonstrates that faculty–student interaction outside of the classroom produces positive outcomes for students, faculty, and institutions (see chapter 9, this volume). Despite this evidence, it is often challenging to cultivate and sustain faculty involvement with RLCs.

We have each worked at different types of institutions, with enrollment ranging from 7,000 to 29,000. Collectively, we have just over 40 years' worth of experience (Jamie has 25 years, with more than 15 spent working directly with RLCs in student life positions, and Shannon has 16 years, with

6 spent serving as a live-in faculty member and another 6 overseeing RLCs in academic affairs positions). With our professional backgrounds, we offer tested knowledge and experience in the complexity of faculty involvement in RLCs. We know that positive outcomes associated with faculty–student interactions outside of the classroom are not always sufficient for motivating individual faculty to engage with students via an RLC. With varying teaching, research, and service expectations for faculty, the weight assigned to each of these expectations at a given institution can influence faculty members' openness to student mentoring beyond course instruction and undergraduate research. For example, a faculty member at a research-intensive university may be reluctant to advise or direct an RLC because of the time it could take away from their research and teaching. Even within a single institution, we have seen wide variation in faculty members' ability and willingness to be involved in RLCs, so the weight of expectations on research, teaching, and service alone cannot predict faculty engagement in RLCs. How can we explain such variation in faculty involvement at similar institutions? And how can we account for such variation in faculty engagement within a single institution? We address these and other questions in this chapter as we seek to explain the factors related to faculty engagement in RLCs.

Using the literature on RLCs and faculty–student interactions outside of the classroom, we introduce a conceptual model of faculty engagement in RLCs. Our model organizes factors influencing faculty engagement in RLCs into four spheres: (a) institutional context, (b) organizational structure, (c) professional motivations, and (d) personal motivations. The model explains how factors included in the four spheres—such as alignment of faculty involvement in RLCs with institutional priorities (institutional context), clarity of RLC goals (organizational structure), the rank and tenure status of the faculty member (professional motivations), and extrinsic benefits associated with faculty participation in RLCs (personal motivations)—affect the degree and scope of faculty involvement in RLCs. This conceptual model provides helpful information for faculty, student affairs practitioners, and university leaders who would like to develop strategies to improve the recruitment and retention of faculty in various RLC roles at their respective institutions. It will also prove useful for individual faculty who are considering involvement in an RLC. Finally, the model contributes to a burgeoning research agenda related to the impact of faculty involvement in RLCs.

RLC Faculty Engagement Model

Several factors pertaining to faculty engagement become evident when considering our own direct experiences with RLCs alongside the literature on out-of-class faculty–student interaction and faculty involvement in RLCs.

We organize our discussion of these factors through a new conceptual model of RLC faculty engagement, similar in design and purpose to Wade and Demb's (2009) faculty engagement model for community outreach. Our model categorizes the factors that can affect the degree and scope of a faculty member's engagement in RLCs into the four spheres mentioned earlier (i.e., institutional context, organizational structure, professional motivations, and personal motivations). Although these spheres are distinct, they are dynamically related. Factors in one sphere can influence the factors in another, and we must consider both the individual factors in each sphere as well as the dynamics among them when seeking to explain faculty engagement in RLCs (see Figure 3.1). By synthesizing previous research and practice in the areas of faculty–student interactions, collegiate experience outcomes, and RLCs, the RLC faculty engagement model (RLC FEM) offers new insight into the myriad of factors influencing faculty participation in RLCs.

Figure 3.1. Residential learning community faculty engagement model.

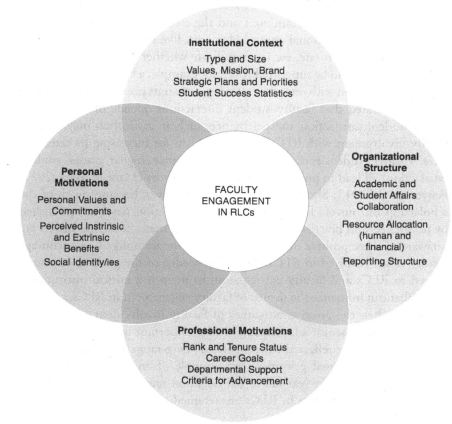

Four Spheres Influencing Faculty Engagement in RLCs

The *institutional context sphere* is characterized by factors pertaining to the individual institution. The institution type, its goals, mission, and outcomes are at the heart of this sphere.

As Cox and Orehovec (2007) suggest, institutional cultural norms need to be examined to determine the value an institution places on faculty engaging with students outside of the classroom generally and within RLCs specifically. Institutional culture is conveyed by institutional values and the degrees to which constituents (faculty, staff, students, etc.) appreciate those values. Institutional values and commitments to faculty engagement in RLCs can be gleaned in part through brand identity (e.g., "a premier institution for experiential learning") and explicit statements about an institution's mission and values (e.g., "the university inspires a passion for learning beyond the classroom"). Examining long-range strategic plans and annual institutional priorities to discern the emphasis placed on students' cocurricular learning and out-of-class engagement with faculty can reveal institutional support of faculty involvement in RLCs. But we also know that institution type (private, public, Carnegie classification, etc.) and the student body size, considered alongside other institutional context elements, like student success statistics (retention, graduation rate, etc.), can indicate whether faculty RLC involvement could or should be supported. Take, for example, a large public research-intensive institution with retention rates lower than its peers. Because research has demonstrated that faculty–student interactions outside of class lead to higher student satisfaction and persistence, such an institution may support faculty involvement with RLCs as a mechanism for increasing its retention rates. Positive student success outcomes (persistence, higher grades, student satisfaction) all lead to positive institutional outcomes (Mara & Mara, 2011; Penven et al., 2013; Shushok et al., 2011). However, because much of the scholarship on out-of-class faculty–student interaction has been published by researchers and practitioners in student affairs, many academic leaders are unaware of these positive outcomes and therefore are unlikely to encourage faculty to get involved in RLCs. Thus, knowledge of the positive outcomes related to RLCs and faculty participation in them is a critical institutional factor that can influence the degree of faculty engagement in RLCs.

Even when the positive outcomes of faculty involvement in RLCs are widely known by senior administrators, it is important to consider whether those outcomes are reflected in the goals of long-range strategic plans and short-term institutional priorities. For example, if an institution is trying to improve its new first-year fall-to-fall retention rate and institutional data demonstrate that students in RLCs are retained at a higher rate than their peers, institutional leaders may seek to expand student participation in RLCs. Thus, faculty members' efforts with first-year RLCs could be described as advancing an institutional priority. This knowledge could assist with the recruitment of new faculty into RLC roles and with garnering academic departmental support for those faculty members.

Understanding how institutional context factors may influence faculty engagement in RLCs is important, but the literature demonstrates that we must also consider how RLCs are organized and administered when examining the participation and roles of faculty in RLCs. The *organizational structure sphere* of our model considers the relations between people across different divisions related to RLCs and the arrangement of human and financial resources pertaining to RLC infrastructure.

Data collected by the National Study of Living Learning Programs demonstrate that the majority of RLCs are administered through some combination of academic and student affairs partnership (Inkelas et al., 2007). Brower and Dettinger (1998) noted that RLCs bring together faculty, staff, and students and "they need each other to accomplish their learning objectives" (Bergman & Brower, 2008, p. 85). Although cross-divisional partnerships between student life and academic affairs are critical for well-functioning RLCs (Inkelas et al., 2004, 2007, 2018), scholars caution leaders against quickly formed collaborations (Magdola, 2005). Genuine collaboration entails partners coming together and codeveloping an initiative. Yet there is a cultural divide to traverse between the divisions of academic affairs and student life, meaning that faculty and student life staff partnerships are not easily created or sustained (Bergman & Brower, 2008). When looking at whether and how faculty are engaged in RLCs, it is important to consider how these cultural differences affect cross-divisional collaborations that are foundational for strong RLCs. Bergman and Brower (2008) observed that the cultural divide between these two divisions (as well as between faculty and staff in general) can impede faculty involvement in RLCs.

The most common cultural differences between faculty and student life staff include time management, work cycle, decision-making, organizational reporting structure, conditions for professional advancement, and communication style. These cultural differences can make it difficult to form productive partnerships in working with RLCs. Given that the domains of student life and academic affairs often promote subcultures within the same institution with different socialization processes, values (Haynes & Janosik, 2012), reporting structures, decision-making schemas, implementation mechanisms, and general purposes, this cultural split can impede faculty members' participation in RLCs. These divides can run so deep that even when faculty are engaged in RLCs, they may not even be aware of the presence or role of student life staff who also work to support those same RLCs (Jessup-Anger et al., 2011). Onboarding and development programs for RLC faculty and staff that work to raise awareness of the divisional cultural differences that could otherwise impede faculty–staff collaboration can help foster and sustain strong faculty RLC engagement.

In addition to considering barriers to faculty engagement, it is important to investigate the organizational structure and coordination of RLCs themselves because the structure and management of RLCs have been found to affect substantive faculty–student engagement (Inkelas et al., 2007; Kennedy, 2011). Through data collected in a national study of more than 600 living–learning programs (Inkelas et al., 2004, 2007), Inkelas et al. (2008) developed a structural typology of RLCs consisting of three organizational types: (a) small, resource deficient, primarily run by residence life/housing with limited faculty or academic affairs involvement; (b) medium-size, moderately resourced, with some faculty and academic affairs partnerships; and (c) large (approximately 300+ students) programs, well resourced with robust faculty involvement and academic–student life collaborations. The structural typology identifies six key organizational factors that influence the degree to which cross-divisional collaboration is possible within RLCs: (a) funding structure, (b) who and how many people are involved in administering RLCs, (c) what divisions or departments those people are affiliated with, (d) departmental reporting lines, (e) clarity of purpose and vision, and (f) who is responsible for decisions that affect the programs. These organizational factors that influence cross-divisional RLC collaboration also affect the level and sustainability of faculty engagement in RLCs (Inkelas et al., 2018).

In their book *Living–Learning Communities That Work*, Inkelas et al. (2018) offered a best practices model (BPM) for RLCs that advances the descriptive structural typology developed previously (Inkelas et al., 2007) by delineating components for a successful, high-quality RLC. The BPM consists of 10 components arranged in a pyramid similar to Maslow's hierarchy of needs. It is important to consider whether faculty are engaged at each of the levels of RLC coordination and management described by Inkelas and colleagues in the BPM. Where faculty "fit" in the overall organizational structure is itself a critical factor to consider in terms of recruiting and sustaining faculty engagement in RLCs. Even when institutional context and organizational structure provide a highly supportive environment for faculty involvement, this does not guarantee that all faculty will engage with RLCs. Research and practice reveal that there are additional professional and personal factors influencing faculty engagement in RLCs.

The *professional motivations sphere* directs our attention to the various factors that influence a faculty member's current role and career trajectory, including their professional values and goals, their expectations and responsibilities, and their departmental and institutional standing. Many faculty are unaware of the evidence that faculty engagement in RLCs is related to a wide range of positive student outcomes. But even when they are aware of this relationship, it may not compel them to get involved with an RLC. Because activities in residence halls are not typically considered a faculty responsibility, they are rarely recognized or rewarded by institutions. If the promotion and tenure review process does not recognize faculty engagement in RLCs, a faculty member's participation in RLC endeavors could have negative professional implications (Golde & Pribbenow, 2000).

Cultivating new or sustaining current faculty engagement in RLCs is highly dependent on academic disciplinary expectations in terms of teaching and scholarship and the overarching system of promotion and tenure (Golde & Pribbenow, 2000; Penven, 2016). Kennedy's (2011) study bears this out and revealed additional factors to consider in the professional motivations sphere. Kennedy used motivational systems theory to analyze tenured and tenure-track faculty members' motivations for (and disinclinations toward) RLC involvement at three different institutions. The four main factors that emerged in her research were (a) perception and clarity of role, (b) time commitment, (c) departmental support, and (d) impact on the promotion and tenure process. The first two on this list Kennedy considered personal factors, but we argue they sit more squarely in the professional motivation sphere of our RLC FEM. Kennedy found that if the role for a faculty member in an RLC is poorly defined and the time commitment required is unclear, the faculty member's belief in their own capability to fulfill that role is significantly diminished. Kennedy discovered that the weaker a faculty member's capability beliefs are, the more likely they will choose to discontinue their RLC involvement. RLC roles can be time intensive for faculty. Although serving as a guest speaker at an RLC event may take only 1 to 2 hours, faculty assuming an administrative leadership or live-in role could require a significant increase of time investment at the cost of research, general university or academic department service, and other traditional faculty responsibilities (see Thies, 2003).

Kennedy's (2011) study demonstrates how departmental support and alignment of RLC engagement with the promotion and tenure process strongly influence a faculty member's desire to initiate and sustain RLC involvement. The more weight given to a faculty member's RLC efforts in criteria for professional advancement, the more likely the faculty member is to continue in their RLC role (Kennedy, 2011). Thus, for many faculty members considering involvement with RLCs there are two critical questions they must ask. First, how will their efforts matter in terms of professional advancement and career trajectory? Second, will the time they put into an RLC be commensurate with the potential outcomes of their RLC engagement and how their efforts are "counted"? Although many faculty claim their time among students in residence halls has allowed for significant teaching and learning opportunities, these endeavors are often only categorized as service in the promotion and tenure process (similar to school- or university-wide committee work). Some faculty may pay a penalty if they become involved with RLCs and their department chair or colleagues on promotion/tenure/advancement committees perceive that work as detracting from that faculty member's ability to maintain a robust teaching and research agenda (Golde & Pribbenow, 2000; Inkelas et al., 2018; Kennedy & Townsend, 2005; Shapiro & Levine, 1999; Wawrzynski et al., 2009). The risk of not having one's RLC efforts recognized as extensions of both teaching and service by a department chair, dean, and fellow colleagues may be a sufficient deterrent for sustaining faculty RLC involvement. Indeed, there is often little incentive for faculty to engage students in informal spaces like residence halls as there is often "institutionalized pressure to prioritize some combination of research and [classroom] teaching" (Bergman & Brower, 2008, p. 85). In the same vein, given the research and publication pressure on junior faculty, these scholars are likely to limit their service involvement to more traditional endeavors that have clearly delimited time commitments and fewer, if any, expectations for after-hours interactions with students. Thus, considering a faculty member's career point and probationary status are important professional motivation factors to examine because they can reveal pressures and expectations on a faculty member that may compete with RLC demands and responsibilities.

There are professional benefits to involvement in RLCs, and these can serve as incentives for faculty engagement. When faculty are involved in RLCs they often deepen their knowledge of university resources, services, and operations and can expand their network of colleagues in different units across the institution. Greater understanding of university operations and knowledge of resources, particularly in student life, empower faculty to navigate institutional systems and connect colleagues and students to helpful resources. Thus, a faculty member involved in RLCs may be more willing and able to reach out to students who seem to be struggling because of the faculty member's increased awareness of support services for students on campus.

Increased interactions with students outside the classroom via RLCs not only provide faculty with significant insight into student life but also can also influence their classroom pedagogy (Penven, 2016; Sriram et al., 2011). Indeed, faculty who have served in a live-in RLC role report that their live-in experience has improved their teaching (Penven, 2016; Sriram et al., 2011; Thies, 2003). The impact on teaching includes adapting how faculty engage students in the classroom (based on gaining a more holistic understanding of students) as well as altering the structure of the course itself (from assignment types to due date timelines). After working with students in a cocurricular RLC environment, a faculty member may be more apt to see students as partners in teaching and learning and may work with students in their courses to codesign assignments and assessments (see Cook-Sather et al., 2014). In gaining a more comprehensive understanding of campus life along with a more holistic view of students, faculty involved in RLCs are able to more meaningfully engage students in the classroom and are empowered to navigate university systems and resources more effectively.

Finally, consideration should be given to the alignment of an RLC's mission with the priorities of a faculty member's department. A faculty member is likely to be motivated and adequately supported by their department head to engage with an RLC if their involvement may advance departmental priorities. For example, if the engineering department is trying to increase the number of women majors, the department chair will likely support an engineering faculty member's involvement in a "women in STEM" RLC.

It goes without saying that for these positive professional outcomes to be factors that motivate faculty to participate in RLCs, faculty who have not (yet) directly experienced them need to be made aware of them. Of course, none of these professional motivation factors can sufficiently serve as motivation if a faculty member's personal values and commitments are not conducive to or cannot be integrated with RLC participation. In the final sphere of our model, *personal motivations*, we turn our attention to a faculty member's values, commitments, personal goals, and perceived benefits of RLC engagement.

When recruiting faculty to become involved in RLCs, it's important to remember faculty as holistic individuals. Outside of work, they have a number of competing priorities. A faculty member's personal life situation (e.g., family dynamics and personal commitments) and values can have a strong influence on their decision to engage in an RLC. Programs and events for RLCs are often held on evenings and weekends. As a result, faculty participation in the cocurricular components of an RLC may be limited by the demands, commitments, and flexibility of the faculty member's personal life. For example, a faculty member with children who prioritizes nightly family dinners and assisting children with homework may be less inclined to participate in an RLC that necessitates presence at weekly evening programs. Yet if the RLC encourages faculty to involve their family (e.g., bring partners or children to events), this may help mitigate the conflict. Thus, it is important to consider the weight of a faculty member's personal commitments in determining both their willingness to become involved in RLCs and their level of involvement (e.g., a one-time guest speaker or an RLC program director). Such considerations can lead to designing opportunities to integrate a faculty member's commitments into the RLC experience, thereby increasing the chances that a faculty member will become and remain engaged with an RLC.

Similarly, a faculty member's personal values or aspects of their identity can be a motivating factor for RLC engagement. Consider a faculty member who is a first-generation student and is invited to be a mentor in their discipline to students in the "first-gen RLC." If it is important to that faculty member to help other first-generation students transition into college, this may highly motivate them to get involved with that RLC. Alternatively, a faculty member who values a strict separation of their work and personal lives may find intensive RLC engagement unappealing because of the blurring of those personal and professional boundaries. Nonetheless, that same individual might enjoy the opportunity to attend an event to share their research with RLC students.

In addition to factors pertaining to personal commitments and values, there are personal intrinsic and extrinsic rewards for faculty who engage with students in RLCs. Many faculty members who participate in residential learning environments indicate that a motivating factor for them is the opportunity to engage meaningfully with students outside the traditional classroom setting (Gold & Pribbenow, 2000; Penven, 2016; Thies, 2003). In a traditional classroom, the relationship between faculty and students is mediated by a grade, which often serves as a significant motivating factor for a student's overall engagement with the course and the professor. However, interaction with faculty outside of the classroom in an RLC is (typically) an ungraded activity. Therefore, students can willingly, and without concern about a grade, engage with faculty in this environment for the sake of the interaction itself. Likewise, faculty can engage with students without also having to evaluate and "grade" those interactions. Moreover, faculty–student interactions in RLCs can lead to deeper life exchanges about meaning and purpose and can foster mentoring relationships (Cox & Orehovec, 2007; Sriram & McLevain, 2016). Thus, the quality and content of these faculty–student interactions can become intrinsically rewarding and may lead faculty to seek RLC involvement.

In Haynes and Janosik's (2012) study, faculty more frequently identified intrinsic benefits versus the extrinsic rewards of their RLC involvement. Some of these intrinsic benefits included conversing with students about something other than course material, making a difference in the lives of students, and advancing the educational or academic mission of their institution. The extrinsic benefits faculty cited included receiving funding for dining or social events with RLC members, opportunities for research and scholarship on residential learning environments, and support for participating in professional conferences associated with residential education (Haynes & Janosik, 2012). Other extrinsic rewards reported included reserved parking, partial meal plans, a stipend, additional office space near the residential community, reduced rent or rent-free living quarters, and a course-load reduction. These intrinsic and extrinsic benefits are all personal factors that can influence a faculty member's engagement in RLCs, and all should be considered when exploring faculty motivations to become involved with RLCs.

Haynes and Janosik's (2012) study helps us understand the frequency with which certain extrinsic and intrinsic benefits are experienced by faculty members engaged in RLCs, but the study does not tell us which of the benefits are more motivating than others. For example, the majority of faculty members involved in RLCs at various institutions may receive supplemental meal plans; however, this does not mean the meal plan is a primary extrinsic motivator for all faculty members' continued RLC involvement. Combinations of intrinsic and extrinsic benefits of RLC engagement may be compelling; however, conflicts with other factors in any of the other three spheres may override faculty members' inclination to become involved with an RLC. Thus, we must attend to the ways in which the factors in all four spheres interact with one another to produce favorable or unfavorable conditions for cultivating and sustaining faculty engagement in RLCs.

Dynamic Relationship Between Factors in the Four Spheres

Understanding an institution's context; the organizational structures of an RLC (e.g., RLC infrastructure, resource allocation, etc.); and faculty members' professional and personal commitments, goals, and expectations is important for understanding faculty engagement in RLCs. Understanding how factors in one sphere interact with factors in another to motivate or deter faculty involvement in RLCs is equally important when seeking to explain the degree and scope of faculty engagement in RLCs. The RLC FEM encourages us to holistically explore the dynamic interaction of these factors across all four spheres. We provide some examples that illustrate this dynamic interaction and how it may influence an individual faculty member's willingness and ability to participate in an RLC.

An institution's mission, values, priorities, and strategic plan can have a significant impact on faculty personal and professional motivations, RLC organizational structures, RLC program funding, and cross-divisional collaboration. For example, consider a new faculty member who earned a doctoral degree at a research-intensive university with little pedagogical training who is newly employed at a liberal arts institution. This faculty member is now part of a teaching-centered university that prioritizes faculty–student engagement both in and out of the classroom. This faculty member will be motivated professionally to learn how to engage with students outside of the traditional classroom and would do well to capitalize on opportunities to be involved in some aspect of RLCs given that faculty–student engagement is valued by the institutional culture.

If there is a clear connection between faculty involvement in RLCs and the factors in the institutional context sphere (e.g., advising an RLC focused on first-year women in STEM fields advances the institution's priority of developing a pipeline for women in STEM), a faculty member is likely to be motivated and adequately supported by departmental and university leaders to engage with an RLC. However, even when an RLC is aligned with an institutional priority there may be interactions among factors in the organizational, personal, and professional spheres that may make a faculty member reluctant to engage with that RLC.

Take, for example, a faculty member who is a Black-identified woman with expertise in African and Africana history at a predominantly White institution. She may have strong personal, professional, and institutional inclinations to serve as a faculty mentor to the Africana Studies RLC at her university. However, if there are not many faculty or students of color at her institution, she may already be overburdened with expectations from university leaders to support students of color in addition to her departmental and disciplinary responsibilities (see Louis et al., 2016, and Allen et al., 2000). Given the reality of the cultural taxation experienced by faculty of color at predominantly White institutions, this particular faculty member whose expertise and social identity align with the needs and purpose of the Africana studies RLC may not be able to engage with this RLC. This example illustrates how factors in the institutional context sphere (namely, demographics of the student body and of the faculty) may clash with factors in the personal and professional motivation spheres.

Given the number of factors that can influence a faculty member's ability to engage in RLCs, the primary lesson here is that we need to be flexible and responsive in our recruitment strategies. The RLC FEM does not yield a one-size-fits-all recruitment and retention strategy for faculty engagement in RLCs; however, the model encourages us to look at these four spheres of influence holistically in order to understand why faculty engage in RLCs. The RLC FEM highlights the need to know our institution's mission, values, and priorities and prompts us to examine the degree to which our RLC infrastructure promotes and supports student life and academic affairs collaboration. The model also stresses the importance of getting to know our faculty to understand their personal values and their professional goals in order to determine whether involvement in RLCs would be mutually beneficial for the students, staff, and prospective faculty members involved.

Limitations and Future Research

As a conceptual model, the RLC FEM has explanatory power and can guide faculty, staff, and university leaders in understanding the factors influencing faculty involvement in RLCs as these leaders seek to implement or enhance RLCs at their institution. The RLC FEM can be strengthened and refined if more empirical data are gathered to validate the model. This conceptual model may be used to inform qualitative instruments that aim to describe and assess faculty engagement with RLCs. The model can also be used as a conceptual framework for identifying institution-specific strategies to combat the challenges and increase the level and quality of faculty engagement in residential settings in undergraduate education. Notably, combining the RLC FEM with the living–learning communities BPM (Inkelas et al., 2018) could yield a method for cultivating and predicting, as well as sustaining and improving, faculty engagement in RLCs. Finally, the RLC FEM can be used to further investigate the relationships between various factors and faculty engagement in particular types of RLCs at specific institutions.

Conclusion

Our conceptual model provides a comprehensive explanation of faculty engagement in RLCs. As Kevin Leander described in the opening vignette, involvement in RLCs grants faculty the opportunity to engage with students as whole beings rather than disembodied heads. Likewise, our model invites researchers and practitioners to examine factors influencing faculty engagement in RLCs holistically. Explaining Kevin's decision to continue in his live-in faculty role while going through a traumatic experience in his personal life would prove difficult if we were examining the factors in only one sphere of the RLC FEM. Kevin's story reveals that he was motivated to continue in his faculty head-of-house role despite personal adversity because of the intrinsic benefits he experienced from interacting with students outside of the classroom in their shared residential environment. Looking at Kevin's RLC role in relation to institutional context alone would not give us an accurate explanation for why he got involved or stayed involved as a live-in faculty member in a residential college house. This is where the RLC FEM's explanatory power is illuminating. The model directs us to examine the dynamic relations among several factors across the spheres of institutional context, organizational structure, professional motivations, and personal motivations to understand what shapes faculty engagement in RLCs.

The RLC FEM provides a framework for understanding the "why" behind faculty members' involvement (or lack thereof) in RLCs. The model can be used to create institution-specific plans to cultivate or enhance faculty engagement in RLCs. Contributing to emerging scholarship in RLCs, the RLC FEM serves as a springboard for future research into cultivating, predicting, sustaining, administering, and improving faculty involvement in RLCs.

References

Allen, W. R., Epps, E. G., Guillory, E. A., Suh, S. A., & Bonous-Hammarth, M. (2000). The Black academic: Faculty status among African Americans in U.S. higher education. *The Journal of Negro Education, 69*(1–2), 112–127.

Bergman, C. J., & Brower, A. M. (2008). Faculty involvement in residence halls: Bridging faculty and staff cultures through residential learning communities. In W. J. Zeller (Ed.), *Residence life and the new student experience* (Monograph No. 5, 3rd ed., pp. 83–96). National Resource Center for the First-Year Experience and Students in Transition, University of South Carolina.

Brower, A. A., & Dettinger, K. M. (1998). What is a learning community? Toward a comprehensive model. *About Campus, 3*(5), 15–21. https://doi-org.ezproxy.lib.vt.edu/10.1177/108648229800300504

Cook-Sather, A., Bovill, C., & Felten, P. (2014). *Engaging students as partners in learning and teaching: A guide for faculty*. Jossey-Bass.

Cox, B. E., & Orehovec, E. (2007). Faculty–student interaction outside the classroom: A typology from a residential college. *The Review of Higher Education, 30*(4), 343–362.

Golde, C. M., & Pribbenow, D. A. (2000). Understanding faculty involvement in residential learning communities. *Journal of College Student Development, 41*(1), 27–40.

Haynes, C., & Janosik, S. (2012). Faculty and staff member benefits from involvement in living–learning programs. *Journal of College and University Student Housing, 38*(2), 32–45.

Inkelas, K. K., & Associates. (2004). *National Study of Living–Learning Programs: 2004 report of findings*. http://www.livelearnstudy.net/images/NSLLP_2004_Final_Report.pdf

Inkelas, K. K., Szelényi, K., Soldner, M., & Brower, A. M. (2007). *National Study of Living–Learning Programs: 2007 report of findings*. https://drum.lib.umd

.edu/bitstream/handle/1903/8392/2007%20NSLLP%20Final%20Report
.pdf?sequence=1&isAllowed=y

Inkelas, K. K., Jessup-Anger, J., Benjamin, M., & Wawrzynski, M. (2018). *Living-learning communities that work: A research-based model for design, delivery, and assessment.* Stylus.

Inkelas, K. K., Soldner, M., Longerbeam, S. D., & Leonard, J. B. (2008). Differences in student outcomes by living–learning programs: The development of an empirical typology. *Research in Higher Education, 49*(6), 495–512. https://doi.org/10.1007/s11162-008-9087-6

Jessup-Anger, J. E., Wawrzynski, M. R., & Yao, C. W. (2011). Enhancing undergraduate education: Examining faculty experiences during their first year in a residential college and exploring the implications for student life professionals. *Journal of College and University Student Housing, 38*(1), 56–69.

Kennedy, K. (2011). Understanding faculty motivation to interact with students outside of class. *Journal of College and University Student Housing, 38*(1), 10–24.

Kennedy, K., & Townsend, B. K. (2005, November 17–19). *Understanding tenured/tenure-track faculty participation in residential learning communities at research-extensive universities* [Paper]. Annual Meeting of the Association for the Study of Higher Education, Philadelphia, PA.

Louis, D. A., Rawls, G. J., Jackson-Smith, D., Chambers, G. A., Phillips, L. T. L., & Louis, S. L. (2016). Listening to our voices: Experiences of Black faculty at predominantly White research universities with microaggression. *Journal of Black Studies, 47*(5), 454–454.

Magdola, P. M. (2005). Proceed with caution: Uncommon wisdom about academic and student life partnerships. *About Campus, 9*(6), 16–21.

Mara, M., & Mara, A. (2011). Finding an analytic frame for faculty–student interaction within faculty-in-residence programs. *Innovative Higher Education, 36,* 71–82, https://doi.org/10.1007/s10755-010-9162-8

Penven, J. C. (2016). *What is a collegiate way of living worth? Exploring the costs and benefits of residential colleges as perceived by faculty and chief housing officers* [Unpublished doctoral dissertation]. Virginia Polytechnic Institute and State University.

Penven, J., Stephens, R., Shushok, F., Jr., & Keith, C. (2013). The past, present, and future of residential colleges: Looking back at S. Stewart Gordon's "Living and Learning in College." *Journal of College and University Housing, 39*(2), 114–126.

Shapiro, N. S., & Levine, J. H. (1999). *Creating learning communities: A practical guide to winning support, organizing for change, and implementing programs.* Jossey-Bass.

Shushok, F., Jr., Scales, L., Sriram, R., & Kidd, V. (2011). A tale of three campuses: Unearthing theories of residential life that shape the student learning experience. *About Campus, 16*(3), 13–21. https://doi.org/10.1002/abc.20063

Sriram, R., & McLevain, M. (2016). Developing an instrument to examine student–faculty interaction in faculty-in-residence programs. *Journal of College Student Development, 57*(5), 604–609. https://doi.org/10.1353/csd.2016.0065

Sriram, R., Shushok, F., Jr., Perkins, J., & Scales, T. L. (2011). Students as teachers: What faculty learn by living on campus. *Journal of College & University Student Housing, 38*(1), 40–55.

Thies, C. G. (2003). Reflections on assuming administrative responsibilities as an untenured assistant professor. *Political Science and Politics, 36*(3), 447–450.

Wade, A., & Demb, A. (2009, Spring). A conceptual model to explore faculty community engagement. *Michigan Journal of Community Service Learning, 15*(2), 5–16.

Wawrzynski, M. R., Jessup-Anger, J. E., Stolz, K., Helman, C., & Beaulieu, J. (2009). Exploring students' perceptions of academically based living learning communities. *College Student Life Journal, 28*(1), 138–158.

VIGNETTE

If It Were Easy, It Wouldn't Be Meaningful

Jennifer E. Eidum

When I interviewed for an assistant professor position at Elon University in spring 2015, I learned about the residential campus and faculty-in-residence (FIR) role in passing. I immediately had to learn more: It felt like the perfect fit for my professional and personal life. My academic research on reflective writing and culturally relevant pedagogy—not to mention my teaching focus on first-year students—seemed to align with Elon's vision of FIR. Moving from Seattle, Washington to Elon, North Carolina as a single mom with my then-5-year-old son, I knew that I wanted the connection with and support of a community. I knew that if I came to Elon, I would apply for the job.

Just a year later, I was thrilled to be chosen as the FIR for Elon's global neighborhood. During my time as FIR, I have made long-lasting connections with the many students, staff, and faculty connected with the neighborhood. In my role, I collaborate with our neighborhood's community director, graduate apprentice, and student leaders to plan and execute neighborhood programming, I serve as a liaison with faculty and staff across the university who teach and mentor students within the neighborhood, and I connect with the neighborhood's nearly 600 students directly by mentoring student leaders and planning and participating in neighborhood events.

I have also faced a number of challenges living on campus. Although many faculty and staff see the value in connecting with students outside class, it can be difficult to create programs that students will attend during times when faculty are available. In addition, as the key faculty member working with the neighborhood leadership team, it can be difficult to envision, execute, and participate in events while still maintaining my primary teaching and research commitments. It can be exciting to motivate students and faculty for a single headlining event, but the energy wanes when these events occur every month. Finally, and not insignificantly, I feel like I am in a perpetual battle to keep students out of our designated parking space. Parking doesn't seem like a big deal until you have a carload of groceries, a screaming kid, and no place to park near your building.

Through these challenges, I have found opportunities for collaboration and communication across our neighborhood leadership team and with campus partners. We have created important roles for student leaders to take the lead in event planning, advertising, and execution. We look for collaboration opportunities with existing student groups on campus so that our first-year students learn about the broader campus community. I have explicitly modeled a family-friendly environment so that faculty and staff invited to our programs know their partners, kids, and pets are welcome to join us.

It has taken a lot of work to integrate my family into the global neighborhood community and to connect global students with the broader campus and local community, but boundary-crossing is central to the work faculty should do in living–learning communities. These communities sit at the intersection of the personal and professional. During my time in residence, I have worked toward my professional (research, writing, tenure) and personal goals: While in residence, I remarried and recently gave birth to a daughter. While I often feel like I'm juggling the responsibilities of a professor, FIR, mother, and wife, at the same time I am modeling this life to the undergraduates who surround us. In this work I am reminded that it is by working hard and taking risks that we create meaningful experiences.

4

DESIGNING A
RESIDENTIAL CAMPUS

Faculty Leadership in Developing Strategy, Vision, Partnerships, and Learning

Connie Ledoux Book and Jeffrey P. Stein

Years ago, a Harvard faculty member visiting Elon University's campus in North Carolina was asked how her institution had built an intellectually rich residential campus culture. "Was it the focus on academic rigor?" we asked. "The long-standing tradition, ivy, and gothic architecture? Or perhaps the simple expectations of a Harvard education combined with the accretion of decades and centuries of learning?" Her answer speaks directly to the idea of intentionally designing residential campuses: "What seems seamless and natural is carefully and systematically orchestrated by a host of talented people in every corner of campus behind the scenes, working to engage students, often without the students' knowledge they have even been engaged." In these few words, she provided a rich description for high-quality residential campus work: a coordinated and layered cadre of talented faculty and staff working strategically to engage students to develop socially, intellectually, and interpersonally. Through examples from top-tier programs across the country and stories from our efforts at Elon University, in this chapter (and supplemental online resources) we provide strategies for mapping and designing a residential campus vision, collaborative relationships, programs, facilities, and assessment tools to weave learning and faculty leadership through the residential experience and increase student success.

A more intentional approach to the overall residential experience at Elon began at the outset of a new university strategic plan in 2009. We realized that our campus featured many assets (outstanding and dedicated faculty and staff, deep expertise in engaged and experiential learning, a long history of living–learning communities [LLCs], and more), yet it lacked a clear vision and strategic road map for living and learning. Like many institutions, the university employed numerous aspects of residential living, including LLCs, faculty-in-residence, and linked residential courses. However, these efforts were not coordinated under an overarching vision, and the outcomes of our residential efforts remained disparate. While we considered a range of existing models we quickly learned that to achieve our vision of a holistic effort connecting and deepening student success across the 4-year collegiate experience, we needed to be intentional in the design of a coordinated residential campus vision.

The phrase "residential campus" references a fully integrated living–learning environment, one where living on campus does not diverge from learning on campus. Although there are many elements that colleges and universities might include in their design of a residential campus, such as LLCs, residential colleges, theme housing, or simply learning communities, we use the phrase "residential campus" to refer to a larger overarching vision: one that is less programmatic and not confined only to residence halls and instead is inspired by the vision that students continue to engage in learning beyond the classroom, throughout the day, and in every corner of campus.

Now serving as Elon's ninth president and as vice president of strategic initiatives and partnerships, we understand the critical role faculty have played in partnering with administration and staff (particularly student affairs staff) to create and articulate a vision for the residential campus, to provide leadership in the design and programming offered to achieve that vision, and to develop a model to assess and ultimately sustain the campus's residential goals. Faculty colleagues have partnered across the community to map, design, and connect living and learning on campus in what Elon calls the "residential campus pathway" (RCP; see Table 4.1 and a blank version of the pathway in the online supplemental materials), the foundation for our residential campus plan and for this chapter.

The pages ahead are intended to assist faculty and staff in articulating students' residential learning journey to gain institutional buy-in for their own RCP. Borrowing from leading programs across the country, Elon designed a unique model of eight residential neighborhoods (each leveraging embedded LLCs, faculty leadership, and concepts from residential colleges) that met the goals outlined on our RCP for the 3,300 students living on campus. In this chapter, we offer suggestions for how faculty can provide leadership (through collaborative partnerships with student affairs staff and administrators) to assist their campuses in developing their own distinctive mix of residential experiences and programs led by a layered cadre of talented faculty and staff working strategically to engage students to develop socially, intellectually, and interpersonally.

Articulating a Shared Vision for Living and Learning

Unlocking the potential for learning on a residential campus involves confronting history within the academy: Our aim was to remove unnecessary silos and artificial borders in order to blend student experience into a seamless or integrated whole (Kuh, 1996). Elon University's 10-year strategic plan, the *Elon Commitment* (Elon University, 2009), called for the development of "a bold plan to create a campus with seamless connections among the academic, cocurricular and residential experiences on campus" (para. 3). A residential campus committee, formed with members across campus, was charged with "exploring innovative models for this transformation of the residential experience, including residential colleges, a wide variety of living-learning and academic theme communities" (Elon University, 2009, para. 3), as well as a range of new buildings, classrooms, common spaces, and faculty apartments to support the plan. To meet this charge, the committee wanted to move past thinking of students living on campus as what happens "over there" and the purview of only certain people on campus. We wanted students, faculty, staff, and administrators to view the entire campus as a continuous landscape where students are always learning.

The committee's initial report (Elon University, 2010), couching the rationale for this work in the language of student success, described "transforming the residential experience in ways that seamlessly connect the living and learning experiences of students and . . . consequently, dramatically enhanc[ing] the intellectual and academic climate of the campus" (pp. 3–4). After more than a year of research, focus groups, and site visits to leading campus programs, the committee suggested the campus strive to achieve an "intellectually charged residential community that seamlessly engages students where they live and where they learn," including "residence halls, classrooms, lounges, kitchens, lobbies, coffee shops, sidewalks and benches" (p. 3). Our intentional language—*intellectually charged, seamlessly engaged, living and learning*—underscored the focus on developing a broader, more integrated, less restricted, and richer landscape for learning and student success.

Research has consistently demonstrated the benefits of high-quality residential experiences—increases in satisfaction, belonging, persistence, and perceptions of learning—that support students from a wide diversity of backgrounds, including socioeconomic class, academic preparation, and

TABLE 4.1
The Elon University Residential Campus Pathway

1. Class Year	2. Class Themes	3. Academic and Interpersonal Needs/Outcomes	4. Residential Academic Connections, Mentoring, and Services
First Year	**Transition: Join and Explore the Academic and Social Community** • Transition/acculturation • Belonging/finding your niche • Academic expectations • Learning independent skills • Self-discovery • Multicultural connections • Exploring majors • Exploring student organizations	**Goals:** Make a successful personal/ social/academic transition to academy, develop integrated plan for 4 years • Understanding expectations of academic life • Support groups, friends, mentors • Networking/community • Guidance/orientation • Self-discovery, personal/time management • Exploring differences	• Faculty-in-residence, and faculty connects • Learning communities • Linked classes • Peer mentoring/tutoring • First-year courses • Elon 101 seminar/residential teaching assistants
Sophomore	**Define Purpose/Identity: Choice and Fine Tuning** • Find academic home, major • Take on leadership roles • Identify experiential learning opportunities • Identify extracurricular opportunities	**Goals:** Find academic, social, and personal niches; explore academics; declare a major • Academic discovery • Diversity/worldview • Leadership/student organizations • "Forgotten Class" issues **Needs:** guidance, finding purpose, focus at department level, leadership opportunities	• Advising (academic and experiential) • Meeting department and school colleagues • Making connections • Groundwork for experiential learning • Methods courses in majors
Junior	**Application, Synthesis, Practice, and Independence** • Deep experiences in major and beyond • Experiential learning • Providing leadership and mentoring on campus	**Goals:** Deepen academic and cocurricular engagement Study abroad, internships, research, service-learning, leadership • Professional development • Diversity/life skills **Needs:** practice synthesizing and applying knowledge and skills	• Student professional development center • Study abroad, internships, service-learning, leadership, undergraduate research • Mentoring • Departmental clubs, meetings, and so on
Senior	**Exploration, Preparation, Transition** • Reflection on college career and connection to career or graduate school • Integration of learning in capstones (major and core) • Preparation for lifelong learning/professional life	**Goals:** Contribute to larger causes (campus and beyond) and transition to the world beyond Elon **Needs:** Opportunities to practice giving back to campus/ community, be professional, and gain transition skills	• Departmental leaders • Faculty as colleagues • Group study • Student professional development center • Graduate school applications

Class Year	5. Campus Living Locations and Features	6. Campus Living Experiences	7. Class Events/ Initiatives/ Experiences
First Year	• Students live in the core of campus and near important services (advising, library, tutoring, dining, etc.) • Community spaces • Roommates/doubles	• Learning communities • Common spaces • Academic classes in residence halls • Linked core courses	• Orientation • Elon 101 seminar • Common reading • Convocation • Call to honor • Organization fair • Core 110/English 110/Math and Stats 110
Sophomore	• More study space • A little more distance from campus center/study space/common space for "outpost" services or activities relative to goals for second year	• Collaborative spaces • Cohorts by majors • Meeting spaces for programs relative to second-year goals	• Elon experiences • Courses in arts and sciences • Time in majors • Student organizations • Mentoring first year-students as orientation leaders and Elon 101 seminar teaching assistants • Department meetings
Junior	• Independent apartments • Singles/privacy	• Mentor roles with first-year students. Junior residences with meeting space	• Elon experiences (internships and study abroad/study USA) • Courses in arts and sciences • Celebrations of campus leaders (leaders of 21st century, Omicron Delta Kappa, Phi Beta Kappa, etc.)
Senior	• Station at Mill Point Apts. • Amenities and advanced services (career advising and networking, apartment living lifestyle, networking, etc.)	• Senior living environment with semi-autonomy, self-governance	• Core capstone seminar • Major capstone • Application for employment/graduate school/professional school • Graduation

race and ethnicity (Chickering & Gamson, 1987; Engstrom & Tinto, 2008). Yet to become an even more effective platform for learning delivery, residential campus work requires the same careful planning, learning outcome definition, alignment, and coordination as every other form of engaged learning. All parts of the university have to be connected through clear roles, responsibilities, and learning outcomes (Schroeder, 1995). Just as we scaffold undergraduate leadership and mentoring experiences, we quickly learned the importance of scaffolding learning outcomes in the residential neighborhoods through a range of techniques and pedagogies, including annual LLC syllabi, annual neighborhood plans, and alignment with academic programs and calendars—all through a clear student development model.

Keep Learning at the Center of the Residential Campus

Tackling residential learning first requires understanding not only how students learn but also how students progress and develop intellectually, personally, and socially on campus. The watershed moment that shaped our larger aspirations for the past decade and the decade ahead involved a student–faculty–staff team encountering a campus learning map during a visit to Case Western Reserve University in Ohio. This map of student connections and progression on campus—across academics, residence life, and other campus services—forced us to confront the fact that at Elon we had never articulated the role that living–learning efforts played across a student's 4-year developmental pathway. Developing a residential campus plan necessitated consideration of how a residential campus initiative could connect with other university initiatives and programs and be scaffolded across students' 4-year experience.

Around the same time, we visited Dickinson College and heard their team portray the residential campus as a primary platform for delivering learning and bringing to life central campus goals and values. At Dickinson, core institutional values of diversity, citizenship and service, career development, and sustainability were threaded through their residential neighborhoods. Staff articulated how intergroup dialogues, interdisciplinary first-year seminar courses, local service agencies, sustainability staff, and more were connected to students through their neighborhoods rather than randomly across the entire campus.

Dickinson's focus on the residential neighborhood as a learning platform and Case Western Reserve's developmental pathway were transformative concepts because they situated residential living within a scaffolded 4-year learning model. Like any learning map or ladder, the RCP can assist campus leaders in visualizing the residential campus and individual residential units as platforms for delivering developmentally tailored learning, for connecting with other learning and resources on campus, and for designing living and learning that supports and benefits from the full range of learning occurring on campus.

For each class year, the RCP asks campuses to identify six areas: (a) developmental themes; (b) academic and interpersonal needs; (c) academic connections, mentoring, and services; (d) living spaces; (e) class year events; and (f) unmet student needs. By mapping students' learning and development across their 4 years, the curriculum, and residential spaces, faculty and staff together are able to design and pinpoint specific residential experiences to fill gaps, dovetail with existing campus initiatives, and further support overarching learning outcomes. Regardless of the campus resources, facilities, or even inclination toward LLCs or residential colleges a campus might have, the RCP challenges campus leaders to design an integrated living, learning, and developmental plan that aligns with and strengthens the entire campus learning pathway. This mapping ensures a residential campus plan is strategic, purposeful, campus specific, and based in students' learning and development across the residential campus.

Ensure That Facilities and Budgets Support Learning

Articulating the RCP also altered campus thinking about the role of facilities and shifted us from housing students based on amenities to housing based on class-year–appropriate learning outcomes and developmental needs. Institutions can benefit from creating long-term construction, renovation, and refurbishment plans; financial models; and staffing models. By articulating the ideal learning pathway for students, leaders are freed up to consider how facilities, programs, staffing, student services (career development, academic advising, leadership development, writing skills), and experiences (mentoring, faculty involvement, privacy, support networks, student governance, etc.) can be scaled or targeted to specific age groups and residential neighborhoods.

Building out the vision from the RCP does not happen overnight, and it includes frustrations. It took time for our facilities and budgets to align with the developmental needs of students. At times, we were forced to house first-year students in spaces we thought better fit sophomores or house sophomores in upper-class apartments. Inconsistent facilities, budgets, and staffing models across neighborhoods also caused frustration, particularly as older neighborhoods experienced delays in receiving funding to support nonrevenue-generating spaces for mentoring, academic, and social development. Therefore, university budget committees should be well versed in the goals of the residential campus initiative so they understand the full range of personnel, capital, and equipment requests coming from the residential campus committee.

Engage Faculty and Staff in Collaboration Focused on Learning

The articulation of learning goals and objectives is an important step for an effective collaboration between academics and student affairs. This holistic view of the student learning experience acknowledges each campus unit's role in ultimately producing a graduate of the university. For instance, the library and writing center teams began thinking about how to embed their faculty and staff within neighborhoods and provide scaffolded learning opportunities in first-year housing neighborhoods as well as junior and senior apartments. The campus community began to think about how to connect students, faculty, and staff to that learning. A "campus conversation" helped to gather broader feedback on the RCP and pushed faculty and staff to consider intersections between the residential campus and potential out-of-class experiences that could deepen learning that was introduced in the classroom.

Because of this work, several new collaborations emerged. The Love School of Business developed the entrepreneurship learning community to harness student interest in entrepreneurship and start-ups. Art and creative writing students and faculty designed an arts and letters LLC to support student arts culture and to teach students how people who care about the arts live and engage each other. The African and African American studies minor worked with student affairs to create the African diaspora LLC: exploring Blackness across the globe, which provides students opportunities to explore African, African American, and Black culture and take a deeper dive into their own identities, participate in dialogue surrounding African culture, and get involved in the local community. Other LLCs—sustainable living, interfaith house, disparities in education, gender and sexuality, performing arts, sport management, STEM, polyglot (world languages), outdoors, and paideia: politics and active citizenship—engage students, faculty, and staff in developing learning opportunities for students with different interests along their developmental trajectories.

Develop Syllabi, Learning Goals, and Other Methods to Assess Learning

To clarify the learning aspect of the residential campus, we adopted a new practice of asking faculty and staff involved in the residential campus to create learning outcomes for all their activities. Faculty and staff LLC advisors create LLC syllabi: articulating learning outcomes, expectations, required texts or experiences, and policies. These syllabi were developed as a way to situate advisors' roles with academic language and culture and to make transparent the learning outcomes delivered through the residential campus. These syllabi were quickly integrated into, and became an important part of, the campus plan. Today, these syllabi are developed each semester, some by LLC faculty and some written collaboratively by students, faculty, and staff. Syllabi include experiences, events, and trips designed to meet articulated learning and developmental outcomes and are now an essential tool for assessing the effectiveness of the residential campus.

In addition to LLCs, Elon's residential campus includes another layer of residential organization to capture students and spaces not part of themed LLCs. Elon's residence halls and apartments are divided into eight residential neighborhoods, each with its own neighborhood association composed of students, faculty, and staff, who develop an annual neighborhood plan, mentoring programs, and campus partnerships. Faculty directors in each neighborhood lead the planning with careful consideration of learning outcomes and assessment plans. Neighborhood associations submit their plans to the residential campus advisory committee and residential campus leadership team, including the vice president of student life and members of the provost's office. In order to focus on learning outcomes, Elon's residential neighborhoods either have themes, such as civic engagement, or focus their efforts more squarely on the age or developmental level of their students.

These neighborhood learning and development plans can be tied back to best practices on a number of campuses we visited. For instance, during a campus visit to Gettysburg College, we saw first-year seminars linked to teams of faculty and staff working within "burgs," or neighborhoods. This model had students choosing courses, not housing amenities. Burg students, faculty, and staff were asked to set an intellectual tone; to develop an overall approach for the year; to plan specific events, including TED talks during monthly dinners, "life of a scholar" talks, with significant members of the community discussing their ups and downs as a scholar; and to create developmental extended orientation sessions.

In addition to residential neighborhood assessment, we have used a range of institutional measures to analyze the work of the residential campus initiative, including triangulating data and specific questions from retention and graduation studies, the National Study of Living Learning Programs, the National Study of Student Engagement, student surveys, the Multi-Institutional Study of Leadership, assessments from residentially linked classes, and more. Working with institutional research and effectiveness staff early in the design of each neighborhood's learning outcomes helps in preplanning assessment tools and schedules. The takeaway has been that, like all assessment, early planning of assessment and consultation with institutional effectiveness staff create stronger results. The close pairing of residential and living–learning outcomes with institutional outcomes makes this work easier. In addition, a campus-wide focus on the RCP creates an expectation that faculty and staff will receive formal and informal updates and reports on the progress and effectiveness of these initiatives.

Placing learning at the center of residential campus initiatives takes planning, personnel, and time. The RCP, LLC syllabi, neighborhood plans, and additional assessments centralized the role of faculty and staff in overseeing the integration of curricula, foundational university initiatives, campus traditions, student development, partnerships, facilities, and experiences to support student learning. This articulation and mapping of learning objectives provided faculty and staff with a clearer view of the connections that existed and were still needed to scaffold learning across students' 4-year residential and campus experience. Most important, mapping and assessing student learning paved the way for deep and meaningful engagement of a crucial factor to the residential campus's success: faculty.

Focus on Relationships

A key question for any campus is how to ensure that living on campus is more tightly interwoven within the people, roles, and mentoring relationships occurring elsewhere on campus. Although we believed that robust residential campus learning occurs best in community and through relationships, studying leading campus programs and completing the RCP (particularly the sections focused on connections, mentoring, and experiences) clarified that a key driver of student success includes building collaborative teams and layering important relationships throughout a student's residential experience in support of high-impact and mentored learning. This mapping of learning forced deeper consideration of living on campus as a connected and relationship-driven experience that develops student belonging as well as personal, social, and intellectual development (Felten & Lambert, 2020).

Perhaps more important, investing in students, faculty, and staff ensures the residential campus is a relationship-rich, high-impact practice (Kuh, 2008) powered by student, staff, and faculty mentoring. Integrating the residential campus into student, faculty, and staff leadership roles makes it possible to weave the residential campus through the core functions of campus. In 2014, a widely influential Gallup/Purdue study of 30,000 college graduates drove this point home: Alumni who reported a strong sense of well-being in life after college were those who reported key relationships during college (Gallup, Inc., 2014). Most critically—as faculty consider "why" to invest in a residential campus initiative—just 3% of alumni in the study reported having these relationships (Ray & Marken, 2014). Yet students report forming valuable relationships with faculty and staff through learning communities and residential campus initiatives (Felten & Lambert, 2020; Haynes & Janosik, 2012; Wawrzynski et al., 2009), and the quality of carefully developed out-of-class interactions with faculty actually outweighs the frequency of such interactions (Cox & Orehovec, 2007). Thus, we know that to achieve the learning, connections, mentoring, and relationships identified in the RCP, efforts must be positioned as a central component of the overall campus experience, involving collaborative faculty and staff leadership teams and champions, departments across campus, faculty and staff mentoring, and connections to shared governance and recognition.

Foster Layered Mentoring

A series of visits to residential programs also revealed a rich tapestry of mentoring occurring on campuses around the nation. We saw that faculty played key roles in the success of residential campus initiatives and quickly learned that the more faculty worked side by side with students and staff, the deeper the relationships formed and the more successful the overall efforts. Adding a faculty member here or there was not the answer; instead, campuses were integrating faculty throughout their efforts and interweaving layers of students, faculty, and staff within their programs.

Visiting Vanderbilt, Gettysburg, the University of Missouri, Southern Methodist University, Virginia Tech, Washington University, Cornell, and Dickinson College revealed a wide range of innovative approaches for stacking layers of student, faculty, and staff relationships. Residential college boards (e.g., the residential commons at Middlebury) and residential neighborhood committees (at Cornell, Dickinson, and Vanderbilt) utilized integrated teams of student, faculty, and staff leaders and mentors. Middlebury's commons and Cornell's residential colleges utilized a pairing of faculty deans and residential deans, who led a team of student, faculty, and staff members—all with different roles and responsibilities.

These collaborative and inclusive models resulted in multiple on-ramps for students, faculty, and staff to engage in living and learning that is focused on people and connections. Similarly, Elon's neighborhoods are led by a faculty director and community director, who work with faculty affiliates, faculty-in-residence (like Jennifer, the author of our opening vignette), LLC advisors, student eco reps, resident assistants, learning assistants, orientation leaders, residentially assigned librarians, dining liaisons, and more. Position descriptions for faculty, staff, and student roles in the residential campus all include language focused on relationships and mentoring. Student, faculty, and staff training and development focus on relationships over procedures. The intention is to ensure a student's residential neighborhood serves as their first cohort and their social and intellectual home base from which to build.

In turn, this focus on people and relationships has spread to how we hire new employees. Faculty advisors for LLCs assist in hiring of resident assistants, and every campus interview process for new faculty hires includes an associate provost who explains the importance of mentoring on campus and asks candidates about their interest in serving as a mentor through residential campus initiatives (as Jennifer's vignette at the beginning describes). At Washington University in Saint Louis, just as they recruited faculty for a range of roles, they hired and trained students to serve in a range of roles as resident assistants, academic assistants, and peer mentors. That overarching goal—of ensuring an intensive and multilevel support network for students—helped us understand how integrated and layered leadership played a foundational role in building support for students and pipelines for faculty to connect with the residential campus across varying career stages. These opportunities for different levels of support informed Elon's programming and has been essential as we develop mentoring relationships and leadership pipelines.

Build Collaborative Teams

Leadership matters when it comes to residential campus initiatives. The significant investments in people needed to bring a residential vision to life necessitates allocating resources for faculty and staff time, professional development, and rewards. Investing in people to advance LLCs and a broader residential campus initiative begins with students, faculty, and staff working together to translate essential messages and bring their constituents into the project. These collaborative partnerships among faculty, student affairs staff, and students help each group better understand how to integrate in- and out-of-class learning opportunities and develop a community (Jackson & Stevens, 1990), and these partnerships are critical to moving from siloed approaches to efforts focused on students' actual experiences on campus (Golde & Pribbenow, 2000; Shapiro & Levine, 1999; see chapters 5, 6, and 7, this volume, for more information on partnerships).

Substantial research has shown the value of integrating living and learning leadership to drive student success (Engstrom & Tinto, 2008; Inkelas et al., 2018; Kuh, 1996; Mayhew et al., 2016; Wawrzynski et al., 2009). Inkelas et al.

(2018) articulated that faculty and staff collaboration, based on "clearly articulated goals and objectives" (p. 19), is the foundation of their groundbreaking best practices model in *Living–Learning Communities That Work*. Shapiro (2013) called this collaboration between academic affairs and student affairs the "magic ingredient" undergirding the success of learning communities and requiring greater assessment and research. Building a broad-based campus team also aligned with two of our campus's long-standing beliefs: (a) that wisdom exists within our entire community, and (b) any large-scale institutional effort—whether it be designing a strategic plan, enhancing diversity–equity–inclusion, or combating the spread of COVID-19—requires joining together the expertise and voices of students, faculty, and staff.

Building this collaboration requires more than merely bringing together the usual suspects in residence life and academic affairs staff. As Inkelas et al. (2018) pointed out, such collaborations must be "contextually bound" (p. 19) within the campus culture, and campuses must first build a culture to support the work (Shapiro & Levine, 1999). Thus, it helps to begin the work by intentionally bringing together a broad group of influencers from across campus, including librarians, campus recreation and wellness, academic advising, civic engagement, and student involvement staff. Ask faculty and staff who experienced the benefits of learning in a residential college as undergraduates to share their experiences and explain the gap the university is working to close in order to enhance student success. This process can identify champions who clearly understand and embrace the value of the work going forward. Others may be chosen because they will challenge and strengthen the final product. Seating champions alongside skeptics allows for personal narrative sharing and vision setting for the university's desired outcomes.

Building this deeper bench of engaged and expert faculty and staff helped ensure that conversations about living and learning on campus were happening on a much wider scale on campus, at the colleague, department, division, and school levels utilizing the different languages, values, and epistemologies from across the academy. Elon's group was cochaired by a tenured full professor and a student life dean to model the development of a seamless and integrated approach, and the broad and integrated team first assisted with the development of the campus vision for all residential initiatives. A series of meetings, lunches, and visits to other college campuses in cross-functional teams allowed relationships to build and deepen within this core group of faculty, staff, and students. More important, the team eventually earned campus buy-in for the integration of the living and learning spheres of campus. Touring campus facilities, exploring research on LLCs and residential initiatives, and sharing examples of best practices from across the country increased team competence. We even provided committee members with small stipends so they could invite colleagues for discussion over coffee or lunch. In other words, a broad-based team can work across campus populations to translate how living–learning initiatives mutually reinforce diverse goals across campus units.

We also adapted our initial residential campus committee into layers of ongoing campus committees and structures that were embedded within the university's shared governance model. For example, a residential campus advisory committee, appointed by an academic council and staff advisory council and recognized in the faculty handbook, is composed of faculty and staff from all representative units. This faculty and staff group now officially serves to assess, evaluate, and advise the RCP from across the institution. A leadership group consisting of upper-level administrators from across campus oversees budgets, staffing, and construction related to living–learning efforts.

This broad campus integration across units led to the residential campus becoming part of the interview process and orientation of every new faculty member at Elon. Search committees even identified candidates with residential college experience during the search process. For the first time, new residential apartments and classrooms were designed with faculty feedback. Dining halls and catering services sought faculty feedback and as a result were able to engage faculty in thinking about the community, learning, and food. Each of these transformations required faculty time, the scarcest resource in their bids to promotion and tenure. Thus, the residential campus vision needed to be embraced as an intellectual enterprise, one that fostered the learning goals of the community. Student affairs and academic affairs administrators began writing letters describing the role of faculty in achieving the residential vision to provide written support as faculty worked their way through performance reviews with department chairs and promotion and tenure processes.

Finding the right champions and leaders is crucial. For many years, a distinguished university professor who had led some of our most crucial academic initiatives on campus served as a faculty fellow for the residential campus and regularly spoke at faculty meetings about how these efforts drive student success. Now our leadership team includes a newly formed position at the university, the director of academic–residential partnerships—a joint report to the vice president of student life and associate provost who also has faculty rank—who works with all faculty involved in the residential campus, is a national leader in the field, and currently serves as the cochair and founding member of the Residential College Society. Similarly, the residential campus advisory committee is structured to reflect and support this integrated leadership model and appears in the faculty handbook as an assigned faculty committee. These layers of leadership ensure that the residential campus remains a central focus on campus. Although balancing these layers across multiple academic disciplines can be challenging, these joint structures continually keep us honest by reinforcing the need to bring languages, pedagogies, and people together from across the institution in support of the residential campus.

Sustaining a Residential Campus Initiative

Designing and maintaining a residential campus initiative is a Herculean and ongoing process. Like any strategic initiative, this work requires annual plans, extensive coordination, leadership and accountability, and a great deal of communication across the campus. Faculty leaders benefit from access to ongoing professional development, support, rewards, and recognition. New students, faculty, staff, administrators, trustees, and parents also join the community every year and need help understanding and learning to connect to the campus vision and pathway. Even more challenging can be addressing the impact of aging facilities and furnishings at the same time institutions face additional pressures and tighter budgets.

Sustaining a residential campus requires significant and consistent focus and leadership. It involves constantly updating a residential campus plan and ensuring that decision makers understand the progress and next steps of the plan. Casting a wide net of faculty and staff participants and leaders can help with keeping the residential campus at the forefront of thinking across campus. Every year as we assess and plot our plan, we are reminded of the value of faculty leadership in crafting a residential vision and designing the partnerships, programs, facilities, and assessment to connect learning to every aspect of the student experience. Since we began systematically engaging faculty in leading this work, we have experienced increases in student retention and learning. Along the way, Elon faculty have become the next generation of leading scholars on LLCs and other residential initiatives. These outcomes can be tied back to our first efforts to articulate the student experience, bring learning to all corners of the campus, and engage faculty in designing intellectually charged and seamlessly connected living and learning.

As many colleges and universities across the country are reconsidering and deepening commitments to diversity, equity, and inclusion, at Elon we turned to our residential campus to begin a plan for the next decade to support three central objectives within our next strategic plan in order for our community to thrive: (a) teaching all students to build lifelong mentoring networks; (b) ensuring every student, faculty, and staff member increases their intercultural competencies; and (c) building a culture of well-being bolstered by student, faculty, and staff well-being competencies. In combination with new curricular and learning elements, we believe the platform of the residential campus will be at the heart of students thriving (Eidum et al., 2020) and engaging students more deeply in these essential learning goals. This clear articulation that the residential campus is central to the university's strategic plan for the future builds upon and deepens the success of our initial residential efforts in the last plan.

For colleges and universities across the country, deeply connecting living and learning serves as a multiplying factor in reaching overall campus mission and goals. Utilizing a strategic planning process to advance institutional buy-in and understanding, campuses can develop a residential vision closely tied to campus mission and values; embed the residential campus within shared governance structures, educate faculty and staff, and identify faculty champions for initiatives; enhance mentoring of students by building a cadre or layered set of students, faculty, and staff mentors within residential neighborhoods; increase student success; and achieve central institutional goals and learning outcomes. The process begins with significant investment in developing an integrated team of students, faculty, and staff who can define key outcomes, translate goals to their colleagues, and connect with institutional culture and structures. Faculty must play a key role in leading the development of a residential campus vision and plan, and the vision of fully integrated living and learning environments on college campuses will not be achieved without their participation.

References

Chickering, A. W., & Gamson, Z. F. (1987). Seven principles for good practice in undergraduate education. *AAHE Bulletin, 39*(2), 3–7. https://doi.org/10.1002/tl.37219914708

Cox, B., & Orehovec, E. (2007). Faculty-student interaction outside the classroom: A typology from a residential college. *Review of Higher Education: Journal of the Association for the Study of Higher Education, 30*(4), 343–362. https://doi.org/10.1353/rhe.2007.0033

Eidum, J., Lomicka, L., Chiang, W., Endick, G., & Stratton, J. (2020). Thriving in residential learning communities. *Learning Communities Research and Practice, 8*(1), Article 7.

Elon University. (2009). *The Elon commitment strategic plan: Significantly enhancing Elon's campus with premier new academic and residential facilities and a commitment to protecting our environment.* https://www.elon.edu/u/administration/president/strategic-plan-2020/campus/

Elon University. (2010). *Residential campus committee report: Living & learning at Elon University in 2020* [Unpublished internal Elon University report].

Engstrom, C., & Tinto, V. (2008). Learning better together: The impact of learning communities on the persistence of low-income students. *Opportunity Matters, 1*(1), 5–21.

Felten, P., & Lambert, L. (2020). *Relationship rich education: How human connections drive success in college.* Johns Hopkins University Press.

Gallup, Inc. (2014). *Great jobs great lives. The 2014 Gallup-Purdue index report: A study of more than 30,000 college graduates across the U.S.* https://www.luminafoundation.org/files/resources/galluppurdueindex-report-2014.pdf

Golde, C. M., & Pribbenow, D. A. (2000). Understanding faculty involvement in residential learning communities. *Journal of College Student Development, 41*(1), 27–40.

Haynes, C., & Janosik, S. M. (2012). Faculty and staff member benefits from involvement in living–learning programs. *Journal of College & University Student Housing, 38*(2), 32–45.

Inkelas, K. K., Jessup-Anger, J., Benjamin, M., & Wawrzynski, M. R. (2018). *Living–learning communities that work: A research-based model for design, delivery, and assessment.* Stylus.

Jackson, G. S., & Stevens, S. (1990). Incorporating faculty and staff into residence halls. *Journal of College and University Student Housing, 20*(1), 7–10.

Kuh, G. D. (1996). Guiding principles for creating learning environments for undergraduates. *Journal of College Student Development, 37*(2), 135–148.

Kuh, G. D. (2008). *High-impact educational practices: What they are, who has access to them, and why they matter.* Association of American Colleges and Universities.

Mayhew, M. J., Rockenbach, A. N., Bowman, N. A., Seifert, T. A., Wolniak, G. C., Pascarella, E. T., & Terenzini, P. T. (2016). *How college affects students, Vol. 3: 21st century evidence that higher education works.* Jossey-Bass.

Ray, J., & Marken, S. (2014, May 6). *Life in college matters for life after college.* https://news.gallup.com/poll/168848/life-college-matters-life-college.aspx

Schroeder, C. C. (1995). Student learning: An imperative for housing programs committed to educating students. Association of College and University Housing Officers-International. *Talking Stick, 13*, 4–7.

Shapiro, N. S., & Levine, J. H. (1999). *Creating learning communities: A practical guide to winning support, organizing for change, and implementing programs.* Jossey-Bass.

Shapiro, N. (2013). When the students we have are not the students we want: The transformative power of learning communities. *Learning Communities Research and Practice, 1*(1), Article 17. https://airtable.com/shrqC2qwuTiRtRhB8/tblTC2OhqfZt567Po/viw2cFjBWIf2dkl5r/recYgw0xv7AfP52eZ/fldSRfESKfQ8pms3w/atttk5z31zZiHGnYs

Wawrzynski, M. R., Jessup-Anger, J. E., Stolz, K., Helman, C., & Beaulieu, J. (2009). Exploring students' perceptions of academically based living–learning communities. *College Student Affairs Journal, 28*(1), 138–158. https://epublications.marquette.edu/edu_fac/90

PART TWO

BUILDING EFFECTIVE FACULTY PARTNERSHIPS IN LLCs

Faculty and Residential Life Partnerships

Jennifer E. Eidum and Lara L. Lomicka

This section outlines ways to capitalize on faculty and residential life partnerships for successful living–learning communities (LLCs). Authors focus on key areas of LLC development, including collaboration on programming, codeveloping LLC curricula, fostering broad campus partnerships, and creating the conditions for effective faculty–student engagement. These chapters offer various perspectives from the field to (re)think successful faculty–student engagement programs. The ideas presented will be useful for both new and seasoned faculty, administrators, and student affairs professionals who work with LLCs.

Erck, Duncan, and Garrett (chapter 5) open this section by presenting a four-step collaborative model based on theory and practice that articulates the vision, resources, oversight, and successes that stem from flourishing collaboration efforts by student affairs and academic partners. Next, Krieger (chapter 6) explores the professional pathways of faculty and residential life professionals outside of campus partnerships, offers information for effective selecting and onboarding of faculty partners in LLCs, and sets up communication models for faculty and residential life partners. In chapter 7, Post explores partnerships that are necessary for success between residence life and academic affairs and presents a list of best practices for faculty who may be serving in LLCs or considering working with an LLC. Targeting both faculty and campus administrators, Manz, Ward, and Gundlach (chapter 8) offer ideas for cocreating a curriculum that weaves both classroom instruction with hands-on learning. Finally, Jessup-Anger and Benjamin (chapter 9) propose a framework for faculty–student engagement in LLCs that creates a symbiosis between academic and personal connection, resulting in gains in student learning, development, and satisfaction.

VIGNETTE

Partnering for Success

Terri Garrett

One of the most treasured aspects of my position is to oversee and facilitate the development of new living–learning communities (LLCs) because this involves partnering with faculty and academic affairs. Engaging faculty in this process is certainly priceless because of the academic expertise they bring to the partnership, but it is their passion and enthusiasm for engaging students in our residential communities that really excite me and fill me with hope for the future!

One example of an academic/faculty collaborative that filled me with that joy is Baylor & Beyond LLC, a community that partners with Baylor University's modern languages and cultures academic unit to focus on developing worldwide leaders. We assembled a steering committee to develop the vision with key stakeholders (e.g., faculty, staff, and students), and I cochaired the committee alongside a key departmental academic leader. To establish a shared team approach, it was important to understand the stories of each member and their hopes for a community focused on global engagement. Hearing faculty, staff, and students articulate their perceived needs of students within this type of community was encouraging and exciting. The diversity of opinion aided in developing a vision statement and learning outcomes, such as expanding global perspectives and promoting language acquisition. To benchmark similar LLCs, we went on site visits to observe how various institutions operationalized their program's vision, and this provided precious time away from campus to dream collectively about the LLC we sought to create. Furthermore, this shared time allowed for interactions that led to meaningful friendships that likely would not have formed outside of this collaboration.

Once the vision of Baylor & Beyond was established, we identified how our respective areas would supply resources to actualize the LLC's goals. Planning for program structures and personnel was the longest phase for the steering committee because it involved all prelaunch aspects, such as community location, size, space layout, and recruitment. Walking the committee members through these logistics helped them understand the foundational pieces of an LLC and to appreciate the administrative underpinnings involved in an intentional learning community. Again, that faculty buy-in and opinion sharing was vital because it allowed living and learning to come together to create a seamless experience for students.

Each time I work through this process, I am reminded that faculty and academic partners need to believe that our housing department cares deeply about them as individuals, their academic disciplines, and the LLC's success. I have found that these trusting relationships start in the development and vision stage and grow over time, just like good friendships do. With each passing year, Baylor & Beyond continues to strengthen its partnership across campus to broaden global and cultural engagement opportunities for students. Better yet, along the way I developed some wonderful faculty friends who enhance my personal and professional life in significant ways!

5

STARTING WITH A SHARED APPROACH

Fostering Student Affairs–Academic Affairs Collaboration in Living–Learning Communities

Ryan W. Erck, Leia Duncan, and Terri Garrett

There is nothing quite like the energy felt in a room of colleagues excited to work together on a shared project. The anticipation while waiting to assert a new idea during a lull in conversation, the crescendo of voices offering support when solving a problem, and the laughter at an inside joke steeped in a mutual history of sweaty brows are all part of the shared experience of united efforts. Unfortunately, it can be difficult to imagine this scenario when considering how insular divisions can be at many institutions. It is easy to deflect the efforts of constructing a successful living–learning community (LLC) onto a specific faculty member who has enough enthusiasm for everyone, with the hope that an energetic collaboration will naturally evolve. The sad reality is that this oft-attempted approach is riddled with susceptibility for failure.

Collaboration on LLCs can be challenging, awkward, and sometimes defeating. However, when approached as a truly shared experience, it can be invigorating and inspiring and remind us how our passion for serving students first began. Inkelas et al. (2018) emphasized that "the design, delivery, and assessment of LLCs takes time, creativity, collaboration, and a commitment to integration across areas traditionally siloed" (p. 142). This chapter is a guide to help facilitate LLC collaboration in a way that is true to the concept of "sharing" this process.

The Context of Collaboration

Although collaboration between student affairs (SA) and academic affairs (AA) has become a more popular practice in recent decades, these two institutional functions remain loosely coupled on most campuses (O'Halloran, 2019). AA typically entails a provost positioned over multiple units composed of deans, chairs, faculty, and related roles, such as academic advising or support. In turn, SA often involves a vice president leading departments and staff in areas such as student activities, orientation, or residence life. Although academic roles are specialized, often autonomous, and operate through shared governance, SA is often more hierarchical in structure and follows a centralized decision-making process (Inkelas et al., 2018; Kuk et al., 2012).

In addition to functional and organizational differences, SA and AA often embody vastly different cultures that consist of divergent values, communication styles, and personalities (Golde & Pribbenow, 2000). Such differences cause partnering efforts to fail roughly 50% of the time (Kezar, 2005). Even with a high risk of failure, numerous publications have demonstrated positive benefits, such as student learning, a sense of community, financial efficiency, and reduced waste or redundancy (Arcelus, 2011; Cook & Lewis, 2007; LePeau, 2015; O'Halloran, 2019).

Collaboration is generally framed as a productive practice, but multiple studies have specifically confirmed its importance to LLC success (Brower & Inkelas, 2010; Ellett & Schmidt, 2011; Erck & Sriram, 2021; Inkelas et al., 2008). In fact, Brower and Inkelas (2010) cited strong SA–AA partnerships as the first characteristic of successful LLCs. In their recently published best practices model for LLCs (BPM for LLCs), Inkelas et al. (2018) offered readers a comprehensive empirical framework for understanding, implementing, and evaluating LLCs. Collaboration lies at the base of their pyramid-shaped model within an LLC's infrastructure. Although faculty and hall director partnerships are often the most visible form of LLC collaboration (see chapter 6), additional constituents (e.g., provost, director of housing, dean) and additional functional areas (e.g., student activities, academic support, dining) are often involved.

Inkelas et al. (2018) noted that "Partnerships between student affairs and academic affairs are critical to the success of LLCs" (p. 18). Yet, with limited exceptions (e.g., BPM of LLCs), practical steps for ensuring successful LLC-specific collaboration are lacking. Pulling from our own broad experiences as SA practitioners (who regularly collaborate with AA colleagues), we address this void in the current chapter by introducing a model focused specifically on SA–AA collaboration.

LLC Model of Collaboration

In reference to SA–AA working together, Inkelas et al. (2018) stated that "Without a strong collaborative relationship between these entities, an LLC will not realize true integration in living and learning, and students may be deprived of seamless learning experiences" (p. 32). Although the literature relentlessly espouses their value, Arcelus (2011) still asked, "If student affairs–academic affairs collaboration is such a good idea, why are there so few examples of these partnerships in American higher education?" (p. 61). Some scholars also emphasize the lack of research highlighting effective partnership characteristics (LePeau, 2015; Whitt et al., 2008). Although many elevate the idea of SA–AA collaboration, resources for partnering, especially in LLCs, are wanting.

By weaving together practices from the literature, our own experiences (including those Terri describes in our chapter's opening vignette), and the concept of sharing to promote success, we offer such a resource through the Living–Learning Community–Model of Collaboration (LLC–MOC). In developing this model, we pulled from our more than 40 collective years of practitioner experience, academic research, and conference papers or presentations on LLC faculty involvement and successful collaborations. In addition, our abundant time spent consulting with faculty and administrators from more than 30 institutions on LLC and faculty-in-residence (FIR) planning has allowed us to observe LLC implementation in numerous contexts. The LLC–MOC is a four-stage iterative process, as seen in Figure 5.1.

The model is grounded in current scholarship and proven practices, and it more pointedly pulls from Inkelas et al.'s (2018) BPM of LLCs and Kezar's (2005) three-stage archetype of collaboration that incorporates building and sustaining commitment. The LLC–MOC has four tiers, moving from *shared vision* up to *shared success* (which is both an outcome of collaboration and a launching point for sustained LLC longevity). Because a singular path toward success is unlikely, the side arrows in the figure demonstrate the iterative nature of collaboration. This back-and-forth allows SA–AA partnerships to unfold and continue blossoming as time passes. When changes need to occur (e.g., turnover, rebranding), it is recommended that the four stages of the model are consulted in the spirit of continuous improvement. This model serves as a practical and hands-on resource for pursuing successful SA–AA collaboration in LLCs.

More than 2 decades ago, the document *Powerful Partnerships* made the case that "Only when everyone on campus—particularly academic affairs and student affairs staff—shares the responsibility for student learning will we be able to make significant progress in improving it" (American

Figure 5.1. Living–learning community model of collaboration.

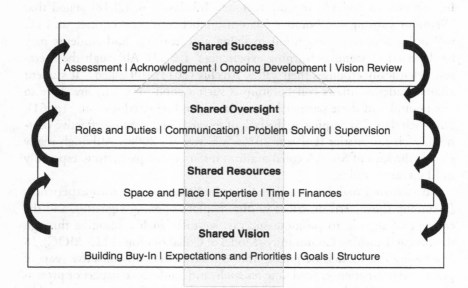

Association for Higher Education et al., 1998, p. 2). Years later, this call to action remains relevant, and the shared responsibility for learning is magnified in the case of LLCs. Although some LLCs have persevered as solely housing ventures, we maintain that SA–AA partnerships should be a cornerstone of these programs to maximize success. Whether a campus has thriving LLC initiatives or is just getting started, the model's four steps—outlined in the sections to follow—help lay the groundwork to ensure collaborative success for the faculty, staff, administrators, and students involved.

Shared Vision

Sharing a vision entails building buy-in, creating expectations and priorities, formulating goals, and defining a structure. These exercises help build the foundation for collaborative LLCs.

Building Buy-In

Many scholars posit that establishing support from campus leadership is imperative to successful partnerships during their inception, especially when they involve faculty members (Cook et al., 2007; Inkelas et al.,

2018; Kezar, 2005; Whitt et al., 2008). However, LLCs bring many layers of complexity and require a wide range of buy-in from various domains. This early buy-in is crucial to success because shared planning and decision-making, in the absence of shared priorities, fall short of true collaboration (Cook et al., 2007).

Top-down mandates are frequently met with resistance, and bottom-up efforts are often sidelined for initiatives deemed more essential. In short, buy-in needs to be shared across all levels and divisions. Sharing buy-in includes higher-level conversations (e.g., provost and vice president of SA), mid-level conversations (e.g., academic deans and directors of residence life), and conversations with those involved on the ground floor of LLCs (e.g., hall directors, faculty partners, program directors). In addition, these conversations should include the departments that will most likely be involved through programming or resource sharing (e.g., leadership development, civic engagement, tutoring resources). Terri's description of the Baylor & Beyond LLC offers an example of this collaborative visioning. Bringing various LLC stakeholders into early discussions offers tiered opportunities to convey a vision and recruit support. An initial step toward finding these stakeholders is understanding the research on LLCs and their associated outcomes. We suggest starting with Inkelas et al.'s (2018) *Living–Learning Communities That Work* as a comprehensive primer.

Another recommendation is to understand the intricacies of the campus culture, which includes learning the local history with similar initiatives and exploring how LLC plans can be leveraged to meet many needs. Erck and Sriram (2021) demonstrated how the diverse and often competing cultures of a university can be mediated by LLCs. It is helpful to show partners how these initiatives benefit their own goals. For example, it might help to demonstrate to the provost how LLCs can encourage students' academic gains. Buy-in is about strategically conveying the LLC message through evidence-informed plans that are backed up by prospects of shared success.

Expectations and Priorities

Setting expectations in LLCs is important (Inkelas et al., 2018), especially when it involves multiple constituents working together. We discuss individual expectations, such as job descriptions, in the "Shared Oversight" section; however, regarding the creation of a shared vision, expectations and priorities need to be established in a collaborative process that stresses the importance of the partnership and resulting programmatic features. These expectations include ensuring an LLC initiative is a significant part of each partner's workload. The work of LLCs can easily get sidelined if partners do not place enough value on the program or have time to focus on expected duties. We recommend early discussions about the bigger picture for involvement through questions such as the following:

- Will faculty partners plan programs, or will more of that expectation lie with staff?
- Will faculty (or staff) teach LLC courses?
- Will faculty partners be asked to serve for a set term, such as 2 years?

Although these questions may seem generic, expectations can quickly escalate to frustration and misperception when left undiscussed.

With distinct cultural norms, it is important to translate expectations into a common language understood by both divisions. In our experience working with a vast number of LLC programs, we have witnessed numerous cases where students lose interest in an LLC when a favorite faculty member leaves. We have also observed faculty investment wane because a new administrator is unconvinced of the value of promoting cocurricular faculty interactions. Therefore, LLC initiatives should have clearly defined and understood expectations for the faculty and staff involved. Furthermore, clear priorities set programs up for longevity, even when personnel turnover occurs.

Goal Setting

Setting LLC goals is a step that occasionally gets overlooked (Inkelas et al., 2018) or is attempted in an isolated way that is detrimental to collaboration. One of the more futile efforts here is to have everyone agree on one primary goal. A second common issue is a complete lack of a unifying goal in favor of appeasing those involved. We recommend splitting the difference between these familiar barriers. For example, academic partners may be unaware of how LLCs positively diversify housing assignments or aid in filling beds. Likewise, residence life colleagues may underestimate how LLCs funnel students into certain majors or give academic units marketing exposure for prospective students. Furthermore, other partnering SA units, such as student activities or a leadership center, may have their own agendas for collaboration. Not only is there a cultural divide between the groups involved, but they also pursue independent goals. Welcoming these competing goals, though, can be an asset to the process instead of a liability, if managed appropriately (Erck & Sriram, 2021).

The beauty of collaboration in LLCs is that the process necessitates both a shared purpose as well as freedom to hold onto individual department goals. This aspect of goal setting is where splitting the difference happens: Partners need to be able to have their own agendas and be given the freedom to pursue them, but they also need to be on board with an agreed upon and shared purpose. Partners should create space to name these goals through initial and ongoing evaluation processes. Inkelas et al. (2018) stressed that participating faculty have a vested interest in shaping the goals and objectives of a community, and knowing why stakeholders are involved helps break down and overcome the myths about involvement, values, and support. In short, goal setting is more in depth than listing hopeful outcomes and should be a shared part of vision casting.

Structure

Inkelas et al. (2008) offered a typology specific to structure, highlighting the size, resources, and extent of SA–AA association. Collectively thinking about the LLC's scope during initial planning helps equalize expectations by getting all parties on the same page. Although it might seem that structure is a result rather than a planned feature, which is often the case, LLC typologies are also helpful planning tools. Our experience creating and sustaining different LLCs and our consultations with multiple institutions on designing LLCs and FIR programs has verified use of such development resources. Planning tools allow for a shared understanding of the vision of LLCs to be established and personalized to individual programs. We posit that beginning with a structural framework in mind helps guide and direct partnership efforts, especially in areas such as resources and oversight, which we discuss next.

Shared Resources

Sharing resources calls for collaborating departments and areas to give willingly from their reserves of physical space, knowledge and expertise, time, and financial capital.

Space and Place

Because "resources" is a broad category, we begin with the most observable: space and place. The residential element of LLCs adds value and seamless integration into the learning community ideal (Inkelas & Soldner, 2012). Regarding facilities, it is important to consider a strategy that serves both sides of the SA–AA partnership, an undertaking most effectively accomplished through a collaborative process. One example of sharing space is making offices (for faculty partners or advising offices) available in the LLC halls themselves. Research shows that student interaction with faculty and staff—even casual greetings outside of an office—can positively contribute to student success (Erck & Sriram, 2022). What better way to do this than meet students in their hall, where they spend significant amounts of time? While residence life might furnish a physical office, academic partners collaborate by placing faculty in spaces that are prone to increased student interaction. Expenses related to features such as furniture, artwork, or office supplies can be shared.

Sharing the resources of space and place should also be emphasized in other community areas that promote interaction. For instance, residence life might provide a designated LLC space for a technology work room, and an academic partner might supply specific equipment for student and faculty use (e.g., 3D printer, laminator). This collaboration also often comes in the form of classroom space. Agreements to allow teaching space in a residence hall can open further opportunities for LLC students to interact with faculty, such as through faculty-led programs or office hours. Eidum et al. (2020) suggest that this additional presence of faculty in LLCs positively contributes to student thriving. However, exchange agreements alone do not constitute collaboration, which is why the LLC–MOC begins with shared vision. Faculty teaching LLC classes are largely ignorant of what is going on regarding residence hall activities (Inkelas et al., 2018). Having faculty in LLC classrooms who understand the rationale behind LLCs (i.e., the value of blending the in- and out-of-class) is critical to a shared underlying assumption about why they are there. Faculty rapport with an LLC's mission is strengthened when they have access to information about events, are invited into planning processes, and are encouraged to bring their students to programs.

Aside from spaces, a deeper commitment to collaboration is a faculty-in-residence (FIR) program, where partnering faculty are provided LLC apartments in anticipation of their continued engagement efforts in and outside of the classroom. Agreements often allow FIRs to fulfill service requirements, develop LLC classes, participate in FIR selection, or reduce teaching loads. A FIR program is a tangible example of collaboration because it moves the process from faculty connection to faculty integration in an LLC. FIR programs are detailed further in Part Three of this book.

Expertise

The knowledge, skills, and abilities that partners bring to the table is critical for successful collaboration. True collaboration, according to Cook et al. (2007), is represented through complementary domains of expertise. Expertise in a vacuum is more likely to breed further division rather than reciprocal labor, and sharing expertise allows partners to draw from the widest pool of knowledge and influence on campus. One example is student recruitment, where an LLC can use its connection to an academic unit to recruit incoming students majoring in that area's discipline to live in the LLC. In turn, the academic unit uses its connection with that LLC to demonstrate an engaging learning opportunity (and perhaps attractive amenity) to prospective students. Collaboratively sharing these areas of expertise can translate to prospective students enrolling within this academic unit and living within this LLC; thus, considered a marked victory for all.

If the previous perspective sounds slightly idealistic, it is because too often siloed divisions do not engage in the sharing of expertise. Loosely coupled divisions need to use imaginative thinking to realize how their expertise, and that of campus partners, can be maximized. Student affairs partners often have expertise in areas such as housing logistics, programming, or risk management. Faculty are expected to have expertise in their fields and their pedagogical craft. Though expertise might differ, learning about the work of colleagues is an evident step toward collaboration through blurring the lines between SA–AA (LePeau, 2015). If expertise is hoarded for personal gain, it is antithetical to the collective mission of LLCs. Realizing each other's expertise, and capitalizing on that, can drive collaborative progress.

Time

LLCs can be time-consuming for SA staff who are constantly reaching out to partners for the community to function effectively (Inkelas et al., 2018). Although the substance of their involvement differs, this burden of time is shared with faculty partners. Faculty often choose to be involved in LLCs in spite of their accountability and reward structures, not because of them (Inkelas et al., 2018). We suggest having SA and AA partners clearly distinguish how much time they are willing, and able, to invest. It is one thing to have an eager faculty member express interest in facilitating programs for a few hours each week. It is another to have them actually find the time, especially if their position is packed with research and teaching duties. Similarly, though a hall director might have a grand vision of cross-country LLC field trips, other required duties might inhibit their time. LLC FIR specifically need an understanding of time expectations. Clear job descriptions for FIR positions (see chapter 10) can help facilitate these expectations.

Another recommendation to facilitate shared time is a *partner programming calendar*. Although most LLCs probably use an activities calendar, a partner programming calendar is a simple way to think about an upcoming semester in terms of the time related to participation for the faculty and staff involved. Such a calendar serves as a project management hub whereby all partners classify their expected time to invest in the community by reflecting on various actions (e.g., meetings, planning, attending programs). With teaching and research demands, it is helpful for faculty to see a map of their semester involvement; however, such a calendar should be created as a joint effort to keep partners accountable to time commitments.

Finances

Regardless of whether a campus has a centralized budget model, charges LLC fees, or has dedicated staffing lines, there are important elements to consider concerning shared finances. First, initiating conversations with partners to spur creative thinking about financial resources is more fruitful than searching for a single funding line. Although these conversations can be challenging, when there is a clear vision and goals, the necessary resources will be evident and will assist with the "big asks." We also recommend connecting these conversations to the wide literature base on effective LLC practices to help with convincing. In short, we encourage boldness and creativity in seeking financial partnerships.

More practically, it is helpful from the early stages of LLC planning to think through financial structure. One advantageous model is initiating student programming fees (e.g., $50/semester), which are then used for LLC activities. Initiatives such as this allow programs to be somewhat revenue self-reliant and provide students with experiences above and beyond a traditional residence hall. If fees are a participation barrier for students, resourceful solutions could include academic unit sponsorships or scholarships.

We can widely contend the value of LLCs for student learning, but it is important to realize these initiatives can become expensive. Because many LLCs are heavily funded by SA (Inkelas et al., 2008), finding those critical academic leaders can help all parties see LLC work as a shared endeavor. In fact, Inkelas et al. (2018) stressed that even small contributions by academic units for faculty participation can go a long way toward ensuring successful collaboration. Other partners, such as dining or parking services, should also be consulted. Reserved LLC parking spaces or dining cards to share meals with students are creative ways to fund collaborative endeavors. Chapter 2 offers additional incentive ideas.

Considering staffing, it is costly for AA to share their faculty's time and focus. Golde and Pribbenow (2000) highlighted academic reward structures as a barrier in this regard. Negotiating with deans and chairs for allowing LLC involvement to count toward university service is one approach. Exploring ways to get LLC involvement to count toward teaching requirements or even research criteria (e.g., through scholarship of teaching and learning) are additional approaches valued by faculty members.

Shared Oversight

Shared oversight requires that partners strategize around effective processes regarding roles and duties, communication patterns, means for problem solving, and supervisory or reporting lines.

Roles and Duties

Unclear roles or duties are a frequent hindrance to collaboration. When people do not properly understand their function, it can cause confusion, isolation, and conflict. Although programming content is important, it is equally critical to think through program logistics, such as who facilitates room bookings and catering, or manages online content, or approves purchases. Although these prompts, and many more, should be explored in the planning process, cultural divides often obfuscate the answers. To overcome this, all constituents should be involved in planning, particularly when designating roles. In addition, as Whitt et al. (2008) emphasized, successful programs designate duties aligned with existing campus culture (e.g., a hierarchical system may necessitate high levels of approval, which is important when considering oversight).

We often see a temptation to delegate program content to faculty and administrative operations to SA professionals. Although SA and AA have different areas of expertise, if they assume only historically distinct roles they risk unraveling a successful collaboration. For faculty, Golde and Pribbenow (2000) posited, collaboration means welcoming SA professionals into conversations about the academic mission, the learning process, and the role they play in contributing to students' intellectual development. In addition to internal roles, it is also imperative to include auxiliary partnerships. For example, consider consulting dining managers for initiatives such as recurrent LLC community dinners, or information technology services for website needs.

Communication

Scholars stress that ongoing communication is paramount to collaborative success (Golde & Pribbenow, 2000; Whitt et al., 2008). This communication in LLC initiatives starts by learning the terminology of each culture (Arcelus, 2011). In addition, recurrent meetings with involved partners is one of the clearest ways to maintain communication. The communication required for good relationships needs to extend beyond informing, exchanging information, or simply cooperating (Cook et al., 2007). With full schedules, it is tempting to avoid meetings, but this can cause serious harm to partnerships. Furthermore, we recommend these relationships go beyond meetings to include social gatherings, coffee hours, or family outings. Without frequent and prioritized (and preferably in-person) communication, values and goals can become unfocused and collaboration diminished.

Partners need to reflect on who should meet and how often. It seems obvious that LLC faculty liaisons should meet with their hall director, but how do mid- to upper-level administrators stay involved? Are there monthly/annual reports or quarterly meetings? How often should assessment meetings occur? Answering questions such as these will help facilitate effective communication lines. Whitt et al. (2008) noted that "trying to create and sustain an effective partnership program in the absence of a history of collaboration or even in the absence of one or two good relationships from which to build is probably fruitless" (p. 247). There is a history of struggle for equitable relationships among professionals from SA–AA units, but genuine partnerships require dialogue from both divisions to develop trust and mutual understanding (Arcelus, 2011). In other words, while *communication* might seem like a catch-all for "updates," it is actually a vehicle for sense-making and sharing values in order to overcome cultural barriers and strengthen partnerships.

Problem Solving

Even with clear roles and strategic communication, problems will undoubtedly still surface. Contingency planning is imperative for healthy LLCs. If issues cannot be resolved effectively, they can harm the delicate balance of a partnership, especially in the beginning. One preemptive approach to problem solving is good training, such as opportunities for partners to develop leadership skills, communication habits, and bias awareness. It is also helpful to consider what university-specific policies may be updated and require ongoing training. If faculty are working in a residential setting, who is responsible to communicate updates for emergency protocols, and what is their role in those situations? If partners are going to be using a new purchasing system, who arranges training and tracks progress? How will roles be divided for onboarding new staff or student leaders?

Answering such questions will help arbitrate issues, but not all conflict can be avoided. As such, it is also important to plan for the process of conflict mediation. In this way, conflict can be welcomed and addressed instead of buried and left to fester. Mediation plans should address various involvement levels, as LLC conflict, though often between hall staff and faculty partners, can easily spread upward or outward if not dealt with internally. It is also critical to think through how all parties will be represented in a resolution. Revisiting the shared vision is a productive way to reorient an LLC's direction, and although these conversations might be awkward, feeling included in the mediation process encourages thriving collaborations.

Supervision

Supervisory and support situations are rife with opportunities for collaboration. Faculty report to their department chair or dean, but FIR who work within a residence hall are also typically supervised informally by a senior housing administrator. Differing SA–AA cultures prompt the need for clear plans in establishing these formal and informal relationships. Informal supervision or support often appears as a "dotted line" on an organization chart, which is common in LLC collaborations or with FIR programs. It is not an official supervisory or management line but more of a knowledge-sharing relationship. The expertise of a housing administrator is invaluable to a FIR for setting boundaries, expectations, and resources for the work, whereas an academic chair may not possess relevant cultural knowledge of the role.

Supervision should also entail distributing resources and administering ongoing training. As an example, an SA professional teaching LLC courses housed within an academic college should be invited by academic partners to participate in teaching seminars or workshops to prepare LLC curricula, learn new pedagogical practices, or develop a philosophy of teaching. Such supervisory and support systems exemplify the benefits of shared oversight, keeping collaborators engaged. In this sense, we encourage secondary and tertiary partners to also be included, not solely the close partners.

Shared Success

As the final stage of the model, shared success entails collaboration with assessment, acknowledgement and recognition, ongoing development, and reviewing a program's vision.

Assessment

Collaborative assessment is not a recent idea. In fact, Banta and Kuh (1998) asserted that "one of the most promising but underused opportunities for collaboration comes in the form of outcomes assessment" (p. 42). Collaborating in assessment should begin early in vision casting, but because the evidence produced through such partnerships can lead to intentional and positive change in LLCs, assessment is part of shared success. Many factors should be considered in designing shared LLC assessment, such as the following:

- Will the focus be on programmatic outcomes (i.e., how well a program functions) or learning outcomes (i.e., what students gain by participating)?
- How can collaborators ensure assessments are designed to be more robust than program head counts?
- Who will conduct these assessments, and do they have the necessary tools and resources?

We maintain that assessment—from determining outcomes, measuring them, analyzing the findings, and making changes based on the results—should be a shared SA–AA process. For example, collaborating in assessment could incorporate partnering with faculty or doctorate students in educational psychology or statistics to perform rigorous analyses. It may also entail tapping into faculty research expertise for coding and analyzing data from focus groups or interviews. Such collaboration should include sharing the findings with SA–AA administrators to both tell the story of LLC experiences qualitatively and convey the benefits of LLC outcomes quantitatively. Furthermore, there are probably existing data sources elsewhere on campus. An institutional research and testing department could offer information about students (GPA, majors, etc.) to help guide LLC planning. In addition, residence life departments may issue regular data collection through external organizations (e.g., Skyfactor or Education Advisory Board), which could be tailored for LLC assessment items and explored longitudinally for trends.

In our experience, we often see a single individual undertaking LLC assessment, which can create a situation where information exists in a vacuum, because partners might not have strong buy-in or, worse, think it is not their concern. Collaborative assessment allows for a shared process of transforming data into new changes or initiatives. By including multiple perspectives and areas of expertise into assessment design, a foundation is set for building a body of evidence to demonstrate effectiveness, meet accountability demands, obtain scarce resources, and facilitate change (Whitt et al., 2008). Additional considerations for LLC assessment can be explored in chapters 1, 4, 5, 6, and 8 of this volume.

Acknowledgment

Acknowledging LLC victories, such as demonstrating positive outcomes (especially those confirmed from a collaborative assessment plan), can greatly benefit future partnerships and support. Considering the time commitment of LLC work, recruiting new faculty can often be a challenge. Sharing LLC success stories is one way to increase awareness and interest, which aids in recruitment. In an SA–AA partnership, Cook and Lewis (2007) recommended that faculty and staff should be appropriately recognized by both divisions for their efforts in promoting student success.

One approach for acknowledgment is harnessing the broad influence of university media and news departments. Awards for faculty involvement or writing detailed letters for tenure and promotion are other creative ways to promote acknowledgment. However, the subcultures of each division should be considered when recognizing partner efforts. For example, a mention in the SA newsletter might be appropriate for a staff member who helped with programming. Conversely, awards and accolades may be more meaningful in an academic culture, such as for a faculty partner who used their research laboratory for LLC-specific opportunities. Although praise should be shared, efforts should align with the norms of each domain.

Ongoing Development

Recognizing success is important, and assessment results point to areas for additional expertise, training, or assistance. It can be helpful to house directions for the future in yearly reports or transition manuals. For example, transition reports can serve as the traditional account for the year but also include fundamental information, such as the status of ongoing projects and wise observations from various partners. Because they provide an opportunity to build on the previous years' plans, these reports should be given to new partners to reinforce vision, increase buy-in, and pass on cultural knowledge. We assert that it is critical to an LLC partnership for such reports to be a collaborative effort. Reflections from faculty partners, partners in other SA areas, residence life staff, student employees, and FIR, to name a few, allow for a complete picture of the strengths, weaknesses, and opportunities within the LLC.

Such accounts, when shared in creation, allow for multiple perspectives of reflection. These various perspectives should be incorporated into the design and delivery of support, training, or realignment as needed for the next semester. In this way, the development of partners is an ongoing process and not a one-time occurrence. As a tool to help guide this reflective process, we offer a series of questions in the supplemental resources for this book.

Reviewing the Vision

Once an LLC is established, collaborators should use data and transition materials, in conjunction with current LLC research, to determine whether and how the overall vision should be augmented to best meet the needs of involved parties. Regardless if any changes are warranted, we recommend reviewing the vision annually or biannually to keep partners and programs aligned with the LLC's intended purpose. AA partners may put more emphasis on academic outcomes (e.g., GPA), and SA partners may put more emphasis on cocurricular outcomes (e.g., sense of community). If evidence suggests changes to the vision to best meet outcomes, a shared discussion between partners will help ensure vision and outcomes stay connected.

It is also vital to consider the LLC's history, how changes may affect the community, and how to maintain support. One way to do this is through reviewing foundational LLC documents (e.g., jointly formed mission statements, end-of-year reports, assessment documentation). Discussing a vision modification might be challenging if personnel have changed since such documents were generated, but in that sense it will also be a convenient time and space to review resources and oversight in the LLC. Moving through these steps brings the LLC–MOC full circle, where SA–AA collaborators can once again consider the elements of sharing a vision and work back through shared resources, shared oversight, and shared success.

References

American Association for Higher Education, American College Personnel Association, & National Association of Student Personnel Administrators. (1998, June 2). *Powerful partnerships: A shared responsibility of learning.* https://www.naspa.org/files/dmfile/Powerful_Partnerships.pdf

Arcelus, V. J. (2011). If student affairs–academic affairs collaboration is such a good idea, why are there so few examples of these partnerships in American higher education? In P. M. Magolda & M. B. Baxter Magolda (Eds.), *Contested issues in student affairs: Diverse perspectives and respectful dialogue* (pp. 61–74). Stylus.

Banta, T. W., & Kuh, G. D. (1998). A missing link in assessment: Collaboration between academic and student affairs professionals. *Change: The Magazine of Higher Learning, 30*(2), 40–46.

Brower, A. M., & Inkelas, K. K. (2010). Living–learning programs: One high-impact educational practice we now know a lot about. *Liberal Education, 96,* 36–42.

Cook, J. H., Eaker, R. E., Ghering, A. M., & Sells, D. K. (2007). Collaboration: Definitions and barriers. In J. H. Cook & C. A. Lewis (Eds.), *Student and academic affairs collaboration: The divine comity* (pp. 17–31). National Association of Student Personnel Administrators.

Cook, J. H., & Lewis, C. A. (Eds.). (2007). *Student and academic affairs collaboration: The divine comity.* National Association of Student Personnel Administrators.

Eidum, J., Lomicka, L., Chiang, W., Endick, G., & Stratton, J. (2020). Thriving in residential learning communities. *Learning Communities Research and Practice*, *8*(1), Article 7.

Ellett, T., & Schmidt, A. (2011). Faculty perspectives on creating community in residence halls. *Journal of College and University Student Housing*, *38*(1), 26–39.

Erck, R. W., & Sriram, R. (2021). Residential learning communities as coalitions: Bridging the gap between customer, consumer, and learner. In F. F. Padró, M. Kek, & H. Huijser (Eds.), *Student support services: Exploring impact on student engagement, experience and learning* (pp. 1–18). Springer Nature.

Erck, R. W., & Sriram, R. (2022). Examining how interactions contribute to thriving for sophomore, junior, and senior living-learning community students. *Journal of College and University Student Housing*, *48*(2), 10–29.

Golde, C. M., & Pribbenow, D. A. (2000). Understanding faculty involvement in residential learning communities. *Journal of College Student Development*, *41*(1), 27–40.

Inkelas, K. K., Jessup-Anger, J. E., Benjamin, M., & Wawrzynski, M. R. (2018). *Living–learning communities that work: A research-based model for design, delivery, and assessment*. Stylus.

Inkelas, K. K., & Soldner, M. (2012). Undergraduate living–learning programs and student outcomes. In J. C. Smart & M. B. Paulsen (Eds.), *Higher education: Handbook of theory and research* (Vol. 26, pp. 1–55). Springer.

Inkelas, K. K., Soldner, M., Longerbeam, S. D., & Leonard, J. B. (2008). Differences in student outcomes by types of living–learning programs: The development of an empirical typology. *Research in Higher Education*, *49*(6), 495–512.

Kezar, A. (2005). Redesigning for collaboration within higher education institutions: An exploration into the developmental process. *Research in Higher Education*, *46*(7), 831–860.

Kuk, L., Banning, J. H., & Amey, M. J. (2012). *Positioning student affairs for sustainable change: Achieving organizational effectiveness through multiple perspectives*. Stylus.

LePeau, L. (2015). A grounded theory of academic affairs and student affairs partnerships for diversity and inclusion aims. *The Review of Higher Education*, *39*(1), 97–122.

O'Halloran, K. C. (2019). A classification of collaboration between student and academic affairs. *College Student Journal*, *53*(3), 301–314.

Whitt, E. J., Nesheim, B. E., Guentzel, M. J., Kellogg, A. H., McDonald, W. M., & Wells, C. A. (2008). "Principles of good practice" for academic and student affairs partnership programs. *Journal of College Student Development*, *49*(3), 235–249.

VIGNETTE

Faculty–Residential Life Partnerships: Productive Relationships

Caleb Keith

During the inaugural year of a residential college (RC), I found myself serving as a first-time student life coordinator alongside a newly recruited faculty principal. My greatest takeaway from this experience is that productive relationships, especially those between faculty members and student affairs staff, rely on mutual understanding and trust. Without these, true collaboration and partnership cannot exist; at best, both individuals may work alongside one another, but toward differing goals.

During the first year of the RC, we did not have a blueprint for how to implement the model within our institutional context. Like many institutions, our university was organized in such a manner as to prevent full implementation of the model on campus, wherein the individual RC would operate as semiautonomous on campus. However, if unable to fully enact the RC model in this manner, we took it upon ourselves to try to act as autonomously as possible. To some degree, this paradigm is essential, because many institutions' organizational structures make it difficult to implement initiatives that "blur the lines" between administrative units. These organizational structures can create an awkward position for the faculty members and student affairs staff members in an RC setting; often, they are trying to please two (or more) administrative leaders with different, or even competing, priorities. It became clear that if we were to be effective in this context, we had to band together and create our own—philosophically, if not structurally—operational unit. This decision stemmed not from an us-versus-them mentality but rather was born out of a mutual desire to ensure the implementation of the RC model was successful and sustainable. As such, we started our own weekly staff meetings within the RC, independent of associated academic or student affairs units. A mutual love for French press dark roast coffee enhanced our meetings. Of course, our relationship also benefited from the inordinate amount of time we spent together, whether moving and setting up chairs in the multipurpose room or attending various late-night meetings of student leadership within the RC.

Although the faculty principal may have surpassed me in rank, we learned early on that the attainment of the model would depend on our collaboration. Our success resulted from a willingness to rely on each other's areas of formal training, the ability to admit our knowledge gaps, and a desire to learn about the other's role. As an example, the faculty principal attended significant portions of residence life staff training. This training provided an understanding of, and appreciation for, the work of student affairs staff in the residential environment. In addition, I attended retreats and weekly staff meetings of the honors program (the academic unit with which the RC was connected). These meetings provided me with an understanding of the academic policies and priorities that guided the faculty members and support staff. Ultimately, knowledge of our respective training, competencies, and priorities allowed us to build a foundation of trust and respect, which we knew could be relied on when fulfilling our respective roles and making decisions, both jointly and separately.

6

LAYING THE FOUNDATION FOR A LIVING–LEARNING COMMUNITY

Building Strong Faculty–Residential Life Partnerships

Carl Krieger

As a student affairs professional, I have come to realize that the most successful living–learning communities (LLCs) are built around strong residential life (RL) and faculty relationships. I did not learn this early on in my career, and there were no books—or in this case, chapters—to give me the context or resources I needed to build the truly collaborative RL and faculty partnerships that are imperative for program success. Much like Caleb describes in the vignette, I learned by trial and error working with faculty-in-residence at Duke University and LLC faculty at Virginia Tech. However, it was not until I worked with the team developing the residential college at Virginia Tech that I truly understood what I did not know. I was called to task by my mentor, Frank Shushok, for writing the faculty principal position description in the same manner as I would an RL staff member role. After that conversation and much reflection, I began to realize that many of the issues I had encountered with faculty partners could be traced back to the mutual lack of understanding about our roles as educators, our positional requirements, or even the basic nature of our purpose at the institution.

Through a great deal of research and many more years of experience, I began to understand what could be done to build strong partnerships between RL staff members and faculty members. Faculty value the work that is being done "on the other side of campus" but know very little about what happens "over there." RL staff know from their experience as students the impact faculty can have, but they often misunderstand the multiple facets of faculty's institutional role. Moreover, as Caleb describes, institutional structures and reporting lines often exasperate these misunderstandings rather than fostering cross-unit partnership. After collaborating in the creation of many LLCs, I have found that the collaborations that were most successful were the ones in which the RL professional and the academic faculty member began their collaboration with a focus on their relationship.

I begin this chapter by exploring the professional roles and context of faculty and RL professionals outside of their partnership within LLCs. I then offer guidance on finding the right fit to effectively select and onboard faculty partners in LLCs. Next, I set up collaboration models that faculty and RL partners might consider for their specific relationship. Finally, I discuss assessment of the LLC and how metrics can be used to guide the success of the program. A guided practice with reflection questions to facilitate conversations between the faculty and RL partners can be found in the supplemental resources online. This chapter can be used collaboratively—by faculty members and RL staff members—as a guide to understand the contexts for your work and to ask the questions that truly matter.

Literature Review

Navigating the literature about LLCs would lead one to believe that our living–learning programs are as divided as our campuses, where faculty and RL staff members operate in parallel but rarely interact. The first area of research focuses on the faculty experience in cocurricular student affairs programs like LLCs. Second, additional research outlines the best practices for building LLCs, often focusing on staff roles and expectations. Just a few studies weave together these two experiences.

Research examining faculty experiences with LLCs has primarily focused on the reasons why a faculty member would want to participate in residential living. Golde and Pribbenow (2000) found that "a chance to know students better, . . . an opportunity to act in congruence with their beliefs about interdisciplinary and innovative education, and . . . a commitment to the residential learning community idea and purpose" were reasons for initial involvement (p. 4). Lack of time, limited desire, or cultural disincentives based on tenure and promotion were often seen as the primary roadblocks to joining the cocurricular program (Golde & Pribbenow, 2000; Inkelas et al., 2018). Research about the relationships built by faculty members while supporting LLCs focuses almost exclusively on student–faculty dynamics and positive outcomes (Armstrong, 1999; Stassen, 2003). Often, when faculty describe their own experiences, they mention RL staff only to praise the administrative and student support provided for students living in the community (Davenport, 2009; Dolby, 2014; Rhoads, 2009). Few studies mention the relationship between the faculty member and the RL staff member (Frazier & Eighmy, 2012; Inkelas et al., 2018; Whitt et al., 2008). The dearth of studies focused on the relationship between faculty and RL staff may reflect the lack of contextual understanding between these entities, which in this chapter I seek to address.

Similarly, research documenting the role and experience of RL staff rarely has discussed the relationship with the faculty member; instead, it has focused on the administrative role of the RL staff (Dunn & Dean, 2013; Inkelas et al., 2018). Unlike their faculty partners, there are very few studies that have examined the phenomenological experience of RL professional staff in general and none that describe their experience within LLCs.

There is a stark difference between the literature about the faculty experiences in LLCs and that of RL staff. The literature related to faculty experiences focuses on their relationships with students and the outcomes that were achieved. When LLC research has mentioned RL staff, it has highlighted the administrative and operations component of these communities (Dunn & Dean, 2013; Inkelas et al., 2018). However, it does reinforce the necessity for a chapter that explores faculty–RL partnerships, taking a closer look at how the relationship is developed between faculty members and RL staff in LLCs.

Although other chapters in this volume discuss important collaborations within higher education (specifically, chapter 5 addresses student affairs–academic affairs partnerships, and chapter 7 explores working with partners across campus) that are needed to build and maintain LLCs, the literature that underpins these chapters is a macro-understanding of collaborative relationships between departments or divisions. In contrast, this chapter focuses on the personal relationships and collaborations between the individual faculty members and RL professionals who enact the vision and direction of the department leadership.

Understanding the Roles of Faculty and Staff

The opening to this chapter touched on the misunderstandings that are rife within the university community, especially surrounding the roles and responsibilities of groups that do not often work together. When entering a partnership, you must take time to learn about your partner's professional context. The historical as well as cultural demands and expectations play a significant role in how your partner will engage in a living and learning program. As Magolda (2005) stated, "faculty and student affairs subcultures subscribe to qualitatively different ideologies, complicating initiatives for collaboration" (p. 20). In this section, I describe the contexts that surround faculty–RL staff partnerships, first by describing the role of faculty members and their experience and second by offering insights into the education and professional experience that influences the ways RL professionals approach their roles. Generalizable context is provided, but it is important for readers to research their own institutions to find the unique obligations and expectations that partners may be confronting in their role.

Role of Faculty Members

Understanding the faculty experience is important for determining when and how to approach them for partnerships with an LLC or any cocurricular partnership. For most faculty, the tenure process guides a faculty member's career. Tenure is an advancement process that, once achieved, provides academic freedom through indefinite appointment in which a faculty member can be fired only for cause. In some people's eyes, tenure reflects lifetime employment, but to most faculty members it represents the intellectual freedom to explore the unknown, unfettered by external dictate. Tenured faculty have the freedom to test new ideas and see just how far their research takes them.

Guidelines for tenure vary from campus to campus based on culture and institutional purpose. However, three guiding areas serve as a focus for new faculty: (a) research, (b) teaching, and (c) service. Known as the *three-legged stool* of the tenure and promotion process, each leg may be thicker or thinner from campus to campus and even academic college to academic college. At many institutions, the research component serves as the primary area for which a faculty member is assessed. Faculty members are evaluated on all aspects of research, but special attention is placed on publications and research funding received. Teaching can also play the primary role in tenure and promotion, especially at liberal arts or teaching institutions. Student evaluations, teaching awards, and peer or department administration observations are used to evaluate teaching achievement. Service is often the most difficult and tenuous component of tenure to define. For some, service may simply reflect being available to students during office hours. For others, service may include positions on internal or external boards, taking an active role in student or local organizations, or supporting cocurricular experiences on campus (Phinney, 2009). This ambiguity often renders service an unimportant amalgamation of any priority for the faculty member that fails to fit within research or teaching.

Faculty members generally enter their position as an assistant professor and are given between 5 and 7 years to achieve tenure. For those on the tenure track, the stress put on a faculty member during these years cannot be understated. A well-known message during this time is "publish or perish," and an unsuccessful tenure process may require that the faculty leave their position at the university entirely (De Rond & Miller, 2005). Although some may seek a new tenure-track faculty position and once again start the tenure clock, for others a failed tenure bid may lead to the end of their academic career. .

Once tenure is achieved, faculty may take several routes in their career. For most, receiving tenure provides the opportunity to truly focus their academic passion. In many cases these intellectual passions do not include cocurricular programming. Others may transition into administration or focus on teaching. The tenure process does not generally include program or administrative responsibilities. Membership on committees, administration of grants, and course development may be some of the only experiences faculty members will have had to develop program oversight skills. It may not be until tenure has been achieved that the opportunity to take on larger roles presents itself.

If service is not recognized as an important aspect of the tenure and promotion process, or if cocurricular partnerships are not allowed to be used within the service or teaching component of their tenure and promotion process, participation in or support of cocurricular programs may adversely affect pretenure faculty, possibly ending their career. Once tenure has been achieved, the faculty member's focus is on their academic passion, which may not include cocurricular program support or development. They may also be in their own developmental infancy for administering program oversight. A common misconception is that faculty do not want to support education outside of the classroom or fail to see the value in it. However, with all that is required of them, it is more likely that they have been told directly or through academic culture to place tenure as their primary focus for their first 6 years of their academic career.

Role of RL Staff

RL staff members are trained extensively, provided specific policies and procedures, and held accountable for meticulously following established guidelines. A traditional route for an RL professional begins as a student staff member: resident assistant, front desk staff, or other administrative jobs. They then transition to graduate assistant, traditionally as a graduate hall director overseeing a residential community (Biddix, 2011). They are taught the federal and institutional regulations that require strict adherence. Failure to follow even one step can result in termination from the position. Their range of responsibilities includes issues of life and death, such as alcohol poisoning or suicidal ideation, and can have a long-lasting impact on their own mental health. Beginning with a case precedent such as *Mullins v. Pine Manor* (1983), institutions have been given the responsibility for creating a reasonably safe campus, and RL student staff members are trained to be one of the caretakers of this expectation (Letarte, 2013). This professionalization process is different from the experience of many faculty members who learn about their academic field or teaching through study, investigation, or experience.

For many faculty members, graduate school is meant to focus their research agenda and gain skills in research and teaching. Most student affairs graduate assistantships include a breadth of experiences and provide opportunities to grow as a professional. However, the RL graduate assistantship is unique in that additional areas are added on to the experience. During an academic year, a first-year staff member can expect to oversee a budget that may include thousands of dollars; directly supervise student staff members; run staff meetings independently; adjudicate conduct cases; respond to emergencies that may include life and death independent decision making; and engage in academic advising, social justice advocacy, program development, and education. They are then held accountable for adhering to the policies and procedures for each of these roles at a level comparable to professional staff members. In some cases, a graduate student may have had more administrative professional experience than a tenured faculty member who is beginning an LLC partnership.

The entry-level RL staff member is a unique position within student affairs. Many entry-level professionals live where they work and are responsible for supporting their community 24/7. The position does not follow traditional hours, and weekend, evening, and on-call hours are expected. It is unsurprising that this level of constant and high-level responsibility for a new professional can result in high levels of burnout. If the staff member does not succumb to burnout, the expectation in the field is that they will move on to a new area in student affairs or move up, advancing to a higher position. With the breadth of the position, many professionals find that their passion lies in one of their additional responsibility areas and not RL itself. Advising and mentoring a new RL staff member can be a daunting task, considering the breadth of professional possibilities and the depth of the emotional and psychological toll.

Finding the Right Fit

Given these varied backgrounds of education and experience, it is not surprising that finding the right fit for faculty–residence life partnerships can be difficult but extremely important. Because LLCs are typically located within RL administrative structures, RL staff and administrators often are tasked with selecting faculty partners. For more established LLCs, faculty may be involved in hiring new RL staff. In this section, I provide guidance for RL staff and administrators for identifying, selecting, and onboarding partners who fit, and I offer questions (available in the supplemental online resource) that potential partners might ask during the selection process.

The Selection Process

Finding faculty partners may be easier than one might expect. Faculty members who are drawn to student support programs are generally seen in the same places: campus-wide cocurricular programs, awards banquets, and program committees, for example. Because the service component of the tenure and promotion process is often the least valued by those making decisions about tenure and promotion, finding a faculty member already engaged in student-centered service roles can signal an intrinsic support and understanding for student programs and a willingness to partner.

The initial meeting between the faculty member and the RL professional is important because in many cases the faculty member is being asked to spend time away from their research and teaching. Faculty members are not often required to take on the responsibility of working with an LLC, and any time devoted to the program is time taken from other endeavors. Both the faculty member as well as the RL professional should be honest about the request from the beginning, which will lay a foundation of trust and goodwill. If needed, support for innovative pedagogical practices; experience directing large programs; and tangible remunerations, such as travel funding, meal stipends, or rent-free living accommodations, are perks that could incentivize a partnership. Additional ways to incentivize faculty involvement are discussed at length in chapter 2.

Not all faculty engagement programs require the same amount of vetting. Programs like the faculty fellow position at Purdue University (n.d.) may take only a few conversations because of the limited role of the faculty member. A faculty-in-residence program like that at Duke University (n.d.) may require additional vetting opportunities, such as meeting with students and support letters from academic department leadership. The faculty head of a residential college like those at Virginia Tech (n.d.-b), for which the faculty member is the leader of the program, should incorporate multiple opportunities for the selection body, as well as students, staff, and senior student affairs professionals, to examine the faculty member's qualifications to serve in the role. In general, the more involvement required of the faculty member, the more extensive the selection process should be. Finding a faculty member who sees their cocurricular partnership as an important aspect of their university role will pay dividends later in the program implementation.

Onboarding a Faculty Member

Often, misconceptions about the faculty member's understanding of RL or university policy and practice can result in an insufficient onboarding plan and can limit the ability of the faculty member to initially succeed. Faculty members sometimes begin their position with little knowledge of student affairs. The understanding they have generally comes from working through student conduct or crisis issues associated with course instruction along with a distant recollection of collegiate life a decade earlier. Therefore, it is important to provide the following five steps outlined in Table 6.1 for onboarding a faculty member.

The first step to onboarding a faculty member is to identify the expectations for the role and then to convey them to the faculty member. It is surprising how often it is assumed that the faculty member will know intuitively what the position entails. The second step is to create a safe experience for the faculty member to first engage with the residential community. The first time many faculty members enter what they consider to be the student's home can be a daunting experience, as they may have only a vague understanding of where the residential community is and what will await them inside.

The third step to onboarding is to provide administrative and policy training. The more responsibility the faculty member has in the day-to-day operations of the program, the more they need to be presented with the policies and practices of the organization. For many faculty members the idea of confronting a residential conduct issue can be daunting and not within their

TABLE 6.1
Steps for Onboarding a Faculty Member

1. Convey role expectations.
2. Provide a tour of the community.
3. Provide administrative and policy training.
4. Introduce faculty to new colleagues.
5. Provide orientation to departmental culture.

position expectations (Rhoads, 2009). Being clear about what is, and what is not, part of the faculty role can put the faculty member at ease and decrease the number of misunderstandings that may occur.

The fourth step to onboarding begins by the RL department determining where the faculty member fits into the organizational chart, if at all, and introducing them to their new colleagues. Professional and holistic introductions with the full-time RL team will not only orient the faculty member to their new colleagues within the department but also reflect the collegiality needed for positive faculty and RL relationships to flourish. The fifth and final onboarding step is to provide a cultural orientation for the faculty member about the RL department. It is important for the faculty member to know the organization values, both the micro as well as macro.

Finding the right fit with the faculty partner remains at the heart of building and maintaining positive relationships between faculty members and RL staff. A well-established foundation will pay dividends as the partners begin to implement the program. Finding and selecting the right candidate and providing onboarding by conveying role expectations, providing a tour of the community, providing administrative and policy training, introducing them to their new colleagues, and providing orientation to departmental culture can have a dramatic impact on the faculty experience and health of the LLC program.

Building the Relationship and Program

Once the faculty member has been identified and onboarded, their role in the community and relationship to the RL staff professional in the organizational chart must be discussed. Inkelas et al.'s (2018) book *Living–Learning Communities That Work* provides a framework described as the "Best Practices Model for Living–Learning Communities" (p. 17). This model reflects the many moving pieces that make up an LLC and points to intentional integration as the pinnacle of success. Much of a community's success, they espouse, is a commitment to the program goals and objectives. The role of the faculty member in creating and implementing program goals and objectives is not outlined, yet it has a great deal of bearing on the relationship between them and the RL professional.

The success of a collaborative faculty and RL program is entirely based on the relationship. That relationship can take many forms, at the heart of which is the question of responsibility for the creation and implementation of the program goals and objectives. In the following section, I describe three types of collaborative relationships for faculty–RL partnerships within an

LLC: (a) the faculty member as a support agent, (b) the faculty member as a collaborator, and (c) the faculty member as the program lead.

Undergirding each of these partnership models is the question "Who is in charge?" Defining the responsibility for program goals and objectives will serve as a guardrail to the traditional pitfalls that happen in the first year of program development and lay the foundation for continued positive, open communication and collaboration. Although intentional integration is seen as best practice, it is not always possible to implement on the basis of institutional culture or resources. Therefore, it is important to examine how varying degrees of faculty support affect the relationship with the RL staff member and the power dynamics that are at play within the LLC program.

The Faculty Member as a Support Agent

Some partnership programs use the faculty member as an academic figurehead representing a link between RL and the academic purpose of the institution. They may have few responsibilities or expectations but their presence in the community is symbolically important. Programs like faculty associates at Washington University in St. Louis (n.d.) may encourage semiregular appearances in the community. Because of their limited role within the community, examples like this may seem to be the simplest partnerships between faculty and RL professionals. However, the faculty member as a support agent requires the least amount of buy-in from the faculty members and can, therefore, be the most difficult to manage.

When the faculty member is a support agent, the RL staff member, no matter their level of experience, will often be seen as the leader. The faculty member will look to the RL staff member to coordinate the program and will rely on them to manage the faculty member's role and guarantee success. Because acting as a support agent requires little time commitment from the faculty member, they often prioritize responsibilities, which will enhance tenure and promotion. Helping the faculty member identify interactions they find important and worth their limited time will help structure and focus their efforts. It is natural for an RL staff member to feel unqualified to lead a faculty member who is older and more experienced in higher education. However, it is important for them to acknowledge their role and, with the help of their supervisor and input from the faculty member, provide the structure for program implementation.

The Faculty Member as a Collaborator

A truly collaborative LLC can result in one of the most fulfilling relationships for an RL staff member. At Virginia Tech in the Galileo and

Hypatia living–learning programs, a faculty member works in tandem with the RL professionals to plan and implement the program (Virginia Tech, n.d.,-a). With the faculty member as a collaborator, the faculty member and RL staff engage with complementary expertise, one providing academic understanding and the other providing knowledge of student development. Having the faculty member as a collaborator can inspire a new RL professional to see the university experience in its entirety and truly understand the impact they are having on the whole student. The faculty member, in turn, is introduced to student affairs practices and gains the skills involved in navigating the breadth of cocurricular student experiences available on their campus.

It is imperative that program success is not identified as the sole responsibility of the faculty member and entry-level RL staff member. Mid- and senior-level RL staff must be part of the team, planning and identifying metrics of program success. Time should be set aside for collaborative creation of program goals and objectives as well as a shared vision. As the year progresses, it is essential to maintain the team dynamic through recurring meetings and check-ins. Finally, it is important to find ways to make the leadership mutually beneficial throughout the year. Faculty can support the RL staff through advocacy and experience. The RL professional can support the faculty member by providing administrative direction and education about the student experience. Reciprocal leadership will reinforce a common focus on the goals and objectives for the community.

The Faculty Member as the Program Lead

In the past 2 decades, many campuses have increased collaboration with faculty partners (Dunn & Dean, 2013; Inkelas et al., 2018). Residential college programs are one type of LLC that is growing quickly and require significant faculty leadership (Jessup-Anger, 2012). As faculty members have become more involved in living–learning programs, so has the need for learning outcomes and course connection (Inkelas et al., 2018). It is then unsurprising that in cases where a great deal of faculty insight is needed, they would be placed as the program lead.

Finding a faculty member to take on this leadership role, especially the right faculty member, can be challenging given that the role may require faculty to live in the residential community or include a course release to devote the necessary time for program leadership and implementation. The type of faculty member tapped for such a program generally has tenure and a wealth of experience in academia. However, granting oversight of what is traditionally an RL-sponsored program bequeaths an inordinate amount of power to someone unaccustomed to RL policy and practice.

RL professionals are not enculturated to share leadership or defer leadership to others (Magolda, 2005). Therefore, given that the faculty member will be the program lead, it is equally important to find the right RL staff member as it is the faculty member. Attributes such as deference, lack of ego, and being supportive, along with an educational mindset, are important and yet rare to find. RL departments are also not accustomed to having foundational policies and practices challenged, and yet an outsider's view, especially one with institutional and programmatic power, will often push against policies and practices that seem arbitrary or archaic. However, this type of outside view can often bring to light administrative inefficiencies.

It is therefore important to provide onboarding akin to all new RL staff members. This onboarding includes a peer relationship with all levels of RL staff and an offer to sit at similar tables and attend department meetings and social gatherings. Although grace must be given to this transition, accountability must also play a role for a faculty member with an LLC program leadership position. It is most important to identify someone to hold the faculty member accountable who has the academic and institutional gravitas they expect, such as a vice president or assistant vice president for student affairs. The most important relationship, however, will be with the RL staff member assigned to the program. As the relationship grows, their daily role will be to supplement the faculty member's understanding of students in the classroom with their knowledge of student development. It is common for almost daily contact to occur between the two. Their mutual understanding of the programmatic and student life community will enhance the outcomes of the program.

Telling the Story

Telling the story of the LLC may seem unusual as a primary facet of building strong relationships between RL staff and faculty members; however, this could not be further from the truth. Faculty culture is built around research and student affairs culture generally focuses on program assessment. Coming to a common understanding of the purpose of program analysis is an important topic to cover early in the program implementation and relationship. In most cases, LLC analysis will be geared toward program assessment rather than research and can be done in simple ways. Sharing stories of student success and highlighting the partnership can be documented throughout the year, creating a mosaic of the community experience. Comparing learning outcomes with current research on similar programs can also be used to prove the impact of the program for students or inform changes that need to be made in subsequent years.

Assessment can take many forms and functions, from generalized student affairs research as guided by *Assessment Practice in Student Affairs* (Shuh & Upcraft, 2001) to learning community–specific assessment (see Inkelas et al., 2018). Institutional and departmental culture will guide the extent to which depth or breadth of assessment is expected and appreciated. Reporting basic program outcomes such as GPA, retention data, and program attendance can be an appropriate starting point. Those with the resources can delve deeper, ascertaining the significant differences between the data for learning community students and their nonlearning community peers. For programs in which the faculty play a greater role, assessment of their impact on the program and the student experience can reflect the power of these types of experiences (Sriram & McLevain, 2016). It is important to reflect on the differences between LLC and traditional residential experiences and to highlight the impact of the unique experience. Highlighting contact hours with faculty members, office hours or meeting times with faculty in the residential community, the number of educational programs, the number of programs presented by faculty members, and visits to the community by academically connected partners are all easy metrics to track and report.

Quantitative data are important, but qualitative data can have a dramatic impact on telling the story for the LLC. Highlighting the success of relationships is the simplest way to spotlight achievements during the academic year. For LLCs that include academic courses, using student reflections in assignments may identify successes or improvements that can be changed in the moment. Finally, although program attendance is not a learning outcome, participation counts for programs can reflect the student buy-in to the LLC. Each of these can tell the story of the success of the community and highlight the success of the partnership.

A final report that weaves the assessment with the stories of student experiences and culminates in metrics that reflect program outcome achievement or lack thereof should be a collaborative effort between the faculty member and RL staff member. This story can be leveraged to support the continuation of the program. Each step tells a story of the student experience and reflects on the relationship between the faculty member and the RL staff. The better the relationship that is built, the better the story that is told.

Conclusion

The institutional headwinds to creating a collaborative cocurricular program with faculty members can be daunting. Understanding the roles and context of our faculty and RL partners takes time and patience. Finding the faculty member and student affairs professional who truly fit in the program can be laborious. Building the relationship that aligns with the type of collaborative partnership takes a great deal of planning, and assessing all of this requires time.

What is often missed, however, is the impact these programs and relationships can have on the faculty members and RL staff. Faculty begin to learn the rhythms of students in ways they never understood, and it can enhance the way they teach. They also grow professionally, influencing their career trajectory. RL staff members learn about the faculty experience through first-person insight. They can gain a mentor who will help them grow professionally and intellectually. These relationships matter, because the stronger the bonds, the more impactful the team will be for supporting and educating our students.

References

Armstrong, M. (1999). Models for faculty–student interaction outside of the classroom: The Duke University Faculty Associates Program. *College Student Affairs Journal, 19*(1), 4. https://eric.ed.gov/?id=EJ612655

Biddix, J. P. (2011). "Stepping stones": Career paths to the SSAO for men and women at four-year institutions. *Journal of Student Affairs Research and Practice, 48*(4), 443–461. https://doi.org/10.2202/1949-6605.6244

Davenport, A. M. H. (2009). *Building university community: A phenomenological study of faculty in residence* [Doctoral dissertation, University of Oklahoma]. https://shareok.org/handle/11244/320242

De Rond, M., & Miller, A. N. (2005). Publish or perish: Bane or boon of academic life? *Journal of Management Inquiry, 14*(4), 321–329. https://doi.org/10.1177/1056492605276850

Dolby, N. (2014). What I learned in Danielsen Hall: Faculty–in–residence programs and the power to shape students' lives. *About Campus, 19*(1), 29–32. https://doi.org/10.1002/abc.21148

Duke University. (n.d.). *Faculty-in-residence.* https://undergrad.duke.edu/intellectual-community/student-faculty-engagement-office/faculty-residence/

Dunn, M. S., & Dean, L. A. (2013). Together we can live and learn: Living–learning communities as integrated curricular experiences. *SCHOLE: A Journal of Leisure Studies and Recreation Education, 28*(1), 11–23. https://doi.org/10.1080/1937156X.2013.11949691

Frazier, W., & Eighmy, M. (2012). Themed residential learning communities: The importance of purposeful faculty and staff involvement and student engagement. *The Journal of College and University Student Housing, 38*(2), 10–31.

Golde, C. M., & Pribbenow, D. A. (2000). Understanding faculty involvement in residential learning communities. *Journal of College Student Development, 41*(1), 27–40.

Inkelas, K. K., Jessup-Anger, J. E., Benjamin, M., & Wawrzynski, M. R. (2018). *Living–learning communities that work: A research-based model for design, delivery, and assessment.* Stylus.

Jessup-Anger, J. E. (2012). Examining how residential college environments inspire the life of the mind. *The Review of Higher Education, 35*(3), 431–462.

Letarte, C. M. (2013). Keepers of the night: The dangerously important role of resident assistants on college and university campuses. *Kentucky Journal of Higher Education Policy and Practice, 2*(2), 4. https://uknowledge.uky.edu/kjhepp/vol2/iss2/4

Magolda, P. M. (2005). Proceed with caution: Uncommon wisdom about academic and student affairs partnerships. *About Campus, 9*(6), 16–21. https://doi.org/10.1002/abc.113

Mullins v. Pine Manor College, 389 Mass. 47 (1983), 449 N.E. 2d 331 (Mass. 1983). http://masscases.com/cases/sjc/389/389mass47.html

Phinney, L. (2009, March 27). *What I wish I'd known about tenure.* Inside Higher Ed. https://www.insidehighered.com/advice/2009/03/27/what-i-wish-id-known-about-tenure

Purdue University. (n.d.). *Faculty fellows.* University Residences.https://www.housing.purdue.edu/ResidentialLife/FacultyFellows/index.html

Rhoads, R. A. (2009). Reflections of a professor on nine years of living in the dorms . . . I mean residence halls! *About Campus, 14*(3), 17–24. https://doi.org/10.1002/aca.291

Schuh, J. H., & Upcraft, M. L. (2001). *Assessment practice in student affairs: An application manual.* Jossey-Bass.

Sriram, R., & McLevain, M. (2016). Developing an instrument to examine student–faculty interaction in faculty-in-residence programs. *Journal of College Student Development, 57*(5), 604–609. https://doi.org/10.1353/csd.2016.0065

Stassen, M. L. (2003). Student outcomes: The impact of varying living–learning community models. *Research in Higher Education, 44*(5), 581–613. https://doi.org/10.1023/A:1025495309569

Virginia Tech. (n.d.-a). *Galileo and Hypatia.* Living Learning Programs. https://llp.vt.edu/llc/galileo_hypatia.html

Virginia Tech. (n.d.-b). *Residential colleges at Virginia Tech.* Living Learning Programs. https://llp.vt.edu/residential_colleges.html

Washington University in St. Louis. (n.d.). *Faculty involvement in residential life.* Students. https://students.wustl.edu/faculty-involvement-residential-life/

Whitt, E. J., Nesheim, B. E., Guentzel, M. J., Kellogg, A. H., McDonald, W. M., & Wells, C. A. (2008). "Principles of good practice" for academic and student affairs partnership programs. *Journal of College Student Development, 49*(3), 235–249. https://doi.org/10.1353/csd.0.0007

VIGNETTE

By Name and Story

Jill Stratton

"Get to know each individual by name and story" is what I kept in mind as I helped to create and build Washington University's residential college (RC) program over the course of 27 years. Most colleges and universities focus their community-building efforts around students, hoping faculty and staff get to know students and students get to know each other. In fact, long-time vice chancellor of students at Washington University (WashU) dean Jim McLeod's mantra was to have every student known by name and story. In the RCs, the community is built around more people than just the residents of the building. We worked together to expand the definition of community to include campus partners from across campus. For example, WashU restructured the maintenance and housekeeping assignments to connect one person on each team to a specific community, instead of a rotating schedule. RC leadership added their name and photo to the RC staff photos near the entrance of the building along with the RAs, college directors, and faculty in residence. RAs created door decorations and helped their residents get to know them as members of the community. As residents built relationships with their maintenance and housekeeping staff, residents also understood how their actions could affect the staff. Because of this change, students saw the community as their home and recognized that "Jean" is not responsible for cleaning up if they left trash behind. Jean is a member of their community. Attaching police officers, career center counselors, or mental health professionals to a specific community are additional opportunities to bring nonresidents into the community and allow students to know the professionals by name and story and vice versa.

Now at Vanderbilt University, I have carried this mantra with me. Developing interpersonal relationships and learning new names and new stories is high on my agenda. I advocate for building relationships intentionally by connecting people around specific interests, involving staff who normally are "behind the scenes" to attend events, providing cross-training, and issuing special invitations for involvement. I strive to model opportunities to learn, grow, and be in collaboration with people from all areas of the university community, because all of us are smarter and more creative than one of us. This intentionality is why the name and story are so powerful.

7

IT TAKES A VILLAGE

Strengthening Campus Partnerships and Developing a Faculty Handbook

Jennifer B. Post

In 2014, Southern Methodist University (SMU) fully transitioned from a traditional residential model to a campus-wide residential college (RC) model complete with 11 faculty-in-residence (FIR) and transitioned from a first-year to a 2-year live-on requirement. An RC is a specific subset of living–learning communities (LLCs) in which live-in faculty play an integral role in the leadership of the program. Founded in the Oxbridge model, RCs integrate academics and residential life and require strong partnerships between academic and student affairs (Residential College Society, n.d.). Although SMU had a few successful themed LLCs with FIR prior to 2014, nothing prepared us for such a large transition all at once. As one FIR put it, we all held hands and jumped into the deep end together.

The catalyst for such an enormous change was a desire by the university's leadership to increase retention, graduation rates, and alumni engagement. Rather than starting with one RC, as other campuses had, we transitioned the entire campus at one time. The university president, R. Gerald Turner, wanted the RC system to be *the* common student experience and did not want to create a situation ripe for "haves" and "have-nots." Although SMU operated successful LLCs, not all students participated, and the LLCs created an unintentional segregation of students. SMU sunset their LLCs to allow all students to participate in an environment that integrates "their academic, residential, and social experiences and, subsequently, cultivates a sense of belonging to the University" (Southern Methodist University, 2020, para. 7).

Leading up to the fall of 2014, SMU built five new residential buildings and converted six more residence halls to include FIR apartments and offices and classrooms while simultaneously defining what an RC at SMU entailed. To facilitate that process, we identified schools that had established or were developing RCs and conducted site visits. Teams of SMU staff, faculty, and students visited Vanderbilt University in Nashville, TN; Rice University in Houston, TX; Washington University in St. Louis, MO (which Jill describes in the vignette for this chapter); Oxford University in Oxford, England; and Baylor University in Waco, TX—sometimes multiple times—to learn how they conceptualized and operationalized an RC program. One big lesson learned was that RCs (and LLCs) all operate differently at each institution for reasons that vary, from the age of the program to campus politics to logistical issues. The site visits also helped identify necessary partnerships we had yet to consider. We had to rethink every process and structure in the department, onboard FIR, and gain buy-in from partners across campus. The challenges of collaborating with partners across campus was (and still is) both difficult and rewarding, and we are still finding ways to create stronger partnerships. In this chapter, I explore the partnerships required for LLCs beyond the relationship between residence life and academic affairs.

Literature Review

Many have written about the increasing complexity and specializations that lead institutions to become more fragmented and siloed (Birnbaum & Edelson, 1989; Lutz, 1982; Schroeder, 2005). Institutions, especially larger organizations, are "loosely coupled independent principalities and fiefdoms each disconnected from the other and from any common institutional purpose or transcending value" (Schroeder, 2005, p. 211). LLCs cannot thrive without strong campus partnerships, making the job of those involved in developing and sustaining LLCs all the more crucial and difficult. Researchers have stressed the need to create a seamless learning environment grounded in the university mission (Schroeder, 2005; Whitt et al., 2008). Examples of initiatives that marshal institutional resources to meet university goals such as orientation, first-year experience programs, diversity programs, and service learning programs can be found on many campuses today (Kezar, 2001; Whitt et al., 2008). Similarly, successful campus partnerships and collaborations can make or break an LLC.

When most administrators consider collaboration and partnerships related to LLCs, they primarily think of the partnership between faculty or an academic unit and student affairs, which is covered extensively in chapter 5. Although that partnership is certainly the most essential, a successful LLC takes a village—a collegiate village, including all the campus community members Jill names in her vignette—to truly thrive. Whether focused on program development or the logistical aspects of running an LLC, working with campus partners, and often asking them to adjust their practices for the benefit of the LLC, is critical to success. Most existing research focuses on academic affairs–student affairs partnerships, but there is a lack of research on partnerships between nonacademic units and LLCs. However, many of the lessons and recommendations learned from research regarding academic–student affairs partnerships can be extrapolated to include partnerships with any entity on campus.

The need for, and type of, campus partners varies depending on the nature of the LLC. Some programs are direct partnerships with an academic department, such as an engineering LLC. Such programs may rely on the department chair to assist with financial, personnel support, and recruitment of faculty involvement. Other programs are more interdisciplinary, such as leadership or entrepreneurial LLCs, or may not have a theme at all, such as some RCs. These programs may partner or collaborate with multiple academic units, other student affairs units, or departments across campus. Consider LLCs with common courses: academic advisors, the registrar, and student housing are just a few of the people and departments involved in the process of enrolling students in the correct courses. Another distinction among programs is whether the LLC has a live-in faculty (and family) or not. Keep in mind, each institution operates differently, and the campus setting changes the nature of collaborations. Large public institutions function differently than small liberal arts institutions. Research institutions and institutions with a strong teaching mission may require a different approach to collaboration as the priorities and campus culture vary (Roberts & Winniford, 2007). Understanding and adapting to the campus environment is a first step toward improving collaboration. In this chapter, I provide general guidelines that will help readers adjust to meet the needs, structure, and culture of their campus.

Partnerships Continuum

For the purposes of this chapter, a *partnership* is defined as a relationship between one or more units to achieve a goal. Partnerships should promote the mission of the university and increase effectiveness (Kezar, 2001). Not all partnerships are created equally; neither is it necessary that they all be the same. One of the challenges in creating partnerships is defining their nature (Schroeder, 2005). A helpful tactic is to consider partnerships in categories of increasing levels of engagement. The Partnership Continuum (Table 7.1)

TABLE 7.1
Partnership Continuum

	Support	Exchange	Cooperation	Collaboration
Definition	Units engage at a lower level, providing support through transactional services, facility use and/or funding,	Units engage in a partnership that results in a mutually beneficial exchange beyond facilities and funding, but does not constitute a long-term, coordinated relationship between units. An exchange in expertise.	Units engage in a coordinated relationship, where roles are designated by independent expertise, where responsibilities are shared over a long-term, reoccurring relationship between units.	Units share full responsibility in an integrated partnership that includes planning and researching, financing, decision-making, coordinating, and assessment of a project or experience. This partnership is often long-term and a sustained coordinated relationship that is mutually beneficial for the units.
Example	• Space rental/ usage • Monetary support	• Inviting faculty, staff, or businesses to speak at/ attend events • One-time events using someone's expertise	• Advisory boards • Advisory committees • Task forces • Teaching academic courses	• Learning communities • Learning abroad • Joint research and project engagements

Increasing ⟶ Engagement

Note. From Multicultural Services, Division of Student Affairs, Texas A&M University. (n.d.). *DMS academic collaboration tracking.* https://dms.tamu.edu/academic-partnership/

was created at Texas A&M University to define and track academic collaborations and is used with permission for this chapter.

The Partnership Continuum starts with the *support* level. These types of partnerships help through transactional services, financial support, or facility use. An example may be use of classrooms or funding support (Multicultural Services, Division of Student Affairs, Texas A&M University, n.d.). One may find that the goals between units at the support level are more loosely coupled than partnerships farther along on the continuum. By involving supporting partners in your LLC activities you may strengthen the understanding of your overall goals. For example, by inviting partners to events, or creating faculty or staff affiliate programs, you can create an understanding of how goals overlap.

Exchange partnerships are mutually beneficial and short term. Examples include inviting faculty or staff to train or speak to students. Exchange partnerships provide opportunities to involve faculty or other members of the university in your LLC. Inviting someone to speak or present a program can serve as a first opportunity for someone to learn about the LLC. For example, a flu shot clinic serves both your residents' and the health center's goals. Many units, such as study abroad or the tutoring center, welcome the opportunity to meet students in their home and spread the word about their area of service.

Cooperation defines a long-term, coordinated relationship in which roles are assigned by specific expertise. These relationships could include teaching academic courses, peer leader programs, or governance groups (Multicultural Services, Division of Student Affairs, Texas A&M University, n.d.). These types of programs can be particularly helpful in an LLC program. For example, academic departments may partner to teach first-year-heavy courses within an LLC, which can both strengthen the LLC and increase the richness of the class by creating cohorts of students who both learn and live together. Peer leader programs create leadership opportunities and give units opportunities to expand their outreach farther. Cooperative relationships often have overlapping but different goals. Unit leaders are wise to establish clear expectations and agreements. A written memorandum of understanding (MOU) will help avoid misunderstandings or miscommunication later, particularly as unit leadership changes over time.

Collaboration is the most involved level of partnerships and includes fully shared responsibility of the planning, financing and budget, decision-making and assessment for the program. Collaborative relationships are long term and mutually beneficial (Multicultural Services, Division of Student Affairs, Texas A&M University, n.d.). Such partnerships are difficult to create and sustain as these partnerships can be time consuming and complex

(Schroeder, 2005). In truly collaborative ventures, participants feel a sense of high investment and a part of something meaningful and innovative. Participants share common purpose, accountability, and strong, ongoing relationships (Schroeder, 2005). Academic affairs and student affairs working together to create an LLC could provide an example of a collaborative partnership. A hall director and FIR working together to lead and support an RC could be another example. Ideally, each partnership understands their role, sets expectations, and shares common goals.

Successful Partnerships

Successful partnerships include "four key elements: trust, communication, a sense of shared interests and goals and defined and clear expectations and roles" (Baldwin & Chang, 2007, p. 28). Each of these components is necessary and important, and the lack of each element creates a barrier to success. Trust is necessary for a partnership to flourish. Individuals who feel as though their partner is opportunistic or competitive may feel exploited and be reluctant to involve themselves in a partnership. Communication improves trust and aids in creating a sense of shared interests and expectations. Shared interests and goals motivate individuals to engage in and maintain partnerships. Key factors of successful partnerships include a shared vision, defined goals, a clear mission and strategy, and inclusive participation in decision-making. Finally, creating clear, defined expectations and roles is critical. Nothing creates frustration faster than unmet expectations created by miscommunication and lack of understanding.

Understanding that LLCs often require partnerships of varying levels from across campus, we can consider additional components of successful partnerships, starting with why people are motivated to create partnerships with other units. Baldwin and Chang (2007) determined that both individuals and institutions are motivated to collaborate to meet goals they could not meet as effectively by themselves. In other words, they cannot achieve their goals alone. The authors identified three underlying incentives for collaboration: "increasing prestige, sharing resources or reducing costs, and facilitating learning" (p. 27). Competition is a powerful motivator. Units may join forces to increase their or their institution's prestige or clout. Units may also combine resources to reduce costs. Budget cuts are a constant source of concern in higher education. Departments may be motivated to combine their efforts to achieve mutual goals while using resources more efficiently. Finally, the quest to enhance learning is a strong incentive in higher education. Determining new methods or insights in an ever-changing environment is a desirable outcome for most campus leaders.

Ultimately, people want to achieve their goals, and they need others to do so (Baldwin & Chang, 2007).

The success of a collaboration is dependent on both individual and institutional competency (Cho & Sriram, 2016). Collaboration is a competency that must be developed and requires certain knowledge, skills, and attitudes (Cho & Sriram, 2016). In successful partnerships, individuals must be able to reach out to others and build successful interpersonal relationships with others. Successful collaborations depend on trust; communication; shared goals; and clear, defined expectations and roles (Baldwin & Chang, 2007). Individuals must see the value of their colleagues and their colleagues' work. A lack of understanding of another's role, perceptions of the other's attitudes and contributions can negatively affect collaborations, creating biases and negative stereotypes (Cho & Sriram, 2016). Building strong interpersonal relations can help overcome barriers such as negative stereotypes and lack of trust.

LLC leaders fight an uphill battle if the culture of an institution does not support and encourage collaboration. Cho and Sriram (2016) found that the greatest predictor of how competent student affairs professionals are at collaborations was the institutional collaborative culture. In other words, a collaborative institutional culture leads to individuals who collaborate well. Symbolically, institutions can place high value on student learning and emphasize that all members of the community are responsible for promoting student learning and a seamless learning environment (Cho & Sriram, 2016; Kezar, 2001; Kezar & Gehrke, 2009; Kuh et al., 2005). However, espoused values alone are not enough. Administrators must enthusiastically promote collaboration through decisions, actions, daily conversations, and discussions regarding scarce resources. Senior leaders must also demonstrate staying power throughout the project. Often, senior administrators heavily involve themselves at the beginning of a new initiative and then leave the implementation to others and wonder why the project lags or fails. If those left to do the implementation have not been taught to collaborate well, or do not possess the necessary decision-making authority, the project will struggle, and those involved will be left frustrated (Cho & Sriram, 2016; Lester, 2009).

Barriers to Effective Collaboration

Collaboration is difficult, hard work (Whitt et al., 2008) with plenty of barriers. One of the most challenging barriers is different cultures between units, particularly between student affairs and academic affairs. Miscommunication, stereotypes, and lack of understanding of each other's roles create cycles that are difficult to change. Terminology, differing styles of communication, and a culture of isolation or silos all contribute to cultural clashes that can prevent effective partnerships. The multitude of acronyms and terms at any university can alone create communication barriers and a lack of understanding. I once told a colleague in financial aid to explain a process "as if I were four years old." He could not restrain himself from using specific terminology and casually referenced laws by vague titles. I never did fully understand the process. I share this example as a challenge to effective partnerships due to communication and lack of understanding about the other's role.

Other barriers include a lack of established, shared goals; unclear job responsibilities; and competition for resources. A lack of support from senior leadership can also prevent or diminish collaboration and partnerships (Cho & Sriram, 2016; Schroeder, 2005). Time is yet another barrier to collaborative partnerships. True collaboration takes time to communicate, build trust, develop shared goals, and gain input for decisions. Finally, an imbalance of power can affect effective partnerships: If one party has more power to make decisions, access to more resources, or in other ways holds more influence, a true collaborative partnership may be difficult (Baldwin & Chang, 2007). Between "personalities, history, expertise and territories that define colleges and universities" (Blimling & Whitt, 1999, p. 18), one finds it amazing that collaboration happens at all. The following best practices may help to overcome barriers.

Potential LLC Partnerships

I remember when our first FIR moved to campus: We thought through parking, mail, and noise issues. What we did not foresee was the particular internet needs of a computer science professor who also ran a consulting business. The issue created a barrier to his success and took significant staff time to resolve, but we learned the lesson well. As we built and renovated additional faculty apartments, we worked with the office of information technology, facilities, and the architects to make sure that technology needs of faculty and staff apartments were incorporated into the design. This example is just one of the lessons learned during that process. The following section is an attempt to learn from the experience of others, including institutions such as University of South Carolina, SMU, Elon University, and Washington University, to name a few, by providing a list of potential partners for your LLC.

On your campus, these LLC partnerships may fall anywhere along the partnership continuum or in multiple areas. An academic department may likely fall into the collaborative partnership area, whereas financial services may fall into a supporting category. Dining services may be supportive or coordinating depending on the relationship and program. For example, providing catering services may fall into a supporting category, and developing a demonstration cooking program could be considered a coordinating program. As you consider potential partnerships, the partnership continuum can guide you as you set expectations and create memorandums of understanding (MOU)s.

A common and imperative relationship for LLCs is that between student affairs and academic affairs. The provost office, academic deans, and department chairs can be strong partners in a variety of ways. First, academic leadership can help student affairs professionals understand faculty culture at their institution. For example, what counts as service? Should faculty seeking tenure commit their time to an LLC, or could involvement potentially hurt their progress toward tenure? In addition, academic leaders can also help with recruitment of faculty to participate in the LLC. Identifying and recruiting the faculty with an inclination to get involved and the skills to work with students in an informal setting is an obstacle that academic leadership can help you overcome. Finally, academic leaders are important partners in incentivizing faculty involvement in LLCs. For example, can involvement in an LLC count toward service in relation to tenure and promotion? The dean or provost may also provide financial or human resources to support an LLC, especially if the LLC supports the academic purpose of their college. An honors LLC may help recruit and retain high-achieving students. Academic departments may be one of your most essential partners, especially for those LLCs tied to a specific academic department. Themed LLCs could center on an academic major, such as engineering, languages, or fine arts, without engaging with that academic department. A more developed LLC will collaborate with the academic department to integrate courses, recruit faculty, and even gain financial support and additional human resources to support the LLC and provide a richer student experience.

Eating together is a societal norm that brings people together in an enjoyable way (Fulkerson et al., 2006), and food is a critical part of any residential life program. LLCs should work with dining services to provide meal allowances for faculty leaders to encourage them to eat with students. Dining together gives faculty and students an informal time to talk and get to know each other over a shared meal. The catering department can also be a necessary partner. Food is a foundational part of socialization and often a part of the programs and events LLCs organize, and catering can provide much of this food. Housing departments may negotiate discounts for these programs as a part of the campus dining contracts.

From developing a pet policy for FIR to creating risk management plans for off-campus programs, risk management can help mitigate risk for both students and the institution. Housing and LLC leaders will need to explain the overall goals and importance of these activities to risk management officers to show why the risk is worth the potential outcomes. At many schools, FIR have taken students sailing on their boat, on public transportation to a museum, and on a variety of off-campus trips. Some schools host study abroad trips through their LLCs or RCs. Understandably, risk management officers may initially resist these trips. Their goal is to keep students safe and minimize risk for the university, which is an admiral goal. Instead of shutting down any risky decision, work toward getting to "yes" in a safe way.

SMU built five new RCs while retrofitting six others with support from development and alumni affairs. The five new buildings were donor named, and the classic buildings were named long ago. One surprise was how involved the donors wanted to be in their RC. They hosted students at their homes, brought cookies for the first day of school, donated swag, and attended events. LLCs are ripe for donor involvement, from naming rights to sponsoring events such as study abroad, or providing scholarships for student leaders. LLCs have the potential to create strong communities, and you may find that your donors want to be a part of those communities. Inviting them to weekly teas or to speak at an end-of-year event are wonderful ways to keep donors involved and part of the community.

Faculty involved with LLCs increase their likelihood of encountering students of concern, students in crisis, and conduct issues. As faculty develop relationships with students, the likelihood of a student sharing problems increases. Faculty should understand the role of the dean of students office and understand the process to report a student of concern and how student conduct works. Similarly, ensure faculty know their legal requirements to report Title IX issues and how the Title IX office functions.

Some LLCs build in opportunities for student research. The office of undergraduate research may be able to assist in providing student research opportunities, manage research grant applications, and support reporting processes. In addition, look for opportunities to work with your office of institutional research to incorporate LLCs into broader university assessment. Chances are strong that your university is already tracking retention and graduation rates and may be collecting data via the National Survey of Student Engagement, Higher Education Research Institute surveys, or others, with valuable data that can be extracted for LLC assessment. Partnering with the office of institutional research to dig deeper and see if LLCs differ from the overall population can help you determine where to make adjustments in your program and tell your story to the larger population.

Peer mentor programs provide additional ways to partner with other groups on campus. Examples could include health and wellness, sexual violence prevention, academic success, and tutoring, just to name a few. LLC leaders should identify opportunities to bring services or learning opportunities to their students where they live and develop partnerships with those offices.

Additional partnerships may include:

- Coordinating with the finance department to make sure your faculty can spend money appropriately for your institution. That includes access to a procurement system, budget accounts, and the knowledge of how they can and cannot use university funds.
- Establishing a good working relationship with public affairs can lead to a win–win situation for your LLC and public affairs. Public affairs partners often search for ways to showcase out-of-classroom student learning or faculty–student interactions for the university website or alumni magazines, which also offers your LLC some positive publicity and an opportunity to celebrate the partnership.
- Managing civic and community engagement can help LLC leaders incorporate service learning into their programs.
- Offering LLC classes that tie into the core curriculum by the curriculum office.
- Soliciting the help of the registrar office or academic advising office for common LLC courses.
- Collaborating with the financial aid office for research or travel grants, or provide other types of scholarships.
- Using teaching and learning technologies to support classrooms or other shared academic spaces in the LLC.
- Recruiting students with the help of the admissions office. Make sure tour guides and counselors understand your LLC's mission and the student experience so they can be good ambassadors for the program.
- Building study abroad or alternative breaks into the LLC experience. These trips may be part of the curriculum or an optional trip within the LLC.

As you can see, campus collaborations and LLCs go hand in hand. A successful LLC involves partners from all over campus. From supporting partnerships to full collaborations, each partnership can enhance your LLC. Take the time to brainstorm a wide variety of partnerships on your campus that can enhance your LLC. Develop relationships with those offices and communicate your common goals. Spending the time to set expectations will only benefit your LLC in the long run.

Live-In Faculty Considerations

As discussed in Part Three of this book, live-in faculty positions can bring unique benefits to an LLC and to students (Browne et al., 2009; Davenport & Pasque, 2014; Shushok et al., 2009). FIR also require additional considerations and collaboration from campus partnerships. Faculty often bring family members (including furry family members), which require even more adjustments. In this section, I outline some of the partnerships that may be necessary to successfully integrate faculty, and their families, into a live-in LLC role.

Integrating FIR

On some campuses, faculty involved in LLCs receive an additional stipend or reduced responsibilities, such as a course reduction. These changes may require coordination with human resources or payroll. A reduction in course load or other responsibilities requires collaboration with the academic department and the provost's office. In some departments, that faculty member may be the only one teaching a specific course, so reducing their course load creates a hardship on their academic department. Every institution operates a little differently, so determine who in your organizational structure is needed in these decisions and processes.

When working with FIR, your facilities staff will be a crucial partner. Ensuring adequate spaces for a FIR apartment and offices is the first step. Ensuring the space feels homey is the second. This apartment will be their home, so it is critical for the facilities staff to create an environment closely consistent with an off-campus home. If possible, account for an exterior entrance, residential grade finishes, and personalized paint colors. One staff member from a large, public university shared the importance of anticipating needs for the FIR, FIR family, and students. For example, at her institution they added a screen door to the FIR apartment entrance, which created a more welcoming environment. FIR would leave their primary door open during programs or open hours to encourage students to visit. Students knew if the primary door was open they were welcome to enter the FIR apartment. Similarly, a FIR at another institution requested a screen door so they could leave their primary door open while keeping their pet from escaping their apartment.

Earlier, I shared an example about insufficient Wi-Fi capabilities for a computer science FIR who also managed a consulting business, a practice encouraged among engineering and computer science faculty on our campus. In his situation, the issue was not just bandwidth but also security for his clients. The office of information and technology is another relevant partner for live-in faculty.

Families

Many FIR come with families. Kids and dogs are the best icebreakers between faculty and students! One FIR's kids made and distributed "art" at dinner for students to hang in their rooms. Other FIRs recall distressed students asking to come by for puppy time. The FIR families should be considered full members of the community. In chapter 11, Sriram discusses FIR families in more detail, but a chapter regarding campus partnerships would be incomplete without considering the additional needs and considerations of FIR families (both human and furry). The following paragraphs include a few considerations for LLCs with FIR families who may include human and fur children.

Your office of risk management can help determine expectations and requirements to ensure safety for all, such as supervision of small children on campus or insurance and vaccine requirements for Fido—not to mention renters insurance for the FIR and FIR family. Background checks for adults living on campus is another consideration that your office of risk management and legal affairs or human resources can help you navigate.

As previously mentioned, sharing meals is integral to building community, and that includes the FIR and FIR family. Including a small meal plan for family members allows them to eat with students. You may also want to work with dining services on family policies such as reduced prices for young children. Be sure to work with your tax office: Some campuses consider family meals additional compensation and either disallow meals or report them for tax purposes.

When faculty members consider moving their family to campus, they consider how much of a sacrifice they and their families will make in comparison to how much they will gain. Offering FIR and their families as many of the amenities they would have if they were living off campus will make recruiting FIR easier. Access to campus services, such as the library, campus recreation center, campus IT network services, and reserved parking are examples of amenities that FIR families may expect. Again, relevant partnerships may vary from campus to campus. At some urban campuses, few people drive, so parking is not expected. FIR in other locations rely on cars and park in front of their house if they live off campus, so providing reserved parking is a greater need.

Best Practices for Starting an LLC

When consulting with colleagues on other campuses considering starting a new RC or LLC, I am often asked for suggestions and guidance. Based on a review of the literature, the Partnership Continuum from Texas A&M, and my own experience, I cultivated a list of best practices:

1. Before starting a new initiative from scratch, begin by modifying current programs and initiatives to involve more faculty and collaboration from other units (Cho & Sriram, 2016; Consolvo & Dannells, 2009; Whitt et al., 2008). Strengthening collaboration within existing programs may be easier than starting a new program.

2. Model programs of best practice from other campuses, particularly those that are similar to your campus or share your goals (Consolvo & Dannells, 2009). Using a respected aspirant or peer institution as an example can build trust and reassure skeptics. Conducting site visits with a variety of stakeholders can be particularly helpful as well, especially stakeholders at the collaboration level on the continuum.

3. Take the time to create a shared purpose, vision, mission, and values. Involve joint cross-functional planning and implementation teams (Schroeder, 2005). A lack of shared vision and goals creates one of the biggest barriers to successful partnerships. Spending time creating shared understanding in the beginning will save time and effort in the long run. This step is relevant for partners at all levels of the continuum, but even more so for those at the collaboration level.

4. Demonstrate how the program advances the institution's mission and goals (Cho & Sriram, 2016). Linking your LLC outcomes to recruitment, retention, or graduation rates, for example, may incentivize others to lend support. This step can be especially impactful for campus partners on the lower level of the continuum. Although your immediate goals may not overlap, the mission of the institution should be shared by all members of the community.

5. Recognize organizational culture and the influence culture has on collaboration, both at an institutional and unit level (Cho & Sriram, 2016). Take risks and step out of your collective comfort zone (Schroeder, 2005). I especially like this quote:

   > Tyranny of custom prevents us from challenging prevailing assumptions . . . [if we are] so focused on the traditions, norms, and customs within our organizational boundaries that we fail to recognize distant opportunities for enhancing . . . student learning. (Schroeder, 2005, pp. 209–210)

We often think that a change will not work or cannot work because "That's not how things are done here," or "We've always done it this way." Take the time to reflect on your institutional and unit culture and recognize how culture colors your perception of the possible in ways you may not realize.

6. Create MOUs to document expectations, roles, functions, and resource allocation among partners. As the leadership of and individuals participating in the partnerships change over time, written MOUs are invaluable. This step is just as critical for partnerships at the lower end of the engagement scale as it is for those full collaborating partnerships.

7. Engage in assessment of the partnership (Whitt et al., 2008), and share the results widely. Continue to demonstrate how the program advances the institution's mission and goals (Cho & Sriram, 2016).

8. Publicly celebrate successes and recognize and reward involved partners. Affirmation and recognition will encourage future collaborations.

9. Be a strong and vocal advocate with a commitment to building and sustaining relationships (Schroeder, 2005) and creating excitement around a shared vision (Cho & Sriram, 2016).

As you can see, and as Jill's opening vignette for this chapter suggests, a successful LLC takes a village to run! This is by no means a comprehensive list, but I hope this list will get you in the right frame of mind to create the most appropriate list of partners for your LLC at your specific institution. The sky's the limit when thinking creatively about opportunities for partnership, and your program will only be richer for these collaborations.

References

Baldwin, R. G., & Chang, D. A. (2007). Collaborating to learn, learning to collaborate. *Peer Review, 9*(4).

Birnbaum, R., & Edelson, P. J. (1989). *How colleges work: The cybernetics of academic organization and leadership.* Jossey-Bass.

Blimling, G. S., & Whitt, E. J. (1999). *Good practice in student affairs: Principles to foster student learning.* Jossey-Bass.

Browne, N. M, Headworth, S., & Saum, K. (2009). The rare, but promising involvement of faculty in residence hall programming. *College Student Journal, 43*(1), 22–30. https://scholarworks.bgsu.edu/cgi/viewcontent.cgi?article=1010& context=econ_pub

Cho, A. R., & Sriram, R. (2016). Student affairs collaborating with academic affairs: Perceptions of individual competency and institutional culture. *College Student Affairs Journal, 34*(1), 56–69. https://doi.org /10.1353/csj.2016.0003

Consolvo, C., & Dannells, M. (2009). Collaboration with academic affairs and faculty. In M. J. Amey & L. M. Reesor (Eds.), *Beginning your journey: A guide for new professionals in student affairs* (3rd ed., pp. 89–108). National Association of Student Personnel Administrators.

Davenport, A. M., & Pasque, P. A. (2014). Adding breadth and depth to college and university residential communities: A phenomenological study of faculty-in-residence. *Journal of College and University Student Housing, 40*(2), 46–65.

Fulkerson, J. A., Neumark-Sztainer, D., & Story, M. (2006). Adolescent and parent views of family meals. *Journal of the American Dietetic Association, 106*(4), 526–532. https://doi.org/ 10.1016/j.jada.2006.01.006

Kezar, A. (2001). Documenting the landscape: Results of a national study on academic and student affairs collaborations. In A. Kezar, D. J. Hirsch, & C. Burack (Eds.), *Understanding the Role of Academic and Student Affairs Collaboration in Creating a Successful Learning Environment* (New Directions for Higher Education, no. 116, pp. 39–52). Jossey-Bass. https://doi.org/10.1002/he.32

Kezar, A., & Gehrke, S. (2009). Supporting and enhancing student learning through partnerships with academic colleagues. In G. S. McClellan & J. Stringer (Eds.), *The handbook of student affairs administration* (3rd ed.; pp. 435–455). Wiley.

Kuh, G. D., Kinzie, J., Schuh, J. H., & Whitt, E. J. (2005). Never let it rest lessons about student success from high-performing colleges and universities. *Change, 37*(4), 44–51. https://doi.org/10.3200/CHNG.37.4.44-51

Lester, J. (2009). *Organizing higher education for collaboration: A guide for campus leaders.* Wiley.

Lutz, F. W. (1982). Tightening up loose coupling in organizations of higher education. *Administrative Science Quarterly, 27*(4), 653–669. https://doi .org/10.2307/2392536

Multicultural Services, Division of Student Affairs, Texas A&M University. (n.d.). *DMS academic collaboration tracking.* https://dms.tamu.edu/academic-partnership/

Residential College Society. (n.d.). *Definition.* http://residentialcollegesociety.org/definition/

Roberts, D. M., & Winniford, J. C. (2007). Campus partnerships. In R. L. Ackerman (Ed.), *The midlevel manager in student affairs: Strategies for success* (pp. 255–274). National Association of Student Personnel Administrators.

Schroeder, C. C. (2005). Collaborative partnerships between academic affairs and student affairs. In M. L. Upcraft, J. N. Gardner, & B. O. Barefoot (Eds.), *Challenging and supporting the first-year student: A handbook for improving the first year of college* (pp. 204–220). Jossey-Bass.

Shushok, F., Jr., Henry, D. V., Blalock, G., & Sriram, R. R. (2009). Learning at any time: Supporting student learning wherever it happens. *About Campus, 14*(1), 10–15. https://doi.org/10.1002/abc.278

Southern Methodist University. (2020). *History of residential life.* https://www.smu .edu/StudentAffairs/ResidenceLifeandStudentHousing/About/History

Whitt, E. J., Nesheim, B. E., Guentzel, M. J., Kellogg, A. H., McDonald, W. M., & Wells, C. A. (2008). "Principles of good practice" for academic and student affairs partnership programs. *Journal of College Student Development, 49*(3), 235–249. https://doi.org/10.1353/csd.0.0011

VIGNETTE

The Impact of Experiential Learning

Tim Knight

W hen I meet parents of prospective students, I tell them that participating in College Park Scholars is similar to having children in that, no matter how much you prepare yourself, you understand it only after doing it. I have been with the environment, technology, and economy program of College Park Scholars for 7 years, as director for the last 4. College Park Scholars is a group of 12 living–learning programs, each with a unique academic focus. Our academic focus is on sustainability, but we use experiential learning and discussions to teach critical thinking and civic engagement at the same time. When students live together and participate in experiential learning, the impact on their lives is far greater than they expect from 15 credits. As one student wrote in a reflection paper after the first semester:

> [The environment, technology, and economy program] was not what I expected it to be . . . I did not think that there was going to be a lot of work or meaningfully impact me, especially since the class itself was only a one credit colloquium. The experiences of the class, because it involved hands-on learning and [was] taught by people with a mission and passion for the topic, opened my eyes to sustainability and our place within an environment and community.

The experiential learning aspect of our curriculum increases the impact we have on students and the connections between students and instructors. We can learn about waste sorting in class, but it is a completely different experience to pull on rubber gloves and to sort the three waste streams (landfill, recycling, compost) from the student union in our annual waste audit. Students report that these experiences have lasting effects on their behavior and their understanding. By removing learning from the formal classroom setting, it also relaxes some of the separation between students and faculty. It builds social bonds among students as well as between students and faculty.

This translates into the classroom, where students become more willing to participate in discussions as we build trust and relationships.

Because many of my students major in disciplines that are not directly related to our academic focus, we use sustainability as a lens through which to view their lives. We also center civic engagement and what it means to be a responsible citizen. To this end, we partner with a number of groups, on and off campus. The waste audit, for example, is conducted in partnership with the campus waste management group. This demonstrates how experiential learning creates a mutualistic relationship between student learning and university maintenance.

There is a synergy that happens when students live and learn together, even when that learning is such a small part of their total experience. They develop relationships that last past their time in the program, or even in college. Instead of assigning a textbook, I use articles that relate to our themes each week, which allows me to keep the readings very topical. Students report discussing our class topics over meals and even arguing over the more controversial ones in the hallways and their rooms. They develop habits of engaging with the news and society, assessing the impacts of their actions and discussing them with their peers. There is a sense of belonging and mutual support that comes from a living–learning program that leaves a lasting impact and, I believe, helps to account for the positive outcomes that we see in the research.

8

"MINE" THE GAP

Connecting Curriculum, Courses, and Community

Jonathan W. Manz, Mark Daniel Ward, and Ellen Gundlach

As the professor wraps up the introductory animal science class discussion, she reminds students to meet in front of their residence hall on Saturday at 10:00 a.m. When they meet on Saturday, the professor, her class, and the two resident assistants (RAs) who live on the same floor as the students travel by bus to a neighboring state to visit a horse farm. At the farm, the staff show the students how to feed and care for the horses. The students also learn about the overhead costs related to operating the farm and the profit margins made from the sale of the animals. This trip is just one of many beyond-the-classroom learning experiences the professor has written into the curriculum for her agriculture course associated with the living–learning community (LLC) she supports.

We share this as an example of a course curriculum intentionally designed for the LLC because it provides both social and educational learning beyond the classroom. Students participating in this LLC are actively engaged in their field of study and experience the communal bonding with peers and faculty. The authors of this chapter have participated in similar learning communities as faculty and administrators and can attest to the powerful impact they have on students. Tim Knight's vignette for our chapter offers an additional example of this impact.

The purpose of this chapter is to share recommendations and insights into curriculum and course designs for LLCs. First, we provide an overview of the literature and introduce recommendations from the Washington Center for Improving Undergraduate Education (Lardner & Malnarich, 2008) to frame the discussion. We share our experience creating and leading The Data Mine—a large-scale LLC, featuring a curriculum that weaves classroom instruction with hands-on learning—as a case study of a comprehensive curricular design of LLCs. We target both faculty (those interested and those already engaged in LLCs) and campus administrators who are cocreating these experiences. The chapter concludes with a discussion on implications and steps that a faculty member or campus administrator can take.

Mining the Literature

Kuh's (2008) report for the Association of American Colleges and Universities indicated that learning communities, where students take linked courses together and work closely with each other and faculty, represent one of 10 high-impact practices in higher education. He noted that the integration of linked courses (associated with the program and overlapping in their curriculum to some degree) provides the impetus to investigate large issues that surpass the bounds of any one course. Furthermore, learning communities provide students and faculty the opportunity to share discussions around a central theme and can help build relationships that are complemented by activities that take place outside of the classroom (Kuh, 2008). These opportunities are expanded when learning communities have a residential component.

Demonstrating the benefit of combining the curricular and residential experience, Purdie and Rosser (2011) found that students participating in an LLC with linked courses persisted from their first year to their second year at rates higher than students participating in LLCs without linked courses. Underrepresented, first-generation, and at-risk students persist at higher rates than their peers when participating in LLC experiences that focus on the success of these particular populations (Nosaka & Novak, 2014). Stassen (2003) studied three types of LLCs with varying degrees of structure, and all three types had positive impacts on participating first-year students' GPA when compared with peers. Little research has focused on curriculum and course design for LLCs beyond the first year, but there has been some mention of positive benefits of sophomore involvement in LLCs (Gaff, 2000; Parker & Ward, 2019).

Although studies have documented that students benefit from participating in LLCs, they do not always make a statistically significant, positive difference for students' academic performance. For example, a single-institution study found that a cohort of students jointly enrolled in dual courses did not perform significantly better than their non–learning community peers taking courses individually (Smith & Lovgren, 2018). At another institution, students who participated in LLCs with academic themes, but no affiliated courses, did not demonstrate significantly higher GPAs or retention rates compared with their peers (Purdie & Rosser, 2011). In a single-institution study, some students participating in linked courses within a nonresidential learning community reported that the relationships within the community were strained because of the excessive amount of time spent together among the multiple courses (Virtue et al., 2019). It is important to acknowledge that there are a few cases where LLCs were not impactful. However, there are multiple strategies, including the use of a residential curriculum (Blimling, 2015) and faculty engagement with students (Wawrzynski et al., 2009), that enhance learning and the residential experience.

Residential Life Curriculum and LLCs

Curriculum, which was once exclusive to the classroom, has become en vogue for housing and residence life departments in their approach to educating students living on campus. A small number of broad learning goals, such as developing engaged citizens, are usually the focus of a residential curriculum. Typically, a semester is mapped out with learning outcomes and strategies to help meet the learning outcomes (Blimling, 2015).

As early adopters of this model, housing administrators at the University of Delaware utilized structured and sequenced learning approaches in the residential environment. The purpose of this approach is to blend research on student development with learning theory and pedagogy to be intentional in educating students (Kerr et al., 2017). Blimling (2015) emphasizes that, when utilizing a residential curriculum, student affairs administrators should partner with faculty in the development process.

In general, many campuses reported a 30% to 50% reduction in conduct interventions due to better communication of responsibilities of living within a residential environment focused on learning. Housing administrators have also reported greater student persistence, sense of belonging, and satisfaction (Kerr et al., 2017).

Faculty–Student Engagement

Both students and faculty benefit from the enhanced connections made possible in LLCs from associated faculty and courses. At one institution, students perceived that academic LLCs provided environments that encourage learning as a community and where faculty and staff are welcome (Wawrzynski et al., 2009). Students also benefit from interacting with faculty, especially those faculty who have physical office space within the residential environment of the LLC (Wawrzynski et al., 2009).

In a large, multi-institutional study representing 34 institutions and 297 LLCs, Inkelas et al. (2008) examined typologies of LLCs, according to their research from the National Survey on Living–Learning Programs. The three typologies, based on size and resources, represent varying degrees of faculty integration and student participation. Through self-reported data, the study examined students' growth in critical thinking abilities; their ability to apply critical thinking to new ideas and ways to apply their knowledge; and their appreciation of and openness to multiple, diverse viewpoints. Interestingly, the typology representing LLCs with the least amount of resources and faculty integration yielded higher results in the three areas of student growth than the typology representing LLCs with the most resources. However, the researchers cautioned that the reason behind the lack of difference between the two groupings is not established, and (to date) we are unaware of any further studies that have investigated this matter.

Despite these benefits of faculty–student involvement, it may be surprising that the National Survey on Living–Learning Programs data show a lack of faculty involvement in many LLCs. Nearly 25% of the LLCs in the study had no faculty involvement, and 64% of the LLCs in the study had at most three faculty members involved. To provide perspective, the size of LLCs in the study ranged from 10 to more than 1,000 students participating, with 50 as the common enrollment size (Inkelas et al., 2018). In chapter 6 of this volume, Krieger discusses strategies for engaging faculty in LLCs and addresses potential barriers that may limit their involvement.

LLC Academic Environments

Inkelas et al. (2018) recommended that the "academic environments" in LLCs include four key elements: (a) courses for credit, (b) faculty advising, (c) academically supportive climates, and (d) socially supportive climates. Courses for credit can range in the number of credit hours and are either offered directly to students in the LLC or colisted with an academic department. Faculty advising pertains to LLC faculty offering academic advising to their students. Peer-to-peer interactions in the residence halls help create both academically and socially supportive climates, as reported by students participating in LLCs (Inkelas et al., 2018). Depending on the reader's institution, these four areas recommended by Inkelas et al. (2018) may already be common practice, or they could be novel ideas. Residence halls hosting LLCs should be not only socially supportive climates (which is more common) but also academically supportive climates (Inkelas et al., 2018). Based on our experience, academic support manifests itself in both physical structures (e.g., collaboration spaces, quiet study areas) and a strong presence from faculty and academic support staff. Finally, when campus leaders develop LLCs, credit-bearing associated courses (i.e., linked courses) should be considered as an avenue for learning and faculty and student engagement. These recommendations are part of Kuh's (2008) description of learning communities as a high-impact practice.

In general, linked courses occur when faculty intentionally design their curricula with the other linked course(s) and the goals of the LLC in mind. Ideally, the faculty are collaborating with the other linked course instructors or LLC administrators. Linked course design elements often include shared assignments, in addition to a shared topic, for instance, a smaller introductory oral or written communication course using engineering topics for projects while linked with a larger introductory engineering course. This linkage helps engineering students recognize the need to effectively communicate their engineering designs. In practice, the strength of the course linkage may vary, with some programs offering a partial overlap at certain times of the semester (Luebke, 2002) and others having an extensive collaboration throughout the semester or even the academic year (Brown et al., 2018). The logistics of linked courses require even more faculty coordination and planning, particularly if the courses are going to share space or overlap in other ways (Williams, 2015).

Although students do find benefits in participating in linked courses, particularly in overlapping topics between the courses and the social nature of sharing multiple courses with the same peers, the academic benefits are mixed. One study found a nominal increase in students' GPA when a linked course was associated with their LLC (Purdie & Rosser, 2011). Results from a different multi-institutional study demonstrate that linked courses did not have a significant impact on students' academic performance, relationships, or psychological well-being (Eidum et al., 2020). Williams (2015) found that students participating in linked courses at the University of West Florida demonstrated objectively more learning and showed greater improvement over the course of the semester than their peers in nonlinked versions of the courses. However, those same students in linked courses self-reported lower competence. Results from another study were unclear as to whether students learned more in linked courses compared with their peers in nonlinked versions of the same courses (Luebke, 2002).

However, despite the results of these studies, we recommend that a credit-bearing course be associated with an LLC, if possible, as one of the many pathways for faculty–student engagement. When using linked courses in an LLC, students should coregister in these courses (Inkelas et al., 2018) as an LLC cohort. Having courses associated with LLCs allows for students to synthesize knowledge both in and out of the classroom. The animal science story in the introduction of this chapter reflects this strategy. At Central Michigan University, students participating in an education LLC with three linked courses reported appreciating the social and academic community feel, the group projects, and having all three linked courses taught on the same day (Brown et al., 2018). The faculty regularly communicated about the LLC, shared collaborative assignments among the three courses, and supported the general well-being of the students. The faculty reported that this frequent communication provided a stronger support system for their students because they were able to demonstrate support in multiple settings, for example, through the three classes and after-class interactions (Brown et al., 2018).

Although Eidum et al. (2020) found that linked courses do not have a positive or negative impact on students, faculty involvement as a whole does have a positive impact. Linked courses are one of the easiest ways to get faculty involved in LLCs; therefore, these courses are still a worthwhile strategy. Credit-bearing linked courses provide ways for students and faculty to connect within the classroom and create opportunities for learning beyond the classroom. As we describe in the next section, linked courses have been a crucial element to the success of the LLCs we have created and led.

Entering the Mine: Moving to Practice

We look to recommendations from seasoned faculty and administrators to frame our discussion on the implementation of LLC course curricula. The Evergreen State College houses the Washington Center for Improving Undergraduate Education, which includes personnel support for learning communities, among other initiatives. Washington Center leadership recommends three broad aspects to be included in every course associated with a learning community (Lardner & Malnarich, 2008):

1. The curriculum should be created to meet the *learning outcomes* of the program.
2. The curriculum should include *integrative assignments* that utilize public knowledge, so that students learn how to integrate knowledge from multiple disciplines.
3. Faculty are encouraged to take advantage of *campus resources*, such as events and support centers, and incorporate these resources into their syllabi.

In this next part of the chapter, we examine each of these recommendations with examples from our experience, followed by a section on logistical considerations. As a reminder to the reader, we add the residential component to these learning communities to make them LLCs.

One example of an LLC that follows these recommendations is The Data Mine at Purdue University. The Data Mine started as the groundbreaking National Science Foundation–funded statistics LLC, which provided data science coursework and research opportunities for Purdue University sophomores (Gokalp Yavuz & Ward, 2018; Gundlach & Ward, 2021). At the conclusion of the 5-year grant, the LLC leadership expanded opportunities for students to participate. The Data Mine LLC (Purdue University, 2022) has more than 1,000 students from majors all over campus, at any point in their undergraduate or graduate academic career, who share an interest in learning data science skills. Special effort is made to recruit students who are female or underrepresented minorities. The Data Mine is funded by the office of the provost and corporate partner donations. All first-year students, and many continuing students, live in one residence hall, shared with two smaller LLCs. Data Mine faculty and staff members have offices in the residence hall to maximize both formal and informal interactions with students. The facility also includes collaboration and study spaces, a dining hall, and meeting rooms. The office of the provost and division of student life collaborate to oversee the LLC, with housing staff supporting Data Mine faculty, staff, and students with course registration, facilities, and planning.

The Data Mine is an umbrella LLC that combines 20 smaller LLCs. In addition to the common data science seminar, most Data Mine students also choose a specialty cohort, where the students put their data science skills into the context of an academic or career field that interests them. The academic cohorts involve the colleges of agriculture, education, engineering, health and human sciences, liberal arts, management, science, and technology. For example, the actuarial science cohort, where students analyze actual insurance company data, is associated with the College of Science. The academic cohorts each have 10 to 50 students involved. However, the corporate partners cohort is not associated with an academic department; it had approximately 150 students in its first year and 400 students in its second year. In the following section we discuss how The Data Mine successfully incorporates learning outcomes, integrative assignments, and campus resources.

Curriculum and LLC Learning Outcomes

One common element for all Data Mine students is the weekly one-credit-hour seminar (both fall and spring terms). The seminar directly addresses the learning outcomes for the program, which were developed by The Data Mine's faculty and staff.

The learning outcomes (LOs) for The Data Mine are as follows:

1. Students will discover data science and professional development opportunities in order to prepare for a career.
2. Students will explain the difference between research computing and basic personal computing data science capabilities in order to know which system is appropriate for a data science project.
3. Students will design efficient search strategies in order to acquire new data science skills.
4. Students will devise the most appropriate data science strategy in order to answer a research question.
5. Students will apply data science techniques in order to answer a research question about a big data set.

Each week in the seminar, students share a meal in the residence hall's dining court while working on small data science projects. The goal of these projects is for the students to learn how to learn new data science skills (LO3). From the very first day of the fall semester, the students work with real-life, large data sets in a research computing environment (LO2, 5). For example, students might be working with all the New York City taxi data since 2009 or scraping data from the Internet Movie Database (IMDb) website. Instead of a formal lecture, the students are self-guided through examples, with help from their peers, faculty, and teaching assistants. Using active learning, real data sets, appropriate technology, and frequent authentic assessments are all best practices in statistics education (GAISE College Report ASA Revision Committee, 2016). Students are exposed to different data science strategies and techniques because data scientists need a wide array of tools in their toolbox. It is imperative that data scientists learn how and when to flexibly apply these tools (LO4, 5). Students receive help through the Piazza online discussion board (https://www.piazza.com) and in dozens of office hours available each week (including evenings and weekends) in the residence hall.

Students can participate in the LLC for multiple years, working on more advanced projects each year. The LLC has been approximately evenly split between first-year and continuing students. Both advanced and beginning students meet for a seminar in the same room at the same time so that they can benefit from working collaboratively. Advanced students also have the opportunity to apply to be teaching assistants and peer mentors. Although the one-credit seminar does not directly apply to any major, it counts toward the university's applications in data science certificate.

Integrative Assignments

The Washington Center's second recommendation is to integrate multiple disciplines and public knowledge into assignments for the LLC. One way of achieving this is by having multiple linked courses that approach the theme of the LLC from different domains of expertise. In each academic cohort of The Data Mine, a department selects additional coursework, either as part of a major or as an elective, ranging from one to six credit hours each semester. Lower course requirements are easier for students to add to their schedule. These additional classes could be formal lectures, discussion sections, or research projects. Some courses are open only to LLC students, whereas others are open to all.

In the corporate partners Data Mine cohort, two dozen companies provide mentors and interesting, complex, applicable data science projects for the students to work on. The students are organized in teams of up to 25 students each throughout the academic year. Students have weekly (usually virtual) meetings with their corporate mentors and additional work sessions with teammates. Project topics include anomaly detection, computer vision, social media sentiment analysis, flight pattern analysis, and natural language processing. Students learn about corporate culture, workflow processes, security, and data science tools. Some groups visit corporate headquarters. Most mentors visit campus at least once during the academic year, often staying in an apartment in the residence hall. At the end of the academic year, as part of a symposium, student groups create professional quality posters of their work, record presentations, and host sessions where members of the public and staff members from the companies can ask questions about their work. Students reflect on their experiences every 2 weeks and at the end of each semester.

Utilize Campus Resources

The Washington Center recommends that LLCs take advantage of campus resources outside the classroom to create a rich learning experience. These campus resources may be found through support centers, arts organizations, and alumni centers, or within the residence hall. As previously noted, housing professionals have begun creating curricula tailored to the residential environment (Blimling, 2015). Connecting the residential and LLC curricula is a great way to further integrate the "living" and "learning" of LLCs.

Although not directly linked, all Purdue LLCs (not only The Data Mine) overlap with the residential curriculum. For example, students serving in the RA peer leadership role and their supervisors interact regularly with the faculty partners for the LLCs represented in their communities.

Furthermore, RAs have regular "intentional interactions," using a loose script, with the residents in their communities, including engaging LLC students about their experiences. Faculty and RAs work together to give students wraparound support.

The Data Mine strives to take advantage of programs, speakers, and events already happening on campus. Data Mine students are all required to attend three outside events each semester and write a one-page reflection about each experience. Their reflections include a summary of what they learned and a discussion of what new ideas they now want to explore.

Examples of the outside events include guest speakers for the residential community or other on-campus events. Topics range from data science careers, applications of data science, professional development, privacy and ethics, storytelling with data, and scientific innovation expressed through the arts. Purdue's Center for Career Opportunities, galleries, Black cultural center, diversity and inclusion, research computing, and convocations (artistic performances) offices have all provided events, in addition to alumni, professional organizations, student groups, and data science professionals. These outside events give the students a broader perspective of why they are learning what they are learning and where these new skills could be useful in a wide range of careers.

The students submit their reflections through the course management system for a grade. The Data Mine staff and/or teaching assistants read these reflections and provide feedback. These reflections help the staff understand students' interests in regard to inviting new guest speakers, planning curricula, and even creating new LLCs. The students have expressed enthusiasm for the opportunity to interact with such a wide variety of professionals, especially when the speakers spend time discussing why they chose their career and how they got to where they are now. Whenever possible, we invite the speakers to share a meal with the students in the residence hall, which the speakers seem to enjoy as much as the students do.

Logistics

There are logistics to consider when creating an LLC curriculum with linked courses. According to Kuh's (2008) best practices involving learning communities, there should be two or more courses linked to the program. Within The Data Mine, we have the seminar course (which all participating students take), and the second course comes from the specialty cohort. For example, students participating in the data visualization cohort take the seminar class in addition to a data visualization course in the computer graphics technology department. Students in the corporate partners cohort take a second research seminar that focuses on a data science project with their assigned company. Faculty should consider which courses would be applicable to the LLC theme and a good fit to the students' overall academic plan.

Working closely with the registrar and academic advisors in the early planning stages is crucial when associating classes with the LLC. The registrar can help enroll LLC students into the relevant classes so that enough spots are reserved and there are no time conflicts with other courses. Academic advisors must be involved to ensure students graduate within 4 years. If the LLC requires too many credit hours or conflicts with a required course, students may be at risk for an overburdened schedule or possibly a delayed graduation. Because of these potential conflicts, students may have to make tough decisions on whether to forgo the opportunity to participate in an LLC.

After determining the course needs, it is worthwhile to review the course offerings at one's campus and see if current courses can be linked to the LLC. Perhaps faculty are excited, and even invigorated, to partner with a colleague from another discipline. If no appropriate course exists, faculty may need to create a new course to fit the needs of the LLC. Creating a new course takes many layers of approval, so using a "special topics" course designation may be an adequate short-term solution. Enthusiasm for the LLC course(s) and the opportunity to work with students in a unique way may be the main motivations for faculty to participate, as often the financial compensation might be only a meal card for the residence hall dining court or a small account to be used for student activities. However, keep in mind that the students' needs and interests must always be the most important consideration for a successful LLC.

The faculty member(s) teaching the affiliated LLC course(s) should also look at the location where the course will be taught. Ideally, LLC classes are taught in or near the residential community, which provides more opportunities to connect with students and demonstrate the "living" and "learning" nature of the program. Data Mine classes were too large for the residential building, but working with dining staff to use the on-site dining space as a classroom allowed the course to still be a part of the residential environment.

Partnering with staff who coordinate course creation, registration, and space management is key to the success of linked courses. For instance, schedule deputies—the academic department staff responsible for working with the registrar to set up courses for student registration—can designate a section of a course for the LLC or, at a minimum, can reserve a select number of seats in the course. If an entire course or section is not reserved for the LLC, it is advisable to think through how the faculty member will get dedicated time with just the LLC students. If the class includes a lab, then perhaps one section of the lab can be reserved just for the LLC students. Dedicated class time with the faculty and LLC students creates opportunities for the faculty member to become a trusted role model and builds camaraderie with the students. For example, faculty may arrange a course assignment based on a trip taken over the weekend. It can be challenging to have this type of assignment when there is not a section of the course devoted to LLC students.

A benefit to participating in an LLC should be that the students are automatically registered for the associated courses. This automatic registration is convenient for the students, but it may take some legwork on the part of faculty and staff prior to the registration period. The registrar's office can determine how these students can be auto-enrolled in these courses prior to the registration periods. This process will likely include an affiliated LLC faculty member or administrator providing the registrar with a list of participating students and their associated university identification numbers. Because the LLC program at Purdue is quite large, information technology staff arranged for the LLC database to communicate with the course registration system, which streamlined this process. There are likely a handful of logistical details that are specific to a faculty member's campus. Including key stakeholders, such as affiliated faculty, support staff, and academic advisors, in the planning process, as well as ongoing feedback, are key steps for success.

Implications

Our experience with LLCs confirms the three broad recommendations from the Washington Center: (a) meet the learning outcomes of the program, (b) include integrative assignments, and (c) take advantage of campus resources (Lardner & Malnarich, 2008). Using The Data Mine as an example, we have shown how courses and program administrators can collaborate to make sure LLC outcomes are being met. In addition, The Data Mine includes assignments that tie in knowledge from multiple courses and connect that knowledge to experiences beyond the classroom. Finally, despite the 1,000-student Data Mine having only a few dedicated administrators, the students are able to take advantage of campus resources and invited guests.

The Washington Center recommendations are helpful guideposts when building a program; however, we advocate for the residential component of the learning experience as well. Living among peers with similar academic interests allows students to have serendipitous conversations over mutual ideas. Faculty enable students to engage with them in multiple ways when they have offices in the residence halls or spend extra time in the residence hall for programs or office hours. Providing these opportunities for connection and learning can assist in creating the academically and socially supportive environments that Inkelas et al. (2018) stated are part of the best practices for LLCs.

With these ideas in mind, it is important for campus administrators to collaborate when creating LLCs. The linked courses or the residential component should not be an afterthought. Instead, both faculty and housing leadership should be involved from the inception and should discuss the three Washington Center recommendations in conjunction with the residential experience.

Next Steps

When planning a new LLC, faculty should be willing to invest time and physical presence in the residence hall to mentor students and get to know them. Faculty and student affairs staff should look within and beyond classroom learning opportunities to support student development. Some of these learning opportunities should be academic, credit-earning courses, but others could involve conversations with RAs, presentations by guest speakers, arts events, trips, research projects, hackathons, and service learning. The academic courses connected to the LLC could be core courses that coordinate with a discipline-specific LLC course, courses that students in a particular major struggle with, or newly created courses for the LLC that tie together big ideas normally siloed in single departments.

Residential life staff should help faculty to think creatively about how to use the residential space to foster both peer-to-peer and faculty-to-student interactions to help develop supportive learning environments (Inkelas et al., 2018). With the aid of peers, faculty, and staff, students can perhaps feel braver about trying more challenging work or taking advantage of opportunities, such as internships, conference presentations, and leadership roles, that might not have been otherwise possible.

Acknowledgments

Mark Daniel Ward's research is supported by National Science Foundation Grants DMS-1246818, CCF-0939370, and OAC-2005632; Foundation for Food and Agriculture Research Grant 534662; National Institute of Food and Agriculture Grants 2019-67032-29077 and 2020-70003-32299; Society Of Actuaries Grant 19111857; Cummins Inc. Grant 20067847; Sandia National Laboratories; and Gro Master. We thank our fellow Data Mine staff members Kevin Amstutz, Maggie Betz, and Justin Gould, as well as many partners at Purdue who continue to support The Data Mine.

References

Blimling, G. S. (2015). *Student learning in college residence halls: What works, what doesn't, and why.* Jossey-Bass.

Brown, J., Hoffman, H., Rouech, K. E., & VanDeusen, E. A. (2018). Launching integrative experiences through linked courses: The Future Educators Learning Community (FELC). *Learning Communities Research and Practice, 6*(2), Article 4. https://washingtoncenter.evergreen.edu/lcrpjournal/vol6/iss2/4

Eidum, J., Lomicka, L., Chiang, W., Endick, G., & Stratton, J. (2020). Thriving in residential learning communities. *Learning Communities Research and Practice, 8*(1), Article 7. https://washingtoncenter.evergreen.edu/lcrpjournal/vol8/iss1/7

Gaff, J. G. (2000). Curricular issues for sophomores. In L. A. Schreiner & J. Pattengale (Eds.), *Visible solutions for invisible students: Helping sophomores succeed* (Monograph No. 31, pp. 47–53). National Resource Center for the First-Year Experience and Students in Transition, University of South Carolina.

GAISE College Report ASA Revision Committee. (2016). *Guidelines for assessment and instruction in statistics education college report 2016.* https://www.amstat.org/docs/default-source/amstat-documents/gaisecollege_full.pdf

Gokalp Yavuz, F., & Ward, M. D. (2018). Fostering undergraduate data science. *The American Statistician, 74*(1), 8–16.

Inkelas, K. K., Jessup-Anger, J. E., Benjamin, M., & Wawrzynski, M. R. (2018). *Living–learning communities that work: A research-based model for design, delivery, and assessment.* Stylus.

Inkelas, K. K., Soldner, M., Longerbeam, S. D., & Brown, L. J. (2008). Differences in student outcomes by types of living–learning programs: The development of an empirical typology. *Research in Higher Education, 49*(3), 335–368. https://doi.org/10.1007/s11162-008-9087-6

Kerr, K. G., Tweedy, J., Edwards, K. E., & Kimmel, D. (2017). Shifting to curricular approaches to learning beyond the classroom. *About Campus, 22*(1), 22–31. https://doi.org/10.1002/abc.21279

Kuh, G. D. (2008). *High-impact educational practices: What they are, who has access to them, and why they matter.* Association of American Colleges and Universities.

Lardner, E., & Malnarich, G. (2008). A new era in learning-community work: Why the pedagogy of intentional integration matters. *Change: The Magazine of Higher Learning, 40*(4), 30–37. https://doi.org/10.3200/CHNG.40.4.30-37

Luebke, S. R. (2002). Using linked courses in the general education curriculum. *Academic Writing.* https://wac.colostate.edu/aw/articles/luebke_2002.htm

Nosaka, T., & Novak, H. (2014). Against the odds: The impact of the key communities at Colorado State University on retention and graduation for historically underrepresented students. *Learning Communities Research and Practice, 2*(2), Article 3. http://washingtoncenter.evergreen.edu/lcrpjournal/vol2/iss2/3

Parker, L. C., & Ward, M. D. (2019). Purdue University: Statistics living learning community. In T. L. Skipper (Ed.), *Aligning support for student success: Case studies for sophomore-year initiatives* (Research Report No. 10, pp. 33–38). National Resource Center for the First-Year Experience and Students in Transition, University of South Carolina.

Purdie, J. R., II, & Rosser, V. J. (2011). Examining the academic performance and retention of first-year students in living–learning communities and first-year experience courses. *College Student Affairs Journal, 29*(2), 95–112. https://search-ebscohost-com.library.lcproxy.org/login.aspx?direct=true&db=eue&AN=67126 988&site=ehost-live&scope=site

Purdue University. (2022). *Home page*. Data Mine LLC. https://datamine.purdue .edu/

Smith, K., & Lovgren, R. (2018). Empirical evidence of deep learning in learning communities. *Journal of Applied Research in Higher Education, 10*(3), 311–321. https://doi.org/10.1108/JARHE-11-2017-0141

Stassen, M. L. (2003). Student outcomes: The impact of varying living–learning community models. *Research in Higher Education, 44*(5), 581–612. https://doi .org/10.1023/A:1025495309569

Virtue, E. E., Maddox, G., & Pfaff, K. (2019). The lasting effects of learning communities. *Learning Communities Research and Practice, 7*(2), Article 6. https:// washingtoncenter.evergreen.edu/lcrpjournal/vol7/iss2/6

Wawrzynski, M. R., Jessup-Anger, J. E., Stolz, K., Helman, C., & Beaulieu, J. (2009). Exploring students' perceptions of academically based living–learning communities. *College Student Affairs Journal, 28*(1), 138–58. https://search-ebscohost-com.library.lcproxy.org/login.aspx?direct=true&db=eue&AN=50803 4139&site=ehost-live&scope=site

Williams, M. H. (2015). Using simulations in linked courses to foster student understanding of complex political institutions. *Journal of Political Science Education, 11*(3), 332–346. https://doi.org/10.1080/15512169.2015.1047102

VIGNETTE

An Indelible Mark

Melissa Shew

My favorite scar runs as a 2-inch diagonal across my right hand. I got it from an enormous oven in the basement of a residence hall where I was making trays of enchiladas with students in my philosophy class. What we were doing that Saturday morning—shopping for groceries together, roasting tomatillos and garlic and onions, assembling trays of enchiladas, them showing me how to do a dance move (and me failing, badly), laughing—was not required, but that morning and others like it were easily the most essential part of the course.

That iteration of a required philosophy class at Marquette University was part of the Dorothy Day social justice living–learning community, where 44 students lived together and took some of their classes together, with the common bond being their dedication to meaningful service. For that class, students performed 3 hours of service each week at the same placement site for the entire year. I reduced the amount of reading and other content slightly to allow for students to have experiences in the community and in the classroom, which was also in their residence hall, by putting them at play with our course concepts and students' own ideas.

Time spent with students in that program often felt intimate, if not sacred. I was privileged to bear witness to and participate in the community through planning retreats, sharing in service, initiating spur-of-the-moment events, and attending events planned by students. All have left an indelible mark on me in terms of what I understand my vocation as an educator to be.

Students from that living–learning community carry the spirit of the program in what they have chosen to do since graduating, with most of them working in service to others in nonprofits, education, health care, law, advocacy groups, and community-based businesses. Of course, they also chose to participate in the Dorothy Day community because they are the kinds of young people inclined to do these kinds of things, as I am the kind of professor who wants to teach in these kinds of ways. Few opportunities on college campuses support these intentional and formative experiences, though, for high-impact teaching practices often require considerable funding, planning, and time along with the collective efforts of so many people.

But they are worth it. I return to the residence hall basement, where students stack trays and I watch, icing my hand. We load the vans, take the food to a women's shelter, serve the residents, play with the kids, and return to our own homes, knowing that we will meet in their residence hall 2 days later, for our class. They will ask about my hand. I will show it to them then. They will ask to see this scar for years to come, when they return to campus as recent graduates often do, with their partners, kids, stories, and full, full lives.

9

FOSTERING FACULTY–
STUDENT ENGAGEMENT
IN LIVING–LEARNING
COMMUNITIES

Jody E. Jessup-Anger and Mimi Benjamin

In *The Undergraduate Experience* (2016), Felten and his colleagues asked readers to imagine a first-year student walking to a faculty member's office hours for the first time. The authors envisioned a long corridor of mostly closed doors that the student must navigate as they make their way to the office. Now imagine the awkward conversation that might ensue. The student could be looking for clarification on an assignment, or perhaps needs to discuss a poor midterm grade. The faculty member might be eager to help but may have difficulty overcoming the power and education differential that too often leads to ineffective communication. A stilted conversation happens, and the student leaves, feeling better but still baffled as to how to navigate relationships with faculty.

Flipping the script, imagine faculty walking into a residence hall. They might get stopped at the front desk and asked for identification. They likely have no idea how to find the dining hall, lounge, or fireside near which they have been invited to chat. Students laze about, relaxing with friends, playing ping pong, gaming, or scrolling through social media, clearly blowing off steam after classes and work. Some students might recognize the faculty from a lecture but are reticent to approach because they fear the faculty might not recognize them. The faculty asks for directions and meanders toward their destination, perhaps a bit nostalgic for their college days, and a bit bewildered by the fact that students do not acknowledge them as they walk through the building.

These hurdles to faculty–student interaction are common. Entering and navigating the context of each other's terrain is sufficiently awkward and decentering that students and faculty alike may avoid it entirely. For faculty, the discomfort may stem from feeling like they are intruding on students' personal space, especially since residence hall space consists primarily of students' bedrooms. For students, having faculty in the places where they might feel most relaxed, where they both engage in and avoid academic work, might feel too revealing. This resulting avoidance is problematic because it limits the potential for meaningful interaction that researchers claim is important for student learning, development, and satisfaction (Felten & Lambert, 2020). As Melissa Shew illustrates in her vignette for this chapter, living–learning communities (LLCs) provide structures that bridge this common divide to help create meaningful interaction—and indelible marks for all involved. In this chapter, we detail current research on faculty–student engagement generally and specific to LLCs. Based on that research, we offer a framework for finding the sweet spot for faculty–student engagement in LLCs—one that creates a symbiosis between academic and personal connection—and ultimately may deepen the gains in student learning, development, and satisfaction. Then, we discuss the implications of the framework for practice, advancing actions that LLC faculty and staff can take to enhance faculty–student interaction.

Literature Review

Often, when postsecondary institutions initiate LLCs, they do so with an eye toward enhancing learning by creating conditions for meaningful student engagement, which Kuh (2003) asserted is "the time and energy students devote to educationally sound activities inside and outside of the classroom, and the policies and practices that institutions use to induce students to take part in these activities" (p. 25). Research on LLCs provides evidence that faculty–student engagement can enhance students' experiences while also providing faculty with greater satisfaction. In the LLC best practices model advanced by Inkelas et al. (2018), the authors identified two elements that pertain to faculty–student engagement as crucial to LLC success: (a) the academic environment, which is intentionally constructed to center academic engagement and includes faculty–student engagement, and (b) a socially and academically supportive climate, which promotes "rigorous academic study, while also being fun and supportive" (Inkelas et al., 2018, p. 21).

Faculty members are critical to both the academic, or "learning," element and the residential "living" element of LLCs. Their involvement can be as intense as living in the residence hall with the students or as limited as visiting the hall for events. Studies suggest that faculty–student out-of-class interactions are beneficial for faculty and students alike. For faculty, benefits include developing more meaningful relationships with students as well as engaging in interdisciplinary and innovative pedagogy (Golde & Pribbenow, 2000; Jessup-Anger et al., 2011; Kennedy & Townsend, 2008). Research on the benefits of faculty–student interaction for students suggests that such interaction promotes students' connection to the institution (Cotten & Wilson, 2006), satisfaction (both academic and social), development, persistence, and graduation (Astin, 1993; National Survey of Student Engagement, 2019). Cotten and Wilson (2006) found that when students engaged meaningfully with faculty, they reported increased effort and motivation in their academic pursuits because of a desire to please faculty. Furthermore, in their study of LLCs, Eidum et al. (2020) found a correlation between faculty–student involvement and student *thriving*, a measure of student intellectual, social, and emotional engagement and psychological well-being that results in overall success (Schreiner et al., 2012). Schreiner et al. (2012) illustrated that this state of thriving is particularly salient for transfer students, sophomores, and students of color. Mara and Mara (2011) suggested that having faculty living in the residential community with the students leads to beneficial interactions. Whether faculty live in the community or participate there periodically, their involvement reinforces the academic element of the program and provides added support for students.

Traditional-age undergraduate students are the primary target of LLC initiatives because they are the students most likely to reside on campus. These students, who are often in their first year of college, are likely just beginning to learn the norms of college life. They may position faculty as "experts from whom knowledge can be received by incompetent novices like themselves . . . [and, thus] view their relationships with professors as transactional and formal" (Inkelas et al., 2018, p. 54). Without intentional scaffolding on how to build meaningful relationships with faculty, students may rely on formulas from parents, pop culture, high school, or experience in relationship-building with other adults in their lives (Baxter Magolda, 2001). For example, from the depiction of professors in film (Fitch, 2018), students might determine that faculty are unidimensional, awkward, and stodgy. They might believe that mentoring relationships are uncommon and all consuming. At worst, students might worry that professors will prey on them or their ideas. As such, it is important to envision how faculty–student interaction happens to identify how to scaffold it toward meaning.

Various types of and purposes for faculty–student interactions occur in these residential settings. Cox and Orehovec (2007), whose study and typology are discussed in our framework later in this chapter, categorized interactions between students and faculty in a residential college (which is a comprehensive LLC) and concluded that five types of interactions were present (listed in order of frequency). Disappointingly, the most common type of interaction was no interaction at all (disengagement). From there, types of interactions included greetings or minor communication (incidental contact); academic matters (functional interaction); personal interaction that was purposeful/not incidental (personal interaction); and mentoring, which included professional assistance, support, and role modeling. However, mentoring was so infrequent that the authors cited only one instance of it. That said, Arensdorf and Naylor-Tincknell's (2016) study of LLC students found that their participants had more noteworthy faculty connections than non-LLC students, suggesting a benefit to using the LLC context for interactions and the possibility that, with intention, these meaningful interactions can be encouraged. Inkelas et al. (2018) encouraged academic advising within the LLC, suggesting that having students meet academic advisors in the LLC may enable students to interact with faculty, which may result in students seeing faculty as possible mentors. Mara and Mara (2011), two live-in faculty, conceded that functional and mentoring interactions are less frequent; however, they indicated a belief that even the lower-level interactions may lead to the more substantive interactions that benefit students. And as Felten and Lambert (2020) suggested, these relationships do not have to result in long-term, one-on-one mentoring, because students also benefit from "mentors of the moment" experiences (p. 6), which can start through incidental interactions.

Interaction Challenges

Challenges to meaningful faculty–student interaction exist for students and faculty. Students may not understand faculty responsibilities or the benefits of informal interaction with faculty, find faculty intimidating because of their authority role and expertise, be unsure if faculty want to interact with them, and need indicators of faculty approachability to initiate conversation (Benjamin & Griffin, 2013; Cotten & Wilson, 2006; Dean, 2019). Time pressures can be challenging, particularly when students do not see a specific need to be addressed through their out-of-class faculty interaction; they may view establishing relationships with faculty as "costly" because they require additional effort on the students' part (Cotten & Wilson, 2006). These challenges may partially explain why Cox and Orehovec (2007) found functional interactions occurring more frequently than personal interactions and mentoring. In addition, some students are hesitant to approach faculty because they perceive that these out-of-class interactions are not really part of the faculty member's job (Cotten & Wilson, 2006).

Faculty also deal with time pressures (see chapters 11 and 12), may feel challenged to balance their professional roles with more personal interactions with students over whom they hold some power, and may find it uncomfortable to enter students' living spaces for fear of crossing personal boundaries (Bergman & Brower, 2008). Inkelas et al. (2018) and Mara and Mara (2011) have identified dining halls as spaces for faculty–student interaction in LLCs, highlighting that when both the student and faculty member have dining plans, it can support spontaneous interaction and simplify scheduling meetings together.

Cox and Orehovec (2007) identified trust as important for these relationships, and frequent incidental interactions between faculty and students outside the classroom may positively contribute to relationship-building. For example, Mara and Mara (2011) mentioned a specific lunch in which students were comfortable inviting the faculty to join their lunch table because they saw these faculty members regularly in their living and dining space. The authors also highlighted their attendance at residence hall council meetings as valuable, stating

> In this "in-between space," hall council leaders and participants seemed at ease and often spoke with the Faculty-in-Residence before or after the meetings. . . . Thus, a formal setting elicited informal interactions, both personal and functional; and students felt comfortable in the space and the professional roles they occupied. (p. 79)

Working With Student Leaders

Although all students living in the hall/LLC may benefit from connecting with faculty outside of the classroom, faculty-in-residence and other affiliated faculty might have their most significant interactions with the resident assistants (RAs) or LLC peer mentors who help faculty enact their roles and whom they may see regularly at staff meetings (Benjamin & Griffin, 2013; Mara & Mara, 2011). These more formal interactions may mean that the small number of student leaders—such as RAs, LLC peer mentors, or student government leaders—who are best positioned to interact with faculty-in-residence or faculty leaders in LLCs, are the ones who benefit most from these opportunities. As a result, these student leaders may need to serve as the conduits between the faculty and the residents for the greatest number of students to reap the benefits of such initiatives, and expectations for that "bridge" function of the student leader position need to be explicitly stated.

Staff meetings can provide interaction opportunities for LLC faculty, as they may hear information or get requests that they can assist with and connect more personally through common informal staff activities, like "highs and lows" (Mara & Mara, 2011), furthering their relationship with the student staff members. Mara and Mara (2011) cited the front desk/lobby as another valuable space for interactions. Seeing RAs working at a lobby desk resulted in more frequent interactions, particularly when RAs were using their desk time to study, because faculty could talk with them about their academics. In addition, the researchers noted the benefits of the lobby/desk area for interacting with groups of students:

> In that space where the resident assistants were performing professional duties and student residents can conduct (limited) official business, we were not authority figures, but simply additional residents, who might need to pick up a package or borrow a film from the LLC DVD collection. (Mara & Mara, 2011, p. 80)

The authors noted that situations in which the students are the experts, particularly when they are in leadership roles, may result in greater interaction since the faculty members have no evaluative role and little influence. They recommend expanding opportunities for faculty to interact with students in spaces where students are "in charge" (p. 82).

As our review of the literature on faculty–student engagement illustrates, such interaction is complex, multifaceted, and important for both student learning and faculty development. However, because of the myriad challenges to meaningful interaction for both students and faculty, it cannot be left to chance. It is not sufficient for LLC administrators to recruit students, find dedicated faculty, and expect magical interaction to happen; instead, clear intentions and structures to promote this interaction should be present. In the next section, we present a framework for envisioning student–faculty engagement in LLCs. We follow the description of the framework with implications for practice.

Toward a Framework for Faculty–Student Interaction

Existing research into faculty–student engagement, when taken together, provides clues about how institutions might conceptualize and deepen faculty–student engagement in the context of LLCs. In Figure 9.1 we use the existing literature to introduce a new a framework for faculty–student engagement in LLCs, situating Cox and Orehovec's (2007) model within the academically and socially supportive climate elements of the LLC best practices model

Figure 9.1. A framework for faculty–student engagement in living–learning communities (LLCs).

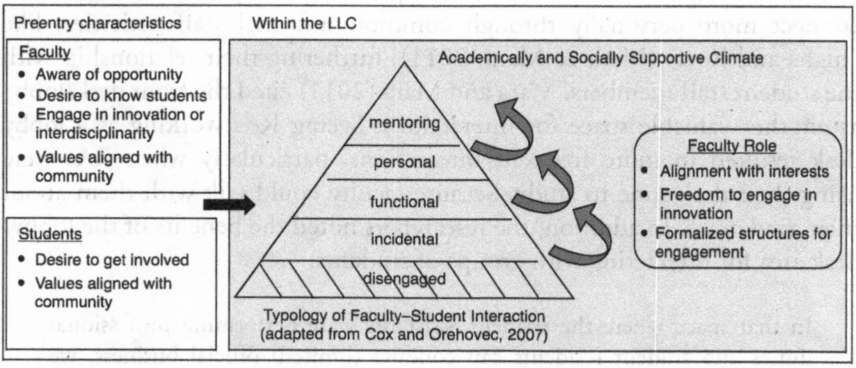

Adapted from B. E. Cox and E. Orehovec (2007). Faculty-student interaction outside the classroom: A typology from a residential college. *Review of Higher Education, 30,* 343–362.

(Inkelas et al., 2018). To explain the framework, we start with the preentry characteristics, which are located on the left side of the figure and are the precursors to effective faculty–student interaction in the community. We then move to the right, describing the elements within the LLC.

As depicted in the preentry characteristics boxes on the left side of Figure 9.1, a precursor to faculty–student engagement in LLCs is ensuring that faculty and students are primed for such engagement. At the risk of stating the obvious, faculty first must know about the opportunity to engage with an LLC and the mechanisms by which to signal their involvement. Administrators who are charged with the LLC's sustainability should regularly provide information to faculty about how to get involved with the LLC, as faculty desire for involvement may shift throughout their career (Golde & Pribbenow, 2000). Lecturers or contingent faculty may need specific outreach as they may not be privy to traditional departmental communication channels. Furthermore, whereas a pretenured faculty member may be preoccupied by the prospect of getting tenure and thus reluctant to get involved or even discouraged from involvement (Golde & Pribbenow, 2000), a tenured faculty member may be attracted to the LLC environment as a place for innovation. Research illustrates that faculty, whether non–tenure track, pretenured, or tenured, are often involved with LLCs because of their desire to have closer relationships with students than the traditional classroom affords them (Golde & Pribbenow, 2000; Kennedy & Townsend, 2008; Wawrzynski, Jessup-Anger, Helman, & Stolz, 2009). They may have had close relationships with faculty in their own undergraduate experiences at small liberal arts colleges or envision LLCs as spaces in which they can engage in interdisciplinary content and innovative pedagogy (Golde & Pribbenow, 2000; Jessup-Anger et al., 2011; Wawrzynski, Jessup-Anger, Helman, & Stolz, 2009). Thus, it is important that faculty are included in the planning of the LLC, especially the goals and objectives, because these may determine whether the community is inclusive of faculty interests. Furthermore, for sustainability as new faculty engage in the community, it is necessary that the goals and objectives remain explicit or sufficiently flexible so that new faculty can align their values with the LLC (Jessup-Anger et al., 2011) and contribute in ways that are interesting to them (Bergman & Brower, 2008).

As depicted in the student preentry characteristics in Figure 9.1, it is important to find and set up students for success prior to their entry into the community. Setting and communicating appropriately high expectations for interaction with faculty and community involvement helps students engage with faculty and peers appropriately (Jessup-Anger, 2012; Jessup-Anger et al., 2020). One way to communicate these expectations is to include questions about expectations on the application to the community. Asking students to think about and articulate how they will engage with each other and be involved in the community as a preentry exercise plants a seed for such engagement once they enter the community.

Involvement expectations are also important and should outline any specific role that an LLC participant has in the community, such as developing and leading program initiatives or performing a requisite number of community service hours. The Dorothy Day social justice community at Marquette University, for example, set the expectation that students plan several social justice–oriented programs for their peers each year. Participation in these activities will lead to more positive developmental and educational gains (Astin, 1993). Finally, the LLC's values should also be clearly articulated to students as they apply to the community so that these students can ensure some alignment among the community's values, the faculty's values, and their values (Jessup-Anger & Howell, 2021).

Developing an Academically and Socially Supportive Climate

An academically and socially supportive climate, as depicted by the gray shading in Figure 9.1, should permeate all aspects of the LLC and will promote engagement between faculty and students. An academically supportive climate is one where academic support for students is embedded in the community through the provision of structures and programs (Inkelas et al., 2018). The physical environment can be particularly helpful in encouraging faculty–student interaction. Faculty offices, classrooms, or other formalized spaces for faculty in the residence halls can provide the "in-between" space faculty need to be comfortable in what otherwise could be deemed a student space. Furthermore, these spaces can create informal interactions between faculty and students, which can help to engender a culture that students deem both scholarly and supportive (Wawrzynski, Jessup-Anger, Stolz, et al., 2009).

The ideal space is one that is specifically designed for such interactions, such as Brooks residential college at Baylor University, which includes a library, faculty offices, and seminar and study rooms. Brooks provides an example of how attentiveness to "how, when, and where learning happens" can aid in the creation of space and increase the likelihood of faculty–student interaction (Shushok et al., 2009, p. 13). However, even spaces that were not originally created for faculty–student interaction can be used for those ends, such as the multipurpose room that is used for an LLC class or an available room that is converted to a faculty office. These spaces can also promote organic interaction between faculty and students.

To promote the creation of an academically supportive climate, faculty must be supported in engaging in the residence halls. Faculty need support from their departments and higher-level academic administrators to maintain relationships. Institutional champions supporting faculty involvement in LLCs can catalyze faculty participation in these programs (Inkelas et al., 2018). Department chairs can help faculty navigate LLC involvement by offering a participation stipend, course buyout, or clarifying what involvement means for promotion and tenure. The variation in faculty status and depth of engagement will dictate the appropriate support. For example, a non–tenure track faculty will not be concerned with issues of promotion and tenure but would likely appreciate a stipend for involvement, given that these faculty are not otherwise rewarded for their time. Kennedy and Townsend (2008) found that once faculty become engaged in an LLC, their continuing involvement rests, in part, on positive or neutral support from their departments. Other factors affecting their continuing involvement included their belief that they were making a difference (Kennedy & Townsend, 2008), quality of relationships built with students and other faculty (Golde & Pribbenow, 2000), and their appreciation for the experimental nature of the community and its effect on their teaching (Golde & Pribbenow, 2000).

A socially supportive environment may also promote faculty–student engagement. A socially supportive environment assists in students' social integration, which is associated with a successful transition to college, sense of belonging, appreciation for difference, and commitment to civic engagement (Inkelas et al., 2018; Inkelas & Weisman, 2003; Jessup-Anger et al.,

2020; Stassen, 2003). Considering Cox and Orehovec's (2007) framework of interactions, a socially supportive environment between faculty and students might include interactions that are classified as personal or mentoring. Sriram et al. (2020) found these interactions in LLCs and labeled them as "deeper life interactions," defined as "exchanges that relate to meaning, value and purpose" (p. 5) between students and faculty and/or staff. To foster these personal interactions, students need to be encouraged to interact with faculty and reassured that these interactions are welcomed (Cotten & Wilson, 2006). Perhaps most critical to faculty–student engagement, a socially supportive environment may provide space for students to explore their shared interests and lead to cocurricular activities in which faculty and students are learning alongside each other at events like guest lectures, service-learning experiences, retreats, or field trips.

Varying Types of Faculty–Student Interaction

The variation in faculty–student interaction within LLCs, depicted in Figure 9.1 by the triangle, is adapted from Cox and Orehovec's (2007) aforementioned typology of faculty–student interaction in a residential college. In their grounded theory case study, Cox and Orehovec explored faculty–student interaction in the community over a 12-month period. Their findings illustrate that the presence of an LLC alone is not sufficient to bring about the faculty–student interaction outcomes that are often sought in LLC environments. At the base of the faculty–student interaction triangle is disengagement, which Cox and Orehovec found was the most prevalent relationship "despite institutionally established conduits through which interaction could occur" (p. 352). The researchers noted that disengagement happened in large part because faculty were absent from events. We depicted the disengagement level with lines through it because it represents an unacceptable form of faculty–student interaction in an LLC.

Moving up the triangle to the *incidental* level, the second most prevalent, which Cox and Orehovec (2007) described as "trivial and perfunctory," incidental contact occurred when faculty and students ran into each other in the residence hall or at an event, greeted each other, and then went their separate ways (p. 352). One level above incidental is *functional*, which "occur[s] for a specific, institutionally related purpose" (p. 353), like addressing an academic question. Functional contact can lead to *personal* interaction, in which "the interaction is purposeful (which distinguishes it from incidental) and revolves around the personal interest(s) of a faculty member and/or student (which distinguishes it from functional interaction)" (p. 354). Cox and Orehovec explained that students who engage in personal interactions with faculty feel valued and important, which ultimately may improve their college experience. At the apex of the faculty–student involvement triangle is *mentoring*, the ideal and least common type of engagement. They used Jacobi's (1991) work to describe a mentoring relationship between faculty and students marked by "direct assistance with career and professional development, emotional and psychological support, and role-modeling" (p. 356).

Often, when administrators and faculty design LLCs, and when faculty and students opt to engage, they do so with a vision for mentoring relationships—those that move beyond the confines of the classroom in context and content alike. This type of interaction is the gold standard, because it can promote student development and learning (Jacobi, 1991) while also providing faculty with a vibrant growth-fostering experience (Jessup-Anger et al., 2011; Wawrzynski, Jessup-Anger, Helman, & Stolz, 2009). However, with so few students experiencing this type of relationship we posit that more needs to be done to intentionally foster faculty–student engagement that can lead to mentoring. Next, we discuss how those affiliated with LLCs might conceptualize faculty–student engagement to facilitate it more effectively.

Promoting Meaningful Faculty–Student Interaction

The arrows alongside the faculty–student interaction triangle in Figure 9.1 illustrate how LLC administrators, faculty, and students might envision deepening faculty–student engagement. Barriers to the faculty–student relationship include difficulty overcoming an unequal power dynamic, students' lack of understanding of the faculty role, time pressures from both parties, and a lack of perceived benefit of outside-of-class interaction. Some of these barriers to faculty–student interaction can be overcome with thoughtful scaffolding to clarify expectations for engagement, develop structures for it, and provide resources to promote it. Being clear about the benefits of faculty–student interaction outside of class and setting this interaction as an explicit goal of the experience during orientation, retreats, and LLC classes will reduce confusion about whether students and faculty should invite this interaction. Furthermore, being mindful of how to transform from incidental toward personal or functional interaction may deepen common, surface-level faculty–student interaction to something more meaningful. Strategies for ensuring deeper interaction include asking faculty to sit with students at dining events (Bergman & Brower, 2008); promoting engagement with students in cocurricular roles, such as student organization advising; and including faculty and students in LLC staff meetings (Mara &

Mara, 2011). Reaching the apex of faculty–student engagement may take additional planning and resources. Integrating faculty–student interactions into student staff job requirements (Benjamin & Griffin, 2013), providing high-quality undergraduate research or other mentoring programs for faculty and students (Cotten & Wilson, 2006; Vandermaas-Peeler et al., 2018), or creating structures for undergraduate research may advance the mentoring relationship that Jacobi (1991) indicated leads to career development, psychological support, and role modeling.

Supporting the Role of Faculty

The box to the right of the triangle in Figure 9.1 highlights important features of faculty engagement in an LLC, which is critical in faculty–student engagement in these communities. Faculty are attracted to and maintain their involvement in LLCs when their work in the LLC is connected to their academic or personal interests. Jessup-Anger et al. (2011) found that, after one semester of experience in an LLC, faculty were energized by opportunities to align their teaching with their interests and to expose students to these interests. This alignment often meant that faculty engaged in innovative pedagogies, such as action research or service learning. Thus, it is important that faculty can see a connection between their interests and their role in the LLC and feel a sense of agency in enacting their role.

Formalized structures for faculty–student engagement ensure that faculty can engage effectively with students. The National Study of Living–Learning Programs (Inkelas, 2007) multiple case study revealed that the two most common forms of faculty involvement in LLCs were (a) teaching the courses associated with the community and (b) advising students in the program. Bergman and Brower (2008) emphasized that faculty academic interests are a driver for their involvement, so connecting these with their role within the hall is vital. Having students and faculty coconstruct community engagement activities that center on faculty expertise yet include students in the planning and execution promotes such engagement. Faculty can tap into their networks to introduce students to industry partners, organize field trips, or engage students in other community-building activities.

In addition, faculty likely need to be alerted to elements of the socially supportive environment that they can capitalize on, such as attendance at hall council where students are positioned as experts. LLC faculty also should be invited to work closely with hall directors and RAs to create a plan for interacting with residents, as the RAs are bridges to the residents. If peer mentors are involved in the program, they should be similarly involved in helping the students and faculty connect. This type of collaboration will require the incorporation of get-acquainted activities between the faculty and student staff to facilitate a partnership.

The faculty–student staff partnership mentioned earlier must be established as an expectation within an LLC-specific RA job description. If the expectation does not already exist, faculty can work with residence life staff to ensure that RAs and hall council leaders have a specified responsibility for creating connections between faculty and residents. This agreement may mean that faculty will need to meet with these student leaders during staff meetings or other structured times to plan approaches. Faculty will also need to signal their interest in and welcoming of informal interaction with students, especially given that students may be intimidated by or lack a capacity to appropriately create relationships with faculty. Having students' peers as a conduit can create a smoother path to incidental or functional interactions as a starting point.

Implications for Practice

When taken as a whole, the framework for faculty–student engagement in LLCs provides some clear implications for practice that LLC administrators can attend to as they design and sustain their communities. Following is a list of these implications, and we encourage readers to revisit the vignette that introduced our chapter because it illustrates the power of faculty–student interaction from the perspective of an LLC faculty member. The following are suggestions to catalyze interactions and move beyond disengagement:

1. Be sure that faculty and students are aware of LLCs. Raising faculty awareness might mean enacting a periodic call for faculty involvement. For student awareness, it might include working with admissions to create advertising videos for specific LLCs or creating student ambassador roles to recruit current students.

2. Ensure that faculty and students understand the values of the LLC and have opportunities to shape the community to align with their interests. Such foundational work might happen at a start-of-the-year retreat and include creating a short mission or vision statement written collaboratively by students, faculty, and residence life staff, creating an LLC "oath," and/or explicitly writing expectations for involvement into the LLC syllabus.

3. Design physical spaces in the community with an eye toward faculty–student interaction. Ideally, there should be spaces that promote formal (classrooms) and informal (multipurpose room, dining hall) interaction.

4. Secure departmental and university support for faculty involvement in LLCs by ensuring that involvement counts for tenure and promotion or is otherwise incentivized. Such incentives might include dining credits, course buyouts or a stipend, or creation of pathways for recognition of the faculty member's work.
5. Invite faculty to participate in the social aspects of LLC life, and ensure they have a role to play. Inviting faculty to start-of-the-year social activities such as retreats or meet-and-greets will send a message that students and faculty developing relationships outside of class is expected.
6. Formalize structures for faculty–student interaction through the provision of service-learning, undergraduate research, and mentoring programs.
7. Work with residence life professional staff to include faculty–student interaction as an expectation for student employment in the halls, and invite faculty to participate in student leadership opportunities such as hall council and RA meetings.
8. Provide faculty with agency to enact innovative pedagogy and cocurricular opportunities to engage students. Such agency might necessitate access to resources to offset costs for field trips, programs, or outside speakers.

In closing, we refer readers back to the vignette at the start of the chapter and to the guiding questions online in the supplementary materials. We believe that the vignette describes the best of faculty–student interaction in LLCs, one that includes academic elements, informal interactions, and deepening connections between faculty and students.

References

Arensdorf, J., & Naylor-Tincknell, J. (2016). Beyond the traditional retention data: A qualitative study of the social benefits of living learning communities. *Learning Communities Research and Practice, 4*(1), Article 4.

Astin, A. W. (1993). *What matters in college? Four critical years revisited.* Jossey-Bass.

Baxter Magolda, M. (2001). *Making their own way: Narratives for transforming higher education to promote self-development.* Stylus.

Benjamin, M., & Griffin, K. A. (2013). "Pleasantly unexpected": The nature and impact of resident advisors' functional relationships with faculty. *Journal of Student Affairs Research and Practice, 50*(1), 56–71. https://doi.org/10.1515/jsarp-2013-0004

Bergman, C. J., & Brower, A. M. (2008). Faculty involvement in residence halls: Bridging between faculty and staff cultures by implementing and extending the features of residential learning. In W. Zeller (Ed.), *Residence life and the new student experience* (3rd ed., pp. 83–96). University of South Carolina Press.

Cotten, S. R., & Wilson, B. (2006). Student–faculty interactions: Dynamics and determinants. *Higher Education, 51*, 487–519. https://doi.org/10.1007/s10734-004-1705-4

Cox, B. E., & Orehovec, E. (2007). Faculty–student interaction outside the classroom: A typology from a residential college. *Review of Higher Education, 30*, 343–362. https://doi.org/10.1353/rhe.2007.0033

Dean, S. R. (2019). Understanding the development of honors students' connections with faculty. *Journal of the National Collegiate Honors Council, 20*(1), 107–121.

Eidum, J., Lomicka, L., Chiang, W., Endick, G., & Stratton, J. (2020). Thriving in residential learning communities. *Learning Communities Research and Practice, 8*(1), Article 7.

Felten, P., Gardner, J. N., Schroeder, C. C., Lambert, L. M., & Barefoot, B. O. (2016). *The undergraduate experience: Focusing institutions on what matters most.* Jossey-Bass.

Felten, P., & Lambert, L. M. (2020). *Relationship-rich education: How human connections drive success in college.* Johns Hopkins University.

Fitch, J. C. (2018). *The cinematic college professor: Conceptions and representations* [Unpublished doctoral dissertation]. University of Kentucky.

Golde, C. M., & Pribbenow, D. A. (2000). Understanding faculty involvement in residential learning communities. *Journal of College Student Development, 41*(1), 27–40.

Inkelas, K. K. (2007). *National study of living-learning programs: 2007 report of findings.* Author.

Inkelas, K. K., Jessup-Anger, J. Benjamin, M., & Wawrzynski, M. (2018). *Living–learning communities that work: A research-based model for design, delivery, and assessment.* Stylus.

Inkelas, K. K., & Weisman, J. L. (2003). Different by design: An examination of student outcomes among participants in three types of living–learning programs. *Journal of College Student Development, 44*, 335–368. https://doi.org/10.1353/csd.2003.0027

Jacobi, M. (1991). Mentoring and undergraduate academic success: A literature review. *Review of Educational Research, 61*(4), 505–532. https://doi.org/10.3102/00346543061004505

Jessup-Anger, J. E. (2012). Examining how residential colleges inspire the life of the mind. *Review of Higher Education, 35*(3), 431–462. https://doi.org/10.1353/rhe.2012.0022

Jessup-Anger, J. E., Armstrong, M., & Johnson, B. (2020). The role of social justice living–learning communities (LLCs) in promoting students' understanding of social justice and LLC involvement. *Review of Higher Education, 43*(2), 837–860. https://doi.org/10.1353/rhe.2020.0009

Jessup-Anger, J. E., & Howell, C. (2021). All are welcome except you: Isolation in a social justice community. *Journal of College Student Development, 62*(2), 113–118.

Jessup-Anger, J. E., Wawrzynski, M. R., & Yao, C. W. (2011). Enhancing undergraduate education: Examining faculty experiences during their first year in a residential college and exploring the implications for student affairs professionals. *Journal of College and University Student Housing, 38*(1), 56–68.

Kennedy, K., & Townsend, B. K. (2008). Faculty motivation to participate in residential learning community activities at research-extensive universities. *Journal of the Professoriate, 3*(1), 29–53.

Kuh, G. D. (2003). What we're learning about student engagement from NSSE: Benchmarks for educational practices. *Change, 2,* 24–32. https://doi.org/10.1080/00091380309604090

Mara, M., & Mara, A. (2011). Finding an analytic frame for faculty–student interaction within faculty-in-residence programs. *Innovative Higher Education, 36*(2), 71–82. https://doi.org/10.1007/s10755-010-9162-8

National Survey of Student Engagement. (2019). *NSSE 2019 overview.* Indiana University Center for Postsecondary Research.

Schreiner, L., Louis, M., & Nelson, D. (Eds). (2012). *Thriving in transitions: A research-based approach to college student success.* National Resource Center for the First Year Experience & Students in Transition, University of South Carolina.

Shushok, F., Henry, D. V., Blalock, G., & Sriram, R. (2009). Learning at any time: Supporting student learning wherever it happens. *About Campus, 14*(1), 10–15. https://doi.org/10.1002/abc.278

Sriram, R., Haynes, C., Weintraub, S. D., Cheatle, J., Marquart, C. P., & Murray, J. L. (2020). Student demographics and experiences of deeper life interactions within residential learning communities. *Learning Communities Research and Practice, 8*(1), Article 8.

Stassen, M. L. A. (2003). Student outcomes: The impact of varying living–learning community models. *Research in Higher Education, 44,* 581–612. https://doi.org/10.1023/A:1025495309569

Vandermaas-Peeler, M., Miller, P. C., & Moore, J. (2018). Considering excellence in undergraduate research in context. In M. Vandermaas-Peeler, P. C. Miller, & J. Moore (Eds.), *Excellence in undergraduate research* (pp. 1–18). Council of Undergraduate Research.

Wawrzynski, M. R., Jessup-Anger, J. E., Helman, C., & Stolz, K. (2009, April 13–17). *An exploration of faculty motivation for participation in a newly developed residential college* [Paper]. Annual Meeting of the American Educational Research Association, San Diego, CA.

Wawrzynski, M. R., Jessup-Anger, J., Stolz, K., Helman, C., & Beaulieu, J. (2009). Exploring students' perceptions of academically based living–learning communities. *College Student Affairs Journal, 28*(1), 138–158.

PART THREE

LIVED EXPERIENCES OF FACULTY-IN-RESIDENCE

Jennifer E. Eidum and Lara L. Lomicka

This section serves as a resource for new and seasoned faculty-in-residence (FIR) who may wish to better understand their roles, as well as the roles and expectations for partners and families living with them in residence, and strive to find a reasonable work–life balance. The chapters detail the lived experiences of FIR—they provide both a theoretical context as well as concrete ideas for new and seasoned faculty members who are serving LLCs. We hope this section will provide valuable evidence and guidelines for faculty considering living in residence or deepening their involvement in an LLC.

As seen in these chapters, there are many studies that attest to the benefits of informal and formal faculty interaction in LLCs, as it can lead to positive outcomes to the student's satisfaction, development, and persistence. Grabsch, Eidum, Penven, and Post (chapter 10) present an overview of FIR programs across the United States, including faculty demographics; FIR program structures; and the benefits to FIR, to students, and to the institution. Part of the lived FIR experience goes beyond the faculty member, including the faculty member's significant other or family members. In chapter 11, Sriram looks at the unique concerns for faculty with families who live in residence on campuses and addresses issues such as balancing work and family, children growing up on a university campus, the importance of community for college students, student–faculty interaction, and spouse/partner integration. How partners/families are viewed by the institution and how they are integrated into residential events, as well as compensation issues, are all factors that weigh on a decision to take on a position of residence. Finally, once in residence, balancing competing demands from home (and family) and work for a faculty member can be a juggling act. In chapter 12, Kennedy provides some concrete guidelines for how FIR can balance work—and life—while living in residence.

VIGNETTE

Shaping Lives in Campus Communities

Nishi Rajakaruna

Campus living is nothing new to me—as a child of a university professor, I grew up on university campuses in Sri Lanka and Japan, and I have lived on or near a campus ever since. Campus communities, wherever I have lived, have shaped my life. That is why I live with students and help them shape those communities where they can also thrive.

I now serve as the faculty-in-residence for the yakʔitʸutʸu residential community (named in honor of and in partnership with the Northern Chumash, the Indigenous Peoples of San Luis Obispo County), where 1,500 California Polytechnic State University (Cal Poly) first-year students reside. I am often the first faculty member students and their families meet when they arrive on campus. I enjoy getting to know my residents and their families, helping students find their way, and connecting students with other faculty and resources on and off campus.

Mentoring students has played a central role in my career: Before joining Cal Poly's faculty in 2017, I taught botany at College of the Atlantic and San José State University for 12 years. In addition to my faculty role at Cal Poly, I cosupervise students at the School of Biological Sciences, North-West University, South Africa. I also have worked with thousands of secondary school and university students in my homeland of Sri Lanka and in India as a Fulbright scholar (2016–2017), sharing my professional and personal experiences as a foreign student in the United States and Canada and giving advice on how best to prepare for higher-education opportunities in North America.

My time mentoring students motivated me to serve as a mentor in a more formal capacity at Cal Poly; that is why I decided to apply for a faculty-in-residence position when Cal Poly announced its pilot program at the end of my first year as a faculty member. With my campus residents, I have created the Plants, Peaks, and Pals Club for hiking, botany, and natural history enthusiasts, and the Camellia Club, a community for tea enthusiasts.

Both clubs provide weekly settings for first-year students and others to get together and interact with each other via regular gatherings and stay connected to the Cal Poly community, even from afar. Both these clubs provide me with informal settings to share with students my passion for plants and give advice—while hiking or sipping a cup of tea—on their academic and professional pursuits, including in finding research opportunities on campus or internships elsewhere. It continues to amaze me how these chats often lead to students finding their place in the campus community and securing life-changing opportunities on or off campus.

I am grateful for the careful mentoring I have received throughout my academic life, and I am determined to be there for students who will need guidance along the way, whether it is on classes to take, on-campus research opportunities, scholarship applications, curriculum vitae preparation, summer internships, study and work abroad programs, or what to do after Cal Poly. I wouldn't be here if not for the caring mentors I have had throughout my life, and that is why having a cup of tea with a student will always be a priority of mine.

10

WHO? WHAT? WHERE? WHY? UNDERSTANDING FACULTY-IN-RESIDENCE PROGRAMS

Dustin K. Grabsch, Jennifer E. Eidum, James C. Penven,
and Jennifer B. Post

In one of the most beloved book series of all time, Harry Potter, author J.K. Rowling takes readers on an adventure replete with magic, young love, and the perfect villain. The school-age wizards and witches in the books live and learn in dormitories on an educational campus not only among each other, but also their professors. This shared living–learning space fosters a key foundation of the novels: the students' relationships with each other and with their professors. Because the Harry Potter series was written and originally published in the United Kingdom, this residential structure mirrors that of a number of British colleges and universities—Oxford and Cambridge in particular—but this model of living and learning is present throughout higher-education institutions across the world in the form of residential colleges, living–learning communities (LLCs), and faculty-in-residence (FIR) programs.

As we have seen throughout this book, faculty involvement in LLCs can include structured interactions with LLC students (e.g., academic advising, teaching a class in the community, or leading academic or social events such as dinners, film screenings, off-campus museum visits, or study-abroad trips) or informal, unstructured activities with students in the residence hall (e.g., sharing a meal, attending social events, or joining casual activities on the students' floor; see chapter 9). The most time-intensive form of faculty involvement, serving as a FIR, blends both structured and unstructured involvement by living alongside students in the residence hall, as Nishi Rajakaruna illustrates with his Plants, Peaks, and Pals Club and Camellia Club described in the vignette (Healea et al., 2015; Shushok et al., 2009;

Sriram & McLevain, 2016). Although we discuss how various campuses define their FIR programs later in this chapter, most broadly defined, a FIR is a university instructor who lives in university-owned housing and has student-facing responsibilities related to their housing. In this chapter, we focus specifically on these faculty and on the contributions and challenges of FIR programs to present the *who*, *what*, and *where* of FIR programs, which show us the *why* underscoring the increasing popularity of FIR programs in the United States, with data gleaned from a nationwide survey of FIRs themselves as well as current statistics on FIR programs.

Literature Review

Integral to student learning and the collegiate experience is the student–faculty relationship (Kuh et al., 1994). Beyond formal interactions between faculty and students (i.e., those occurring in the classroom or laboratory), informal interactions have significant positive outcomes for students. Residence halls, and LLCs in particular, can naturally serve as an environment for these informal interactions to occur (see chapter 9 for more information about faculty–student interaction).

FIR roles are growing in number at institutions across the United States (Bridgeforth, 2010; Sriram, 2015). This growth is partly due to administrators' increasing understanding of residence halls as an "active, vibrant environment for learning" (Penven et al., 2013, p. 124). Bringing together faculty and students in both an intellectual and interpersonal capacity creates a plethora of learning opportunities (Mara & Mara, 2011; Shushok et al., 2009). As interest in FIR programs rises, so too is the number of researchers exploring the experiences of faculty and outcomes of FIR programs (e.g., Browne et al., 2009; Cox & Orehovec, 2007; Davenport & Pasque, 2014; Healea et al., 2015; Penven, 2016; Sriram et al., 2011).

Student and Institutional Benefits of FIR Programs

It is not surprising that the number of FIR programs has grown across the country given that their outcomes often align directly with university goals and benefit students. FIR programs place faculty where students live, increasing opportunities for student–faculty interaction and for informal relationships to develop. When faculty approach students in the residence halls and dining rooms, student–faculty barriers decrease as the students begin to view the FIR as a relatable person (Cox & Orehovec, 2007; Mara & Mara, 2011). This kind of informal student–faculty interaction is associated with positive intellectual, social, and personal interaction as well as increased student satisfaction (Endo & Harpel, 1982). Such interaction also affects students' self-worth, confidence, and academic skills (Kuh, 1995; Kuh, 2008) and has positive effects on persistence to graduation, academic achievement, and student involvement (Andrade, 2007). Research specific to FIR programs has shown that faculty–student interaction outside of the classroom leads to positive outcomes related to student learning, personal development, cognitive thinking, problem solving, student satisfaction, and academic achievement (Healea et al., 2015).

Faculty Benefits of FIR Programs

FIRs are motivated by a variety of factors, including the belief that their work can profoundly influence students (Healea et al., 2015), the goal of getting to know students better, a desire to replicate their own liberal arts education, or a passion for interdisciplinary education (Golde & Pribbenow, 2000). Some faculty are motivated by an alignment of values between them and the specific community (Wawrzynski et al., 2009). Other faculty just want a change of pace or to try something different after finding a stride in academia.

Faculty who participate in a FIR program experience positive outcomes, including "development as educators, further understanding of teaching and learning and a deeper commitment to connecting classroom experiences to life outside of the classrooms" (Sriram et al., 2011, p. 50). Faculty also report increased knowledge of how the university works as a whole and about student success (Humphrey et al., 2015). Perhaps more unexpected for faculty are the benefits to their families (see chapter 11 and Sriram et al., 2011). Living on a college campus offers a more diverse, unique environment and community for families than off-campus residences (Penven, 2016). Finally, FIR programs often include a number of incentives for faculty to live in residence, including subsidized or free housing, partial meal plans, and special access to campus amenities (see chapter 2). Therefore, the FIR position offers a number of personal and professional benefits for faculty members, as suggested by both scholarship and anecdotal evidence.

Challenges of FIR Programs

Although benefits to FIR programs are numerous, there are challenges, particularly for faculty. Faculty have expressed obstacles to residential living ranging from lack of time, limited social skills, and lack of institutional support or incentives—particularly credit toward tenure and promotion (Healea et al., 2015). Other FIR report that building community with and among students requires a significant time commitment (Ellett & Schmidt, 2011; Thies, 2003). In some cases, FIR describe miscommunication between FIR and administrators about desired learning outcomes (Browne et al., 2009). In other cases, FIR are frustrated with a lack of clearly defined faculty roles (Golde & Pribbenow, 2000; Kennedy & Townsend, 2008). Although all faculty involved in LLCs face some of these challenges, FIR often face more of them at a greater magnitude because of their larger commitment to the LLC. Chapter 2 in this book includes a discussion of promotion and tenure for FIR, and chapter 5 includes a discussion of academic affairs–student affairs partnerships specific to FIR. Unique challenges for FIR include balancing professional commitments with family obligations (see chapter 11 and Sriram et al., 2011, for more discussion of families-in-residence) and work–life balance (see chapter 12). Given both the benefits and challenges facing FIR programs, it is important to understand how FIR programs have been operationalized for student success within the United States.

Move to Practice

An analysis of the breadth of FIR program offerings across the United States reveals noticeable trends in the *who, where, what,* and *why* of FIR programs. In this section, we explore each of these elements: (a) *who*—the common characteristics of involved faculty; (b) *where*—the noticeable clusters of programs within particular institutional climates; (c) *what*—the actions taken by programs; and (d) *why*—the commonly espoused program outcomes or goals.

Who—Common Characteristics

When considering distinct institutional types, the eligibility and requirements for sought-after FIR candidates vary. After gathering a variety of position descriptions (collected in November 2020 as a part of a benchmarking process at Southern Methodist University), we reviewed them for themes, ensuring representation by institutional type (e.g., public, private, flagship, regional). Table 10.1 presents representative position descriptions, notable for their variability in academic professional track requirements, prior experience, and other qualifications for FIR.

First, Cornell University's posted position description may reveal an institutional priority to protect or exclude junior faculty, inviting applications from "tenured faculty, clinical professors, and senior lecturers." In contrast, the University of Northern Colorado is much more inclusive of faculty track, inviting "fully tenured faculty, tenure track, associate, assistant, adjunct, or graduate assistants working at the University of Northern Colorado in any college." At the University of Wisconsin—Superior, they

TABLE 10.1

Faculty-in-Residence (FIR) Position Descriptions

Institution	Type	Position Description
Cornell	Midsized, Research, Private	The position of FIR is available to all tenured faculty, clinical professors, and senior lecturers who have demonstrated a commitment to faculty–student interaction beyond the classroom.
University of Northern Colorado	Midsized, Regional, Public	FIR can be fully tenured faculty, tenure track, associate, assistant, adjunct, or graduate assistants working at the University of Northern Colorado in any college. Graduate assistant applicants must have classroom teaching experience. Preference given in selection process to full time faculty. You may also be required to complete a live-on agreement that further outlines your expectations as a live-in staff member.
University of Wisconsin— Superior	Small, Liberal Arts, Public	In the program, a tenured or tenure-track faculty member, teaching staff or student services staff member lives on campus and works closely with residence life, including the hall managers and resident assistants, to provide residents with a variety of thought-provoking, exciting, and educational programs.
University of Southern California	Midsized, Private, Research	FIR must be full-time members of the university faculty. FIR must support the benefits of a living–learning environment, be strongly committed to undergraduate and/or graduate education outside of the traditional academic framework, and have a willingness to make the necessary investment in time and energy in support of the aims of the residential college program. FIR must be excellent communicators in both one–one and group settings; effective programmers (including conception, promotion, implementation, and assessment); able to work collegially and effectively with diverse constituencies, including students, faculty and staff; and accessible and approachable to students.

broaden their description of FIR to include "a tenured or tenure-track faculty member, teaching staff or student services staff member [who] lives on campus and works closely with Residence Life." This broadening of the FIR role may confuse the program goals or result in outcomes that deviate from the research indicating that student–faculty interactions contribute to student persistence (Astin, 1993; Endo & Harpel, 1982; Kuh, 1995; Pascarella & Terenzini, 1991; Tinto, 1992). The positive effects outlined in the research may be less noticeable for student services staff members (e.g., Martin & Seifert, 2011) or graduate students in the case of the University of Wisconsin—Superior or the University of Northern Colorado, respectively. Finally, the position description from the University of Southern California supplies additional insight into specific skills and attributes sought for FIR beyond university position (e.g., full-time faculty), emphasizing their dedication to the mission of the living–learning program and the overall educational mission of the university and a willingness to invest time and energy into extracurricular programming. Rather than focusing on the professional rank of the faculty member, this position description focuses much more on the experience and soft skills of faculty members in connecting with and supporting student life.

Position descriptions are one way to understand the makeup of FIR programs. A recent study by Eidum (2021) surveyed FIR and their partners from institutions across the United States to better understand the experiences of FIR and their families. The survey includes demographic and job-related questions to understand who FIR are and what FIR programs are like, Likert scale and multiple-choice questions about their experiences on campus before and after serving as FIR, and short-answer questions to illuminate the full experience of serving as a FIR. Demographic data from the 75 FIR respondents representing 32 institutions indicate that the typical FIR is a White female with a PhD, who is 45 to 54 years old, heterosexual, married, a parent, and has lived in residence for 2 to 5 years.

These FIR demographic data both affirm and challenge current faculty demographic data: According to the National Center for Education Statistics (2020), the majority of university faculty are White men (41%), followed by White women (35%); however, when looking at lecturers, instructors, and assistant professors, White women are the dominant group (at 44%, 43%, and 38%, respectively)—indicating that the FIR pipeline may trend in favor of women. Moreover, women might be drawn to FIR roles given the natural opportunity to blend work life and personal life. In addition, the numbers of faculty of color in FIR roles echo faculty demographics as a whole, making up 23% of Eidum's (2021) survey respondents and 25% of university faculty in the United States (National Center for

Education Statistics, 2020). FIR programs have an enormous opportunity to expand equity and inclusion initiatives into their program recruitment, especially as increasing faculty diversity (especially faculty of color) yields positive outcomes for underrepresented students (Lundberg & Schreiner, 2004; Ponjuan, 2011; also see chapter 1).

In contrast to data on race and gender, it is more difficult to find nation-wide data on sexual orientation, marital status, and parental status of faculty, but the FIR demographics Eidum (2021) found represent cultural norms in the United States. Importantly, the FIR role brings the family sphere into the workplace. Research has shown that family plays an important role in faculty job satisfaction (Campbell & Prins, 2016; Sherr & Jones, 2007). Therefore, FIR programs should recognize and support different kinds of families and the unique needs of partners and children while living on campus (see chapter 11).

As for professional experience, the vast majority of FIR respondents of Eidum (2021), like faculty themselves, have a PhD (87%), but notably, 13% have master's or professional degrees. Their postgraduate teaching experience varies widely, from fewer than 5 years (9%) to more than 15 (47%). Respondents' time in residence ranges from brand-new to 23 years living on campus, with the most common length of time being 2 to 5 years (45%).

Where—Common Institutional Types

Next, we discuss *where* FIR programs live. LLCs, residential colleges, and other high-impact educational practices most notably are found within higher-education institutions who espouse liberal education principles. According to the Association of American Colleges and Universities (n.d.), liberal education is "an approach to undergraduate education that promotes integration of learning across the curriculum and cocurriculum, and between academic and experiential learning, in order to develop specific learning outcomes that are essential for work, citizenship, and life" (para. 3). Arguably, member institutions of this professional association understand the benefits of integrated functions of housing and academics to enable deep learning practices. Higher-education institutions with strong integration efforts appear to live out the pillars of liberal education—most notably high-impact practices, those that are "specific teaching and learning practices that have been widely tested and shown to be beneficial for all students" (American Association of Colleges and Universities, n.d., para. 6). FIR programs find their legitimacy within liberal education.

Although there is no nationwide registry of FIR programs, a look at the publicly available data on higher-education institutions in the United States reveals that FIR programs can be found at a wide range of institution types, from large public to small private. There are at least 49 higher-education institutions in the United States with FIR programs, including at least 200 FIRs; however, being based only on easily searchable data, this number would likely increase with deeper investigation (Eidum, 2021). Furthermore, the size of LLCs where FIR live and work have a wide range, from under 300 students to more than 2,900 (see Figure 10.1).

There are some beginning efforts (and tools) to better situate the *where* of FIR programs beyond the work for this chapter. For the residential college environment in particular, the Residential College Society (n.d.) maintains the Residential College Mapping Project, which "allows you to search for a RC by institution, dining facility, classes and classrooms and live in faculty" (para. 1). The project also illustrates how some institutions maintain different types of FIR programs and high-impact practices at that particular institution. Another opportunity to formalize the investigation of FIR programs could come from the efforts of the Association of College and University Housing Officers—International, which administers and maintains an annual Campus Housing Index, a tool "that allows campus-based professionals to compare their campus's operations against custom-ized groups of similar campuses" (Association of College and University

Figure 10.1. Residential community size in communities led by faculty-in-residence.

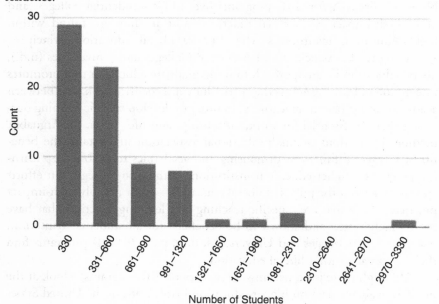

Housing Officers—International, n.d., para. 1). The index enables university housing administrators to self-report campus-level data and to evaluate practices, make decisions, and articulate resource needs using on-demand charts and graphics. At present, the Campus Housing Index does not collect information about FIR programs (e.g., program existence, number of faculty, compensation method). Adding this component to this existing data tool could advance the scholarship and practice of FIR programs.

What and Why: Program Outcomes

Even within the aforementioned FIR position descriptions and program explanations, there are different approaches and strategies for fostering student–faculty engagement. Table 10.2 depicts common behaviors performed by FIRs and the setting where it occurs to cultivate student–faculty interaction. Informed by methods of naturalistic inquiry (Lincoln & Guba, 1985), we used an actor–behavior–setting analysis—the FIR serves as the actor in this model. Their expected behaviors and settings were sourced from flyers, websites, our own FIR experience, and position descriptions from FIR programs.

TABLE 10.2
Faculty-in-Residence Behaviors to Foster Student–Faculty Interaction

Behavior (What They Do)	Setting (Where They Do It)
Work	Building
Mentor	LLC
Engage	Linked course
Advise students	Individual conversations
Discuss	Small group
Support	Casual interactions
Lecture	Programs/events
Instruct	Training
Facilitate	Student leadership meetings
Coach	One-on-one
Teach	Orientation
Develop	Floor meetings

Note. LLC = living–learning community.

Most FIRs seem to be involved in training, advising, mentoring, programming, and supporting students at the individual, group, and community levels. Although the *what* varies, the *why* of the position remains clear: to foster student–faculty interaction.

Central to the purpose of FIR programs are their contributions to student success and retention—achieved through quality student–faculty interactions (Armstrong, 1999; Cox & Orehovec, 2007). The literature has suggested a critical consensus in the motivations, goals, and intended outcomes of FIR programs. We strive to document this consistency in outcomes through excerpts from FIR program websites. To begin, the University of California, Los Angeles posits, "The goal of the Faculty-in-Residence (FIR) Program is to provide both formal and informal resident–faculty interactions through educational programming, classes, individual and small-group advising, and casual association" (UCLA Residential Life, n.d., para. 1).

Duke University's website clearly articulates both a purpose and goal for its FIR program:

> The Faculty-in-Residence Program houses professors in first-year residence halls on East Campus to encourage interaction between faculty members and undergraduate students beyond the classroom or lab. The FIR program affords a broad range of informal and structured opportunities for participating faculty to draw freely on their vocational and professional interests and seek common ground with students in the residential setting. (Duke University, 2022, para. 1)

Appalachian State University similarly expresses, "The [purpose of the] Faculty-In-Residence (FIR) program [is] to provide students an opportunity to interact with faculty members outside of the classroom, as well as encourage faculty to share their academic and personal interests with on-campus residents" (Appalachian State University, n.d., para. 1).

These universities clearly articulate the *why* for their FIR programs— to improve the quality and frequency of student–faculty interactions. These stated goals clearly align with the research on effective FIR programs, foregrounding student–faculty relationships. Perhaps more important than the stated goals of FIR programs are the behaviors and activities that faculty use to reach those goals.

Takeaways and Next Steps

With a shared understanding of the *who*, *what*, *where*, and *why* of FIR programs, we turn to the implications arising from these insights. After reviewing FIR programs and research trends, we have identified several areas for faculty, housing and residence life professionals, and FIR program administrators to address to clarify and strengthen FIR programs at their institutions.

Our first recommendation is a call for FIR program administrators to address the inequity in the demographic makeup of FIRs. Admittedly, the faculty pool that FIRs are drawn from lacks gender and racial equity (National Center for Education Statistics, 2020)—but, acknowledging that FIR recruitment is only as good as the broader faculty recruitment at an institution, it is also clear that there is an important connection between faculty representation and student success, especially in LLCs (Eidum et al., 2020; Lundberg & Schreiner, 2004; Ponjuan, 2011). Tapping diverse FIR candidates at an institution already struggling to recruit faculty with diversity poses challenges to singling out diverse faculty to do all the work. Therefore, FIR program administrators and their supporters must make concerted efforts to consider campus-specific nuances related to equity in the recruitment, selection, and retention of faculty from underrepresented backgrounds, including faculty of color and first-generation faculty. This might include expanding FIR eligibility to include non–tenure track or untenured faculty for FIR roles or working with departments to hire underrepresented faculty directly into FIR positions.

Relatedly, our review of FIR programs supports the calls in previous chapters for tenure and promotion committees to take LLC work seriously when evaluating faculty. We encourage administrators to advocate for their FIR programs as extensions of the teaching mission rather than a solely service endeavor. It is our experience that FIR work is closely connected to teaching and not so distant from research: Mentoring student leaders, advising LLC students, and teaching courses affiliated with one's LLC and/or discipline are examples of FIR work directly connected to teaching. As we highlighted earlier, most FIRs are provided with a teaching release or stipend as compensation for their role. These approved compensation methods may indicate that such time investment, program facilitation, and office hours in the LLC could mirror that of teaching a course. Moreover, many FIR have been able to conduct scholarly research on teaching and learning in their LLCs (e.g., Eidum et al., 2020; Leibowitz et al., 2020). Therefore, administrators working with FIR programs should actively promote the teaching and research components of FIR work to shift campus perception and tenure and promotion guidelines. If FIR programs can dislodge themselves from the service-only pigeonhole they may be able to attract a greater and more diverse cross-section of candidates who could showcase transformative teaching through their work as a FIR. Moreover, incentivizing faculty to connect the FIR role with teaching and research might lead to new forms of out-of-class engagement and new research pathways related to LLCs and FIR programs.

In addition to rethinking FIR recruitment, we have identified several structural areas for both institutions and the broader field to review. Primarily, it behooves higher-education professionals to further define FIR programs, perhaps with typologies like the LLC categories identified in the National Study of Living–Learning Programs (Inkelas et al., 2006). Creating subcategories or typologies of FIR programs will enable a more robust scholarly examination of their impact on student success.

Moreover, we recommend that institutional leaders spend time reflecting on the titles and terminology within FIR programs. In our review of position descriptions, we saw significant differences in the language of FIR titles across institutions and program types (Eidum, 2021). Often, these titles emerge from institutional conventions and are clear within specific institutional settings; however, many of these same titles are used beyond residence life programs (e.g., scholar-in-residence, artist-in-residence, entrepreneur-in-residence, and even FIR) to denote specially funded programs or those hosting external faculty, artists, or practitioners. The variety of titles may lead to confusion about the program mission and function. We urge both the field of higher education, as well as individual institutions, to balance the needs and understandings of both primary audiences—colleagues and students—to use clear titles that show the value and positionality of these roles.

In addition, we find variability in the service term and compensation of a FIR. Terms typically range from 1 to 4 years, with the most frequent across programs being a 3-year appointment. Programs differ in regard to a FIR's eligibility for renewal after a successful initial appointment. Some programs enforce term limits, whereas others do not. Compensation for the FIR position varies widely among institutions. On-campus apartments are an expected form of remuneration given the nature of the role, but the residence's age and bedroom/bathroom count vary across programs. Some programs fund meal plans for FIRs and, in more limited cases, institutions offer FIR family members a meal plan. Another primary compensation method includes teaching releases or course buyouts. In lieu of teaching releases, a stipend ranging from $5,000 to $7,000 is customary. Some programs offer FIR the option of a teaching release or stipend, and others specifically mention budgets for programmatic efforts. These budgets are not always quantified in the position description and range wildly in size. The variability in terms and compensation methods is evident across the field of practice.

Finally, we encourage FIR program administrators to consider the term length of FIR positions. The variability observed in our census could point to different individual needs of the faculty or the institution; however, there is likely a best practice nested within current practice—and it is likely not a 1- or 2-year term. For a faculty member with a family moving onto campus, short appointments may not outweigh the hassle of a move, especially considering children switching schools. Therefore, we recommend a 3- or 4-year initial appointment as a best practice. Regardless, the opportunity for at least one renewal would enable stability for the program, students, and FIR. Program administrators should also couple the FIR position renewal processes with annual performance reviews in order to provide constructive feedback or to encourage underperforming FIRs to transition out of the role prior to the expiration of the appointment period. In some high-impact-practice models, like a residential college, longer appointment periods help with consistency and building traditions from year to year. In summary, a residential student–faculty engagement program should be viewed as a longer, sustained commitment that is critical to the mission of the institution.

Conclusion

In this chapter, we have provided a broad overview of FIR programs in the United States with the goal of understanding who participates, where these programs are located, what FIR do, and why they choose to live on campus alongside students. It is our hope that this chapter can provide a foundation for future research on FIR programs and serve as a resource for FIR program leaders and faculty themselves to advocate for FIR at their institutions.

References

Andrade, M. S. (2007). Learning communities: Examining positive outcomes. *Journal of College Student Retention: Research, Theory & Practice, 9*(1), 1–20. https://doi.org/10.2190/E132-5X73-681Q-K188

Appalachian State University. (n.d.). *Faculty-in-residence program.* https://housing.appstate.edu/faculty-in-residence-program

Armstrong, M. (1999). Models for faculty–student interaction outside of the classroom: The Duke University Faculty Associates Program. *College Student Affairs Journal, 19*(1), 4–16. https://www.proquest.com/scholarly-journals/models-faculty-student-interaction-outside/docview/224809920/se-2

Association of American Colleges and Universities. (n.d.). *Valid assessment of learning in undergraduate education (VALUE).* https://www.aacu.org/value/

Association of College and University Housing Officers—International. (n.d.). *Campus housing index.* https://www.acuho-i.org/campushousingindex?portalid=0

Astin, A. W. (1993). *What matters in college? Four critical years revisited.* Jossey-Bass.

Bridgeforth, J. S. (2010). Residence life and retention: The reemergence of academic programs in student affairs. *Southeastern Association of Housing Officers Fall Report 2010,* 47–48. https://files.eric.ed.gov/fulltext/ED558984.pdf

Browne, M. N., Headworth, S., & Saum, K. (2009). The rare, but promising, involvement of faculty in residence hall programming. *College Student Journal*, *43*(1), 22–30. https://scholarworks.bgsu.edu/cgi/viewcontent.cgi?article=1010&context=econ_pub

Campbell, K., & Prins, E. (2016). Taking initiative and constructing identity: International graduate student spouses' adjustment and social integration in a rural university town. *International Journal of Lifelong Education*, *35*(4), 430–447. https://doi.org/10.1080/02601370.2016.1197332

Cox, B. E., & Orehovec, E. (2007). Faculty–student interaction outside of class: A typology from a residential college. *Review of Higher Education*, *30*(4), 343–362. https://doi.org/10.1353/rhe.2007.0033

Davenport, A. M., & Pasque, P. A. (2014). Adding breadth and depth to college and university residential communities: A phenomenological study of faculty-in-residence. *The Journal of College and University Student Housing*, *40*(2), 46–65. https://www.nxtbook.com/nxtbooks/acuho/journal_vol40no2/index.php#/p/46

Duke University. (n.d.). *Faculty-in-residence*. https://undergrad.duke.edu/intellectual-community/student-faculty-engagement-office/faculty-residence/

Eidum, J. (2021). *Families-in-residence: An analysis of the experiences of faculty and families living on college campuses*. Manuscript submitted for publication.

Eidum, J., Lomicka, L., Chiang, W., Endick, G., & Stratton, J. (2020). Thriving in residential learning communities. *Learning Communities Research and Practice*, *8*(1), Article 7. https://files.eric.ed.gov/fulltext/EJ1251578.pdf

Ellett, T., & Schmidt, A. (2011). Faculty perspectives on creating community in residence halls. *Journal of College and University Student Housing*, *38*(1), 26–39.

Endo, J. J., & Harpel, R. L. (1982). The effect of student–faculty interaction on students' educational outcomes. *Research in Higher Education*, *16*(2), 115–138.

Golde, C. M., & Pribbenow, D. A. (2000). Understanding faculty involvement in residential learning communities. *Journal of College Student Development*, *41*(1), 27–40.

Healea, C. D., Scott, J. H., & Dhilla, S. (2015). The work of faculty-in-residence: An introduction and literature review. *Work*, *52*(3), 473–480. https://doi.org/10.3233/WOR-152189

Humphrey, M., Callahan, J., & Harrison, G. (2015). Living with students: Lessons learned while pursuing tenure, administration, and raising a family. *Work*, *52*(3), 497–501. https://doi.org/10.3233/WOR-152197

Inkelas, K. K., Vogt, K. E., Longerbeam, S. D., Owen, J., & Johnson, D. (2006). Measuring outcomes of living–learning programs: Examining college environments and student learning and development. *Journal of General Education*, *55*(1), 40–76. https://doi.org/10.1353/jge.2006.0017

Kennedy, K., & Townsend, B. K. (2008). Faculty motivation to participate in residential learning community activities at research-extensive universities. *Journal of the Professoriate*, *3*(1), 29–53.

Kuh, G. D. (1995). The other curriculum: Out-of-class experiences associated with student learning and personal development. *The Journal of Higher Education*, *66*(2), 123–155. https://doi.org/10.1080/00221546.1995.11774770

Kuh, G. D. (2008). *High-impact educational practices: What they are, who has access to them, and why they matter*. Association of American Colleges and Universities.

Kuh, G. D., Douglas, K. B., Lund, J. P., & Ramin-Gyurnek, J. (1994). *Student learning outside the classroom: Transcending artificial boundaries* (ASHE–ERIC Higher Education Report No. 8). The George Washington University. https://files.eric.ed.gov/fulltext/ED394444.pdf

Leibowitz, J. B., Lovitt, C. F., & Seager, C. S. (2020). Development and validation of a survey to assess belonging, academic engagement, and self-efficacy in STEM RLCs. *Learning Communities Research and Practice, 8*(1). https://eric.ed.gov/?id=EJ1251571

Lincoln, Y. S., & Guba, E. G. (1985). *Naturalistic inquiry.* Sage.

Lundberg, C. A., & Schreiner, L. A. (2004). Quality and frequency of faculty–student interaction as predictors of learning: An analysis by student race/ethnicity. *Journal of College Student Development, 45*(5), 549–565. https://doi.org/10.1353/csd.2004.0061

Mara, M., & Mara, A. (2011). Finding an analytic frame for faculty–student interaction within faculty-in-residence programs. *Innovative Higher Education, 36*(2), 71–82. https://doi.org/10.1007/s10755-010-9162-8

Martin, G. L., & Seifert, T. A. (2011). The relationship between students' interactions with student affairs professionals and cognitive outcomes in the first year of college. *Journal of Student Affairs Research and Practice, 48*(4), 389-410. https://doi.org/10.2202/1949-6605.6198

National Center for Education Statistics. (2020, May). *Characteristics of postsecondary faculty*. https://nces.ed.gov/programs/coe/indicator_csc.asp

Pascarella, E. T., & Terenzini, P. T. (1991). *How college affects students: Findings and insights from twenty years of research* (Vol. 1). Jossey-Bass.

Penven, J. C. (2016). *What is a collegiate way of living worth? Exploring the costs and benefits of residential colleges as perceived by faculty and chief housing officers* [Doctoral dissertation]. Virginia Polytechnic Institute and State University. https://vtechworks.lib.vt.edu/handle/10919/73608

Penven, J., Stephens, R., Shushok, F., Jr. & Keith, C. (2013). The past, present, and future of residential colleges: Looking back at S. Stewart Gordon's "Living and Learning in College." *Journal of College and University Housing, 39*(2), 114–126.

Ponjuan, L. (2011, Fall). Recruiting and retaining Latino faculty members: The missing piece to Latino student success. *Thought & Action*, 99–110. https://vtechworks.lib.vt.edu/handle/10919/84034

Residential College Society. (n.d.). *Residential College Mapping Project*. http://residentialcollegesociety.org/residential-college-mapping-project/

Sherr, M. E., & Jones, J. M. (2007). Considering family and significant others in the faculty recruitment process: A study of social work recruiting practices. *Advances in Social Work, 8*(2), 275–287. https://doi.org/10.18060/206

Shushok, F., Jr., Henry, D. V., Blalock, G., & Sriram, R. R. (2009). Learning at any time: Supporting student learning wherever it happens. *About Campus, 14*(1), 10–15. https://doi.org/10.1002/abc.278

Sriram, R. (2015). The influences of faculty-in-residence programs on the role of the professoriate: A case study. *Work, 52,* 515–519. https://content.iospress.com/articles/work/wor2194

Sriram, R., & McLevain, M. (2016). Developing an instrument to examine student–faculty interaction in faculty-in-residence programs. *Journal of College Student Development, 57*(5), 604–609. https://doi.org/10.1353/csd.2016.0065

Sriram, R., Shushok, F., Jr., Perkins, J., & Scales, T. L. (2011). Students as teachers: What faculty learn by living on campus. *The Journal of College and University Student Housing, 38*(1), 40–55. https://www.nxtbook.com/nxtbooks/acuho/journal_vol38no1/index.php#/p/40

Thies, C. G. (2003). Reflections on assuming administrative responsibilities as an untenured assistant professor. *Political Science and Politics, 36*(3), 447–450.

Tinto, V. (1992). *Leaving college: Rethinking the causes and cures of student attrition.* University of Chicago Press.

UCLA Residential Life. (n.d.). *Faculty-in-residence positions.* https://reslife.ucla.edu/fir

Wawrzynski, M. R., Jessup-Anger, J., Stolz, K., Helman, C., & Beaulieu, J. (2009). Exploring students' perceptions of academically based living–learning communities. *College Student Affairs Journal, 28*(1), 138–158. https://epublications.marquette.edu/edu_fac/90

VIGNETTE

Growing Up on Campus

Lily Sriram

*M*y oldest daughter and second oldest child, Lily, began living in our residential community when she was 7. Lily was a strong advocate for us moving into Brooks Residential College, where I serve as faculty-in-residence, and she has worked hard to persuade us to stay. Because of what I have seen Lily give and receive in this community, I asked her to offer her reflections in the following vignette. Her story serves as a precursor for my thoughts on engaging families-in-residence.—Rishi Sriram

My name is Lily Sriram, and I am 16 years old. Since I was 7 years old, I have lived on a college campus along with my three siblings and my dog. Living in the community of a residential college is so natural and normal to me now, but it truly changed me into the person I am today. I have gained an incredible amount from this experience. As the only introvert in a family of extroverts, I've learned how to come out of my shell and engage with others while also making time to have to myself and recharge. I've learned to relate to people who are a different age than me and who come from different backgrounds. I've discovered the importance of community in everyone's life and how finding a strong community is rare in today's world.

The experience of living on campus has allowed me to build relationships with people, for which I am so thankful. Many students become some of my closest friends and keep in touch with us long after they graduate. We go to their weddings and get to watch them build lives for themselves. I can talk to the students about my friends, my school, and all about my life, and they offer me advice. Often, they've had similar experiences, and college students are the perfect age because they have had time to reflect on those experiences but not forget about them.

I've gained so much from living here, but I also believe I've contributed a good amount to this community. I believe that my siblings and I make this residential college feel more like a home. Our house is a home for students to go, and several students have told us we remind them of their siblings. Students come from a wide range of family backgrounds, and they tell us how fascinating it is to see a family up close and compare it to their experience.

Along with my siblings, we make events less awkward by starting conversations with people and not being afraid to be the first ones to grab the food or start the activity. I think we also play a part in making students feel welcome. I learn their names and help out on move-in day. Another way we contribute is by giving students the opportunity to mentor and advise someone younger than themselves. Mentoring me gives students a break from being the mentee all the time and provides them the opportunity to teach and counsel, which are important skills to develop. Faculty-in-residence families are crucial parts of an on-campus community, and I am grateful for all that I have received and contributed because a residential college is my home.

11

THE HIDDEN HELPERS

Engaging Families-in-Residence as Resources for Student Success

Rishi Sriram

In the fall of 2019, I was honored to help my institution host the 6th Annual Residential College Symposium—a conference of 150 higher-education constituents who believe that living and learning go hand in hand. Although I served on the executive board of the Residential College Society and as a faculty-in-residence (FIR) in Brooks Residential College at Baylor University, the role I was most excited about was as a spouse and father, encouraging my family to participate in the symposium. My wife, who had our fourth child just days before the symposium began, and our three older children (ages 15, 13, and 11) all registered for the symposium. Having lived in a residential college for 7 years, the symposium was an opportunity for my family to experience firsthand the research and scholarship of living–learning communities (LLCs). My family thoroughly enjoyed going from session to session, listening to scholars and professionals discuss the ideals and practicalities of living–learning communities. They were also delighted to show symposium participants around our home and talk about the role they play in fostering student success within a residential college. It was a pivotal moment for my family because it brought validity to the work they had done over 7 years in residence to contribute to the retention, engagement, achievement, and learning of college students. Lily's vignette for this chapter shares examples of our family's effort to support these goals.

As FIR programs grow in quantity and reputation nationwide, the families that often come into the residential communities alongside the faculty member can remain in undefined and underutilized roles. In this chapter,

I discuss faculty with families who live in residence on campuses. I offer a broader definition of student learning and advocate for the essential roles that community and student–faculty interaction play in the research on college student success. After reviewing this background literature, I explore how families-in-residence influence the campus environment and then provide recommendations pertaining to the people, policies, programs, and places associated with FIR. Thoughtful reflection and purposeful planning can transform families-in-residence into key stakeholders of college student success.

Understanding Learning Across Multiple Dimensions

Understanding the important role families-in-residence can play in undergraduate education requires a paradigm shift of how learning is defined for college students. Shushok et al. (2011) discussed three models that represent vastly different theories about the role residential life plays in student success. The first model, the sleep and eat model, limits the purpose of out-of-class experiences to keeping students alive, safe, and entertained enough to keep them out of trouble. This model isolates learning to the classroom and requires minimum investment into the student experience. The second model, the market model, requires significant financial investment in the out-of-class experience, but not for the aim of student learning. Instead, the market model views enrollment as a competition to attract students who have raised their expectations for what college campuses will provide, leading to an arms race for the latest amenities to attract more students. Therefore, facilities such as recreation centers, residential communities, and student union buildings are designed to impress and attract prospective students while functionally addressing some of the needs of current students.

The third model—and the one advocated by Shushok et al. (2011)—is the learning model. As the name suggests, this paradigm views the entire student experience as a journey toward learning and development. Therefore, every facility on campus, every department and employee, and every hour of the day should work for the purpose of student learning. Experiences outside of the classroom should bring faculty, staff, families-in-residence, and students together in ways that are not possible or practical within the classroom setting. Shushok et al. (2009) unpacked what it means to have a learning model on campus:

> While a few faculty and student affairs educators at our institution and elsewhere may believe that real learning happens primarily either in the classroom or through co-curricular involvement, this thinking is contrary to the

preponderance of evidence that the best learning occurs when the curriculum and co-curriculum are intentionally united, as they are, for example, in the residential college recently developed on our campus. (p. 11)

Embracing a learning model requires two shifts in thinking. First, higher-education leaders should capitalize on all types of teachers on campus: faculty, staff, families-in-residence, and student peers. All play an essential role in the educational experience of students. Second, higher-education leaders should emphasize that learning occurs through relationships, and those relationships occur across three types of interactions: academic, social, and deeper life (Sriram, Haynes, Cheatle, et al., 2020; Sriram & McLevain, 2016). When all types of educators work to create interactions with students across these categories, students flourish.

Chambliss and Takacs (2014) reported that students define their college experience by the relationships they develop with faculty, staff, and peers. Interactions and relationships matter for learning. In addition to whom students interact with, the categories or types of those interactions also matter. Since the publication of Tinto's (1975, 1987) foundational work on student retention, scholars and practitioners have typically divided the student experience into two categories: academic integration and social integration. Although these two categories are well established, recently scholars have challenged the general sufficiency and adequacy of this two-factor model. A third factor—deeper life interactions—is a needed addition. The term *deeper life interactions* was first proposed by Sriram and McLevain (2016) to describe interactions "that occur around life's big questions and meaning-making. Such meaning-making involves awareness of how one composes reality, an ongoing dialogue toward truth, and acting in ways that are satisfying and just" (p. 605). Deeper life interactions are difficult to foster in typical classes or programs because of the personal nature of the interactions, but families-in-residence are well suited for these interactions because of the quantity and quality of time they spend with students outside of formal programming.

Scholars suggest that interactions about meaning, value, and purpose are distinct from academic and social interactions, and quantitative measurements of the three variables validate this claim (Sriram, Haynes, Cheatle, et al., 2020; Sriram & McLevain, 2016). Researchers found that different interactions have unique influences on desired student outcomes (Sriram, Weintraub, et al., 2020). Such research shows that academic interactions with peers, social interactions with peers, deeper life interactions with peers, deeper life interactions with faculty/staff, and social interactions involving time with faculty/staff are all significant and meaningful predictors of students' psychological sense of community. Although Students of Color and first-generation students have lower satisfaction with deeper life interactions with peers, these students do not differ from majority students in their satisfaction with deeper life interactions with faculty/staff (Beckowski & Gebauer, 2018; Sriram, Haynes, Weintraub, et al., 2020; Sriram, Haynes, Weintraub, et al., 2020). Therefore, faculty, staff, and spouses/partners who live in residential communities may be best equipped to facilitate deeper life interactions with underrepresented students.

Universities can best promote student success when campus leaders view learning as something that occurs through interactions both in and out of the classroom (see chapter 2). If relationships that matter most for students occur through academic, social, and deeper life interactions with faculty, staff, and students, and if faculty and staff are best equipped to initiate deeper life interactions with students, then FIR programs are primed to make a significant difference in the lives of students. By living with students, faculty are more likely to encounter moments in the lives of students that can lead to conversations about meaning, value, and purpose. In addition, FIR offer an additional resource to campus for student interactions: families.

How Families-In-Residence Influence the Campus Environment

Families-in-residence refers to all family members who live on campus as part of a FIR program (see chapter 10). Although research related to FIR on college campuses is sparse, studies of families-in-residence are almost nonexistent. A review of the literature does provide some information on families-in-residence, even if families are not the focus of what was studied. Golde and Pribbenow (2000) conducted one of the first studies on faculty involvement in residential communities. Through interviews with faculty members in two residential learning communities at the University of Wisconsin— Madison, they explored the experiences and motivations of 15 faculty members who became involved and stayed involved in these programs. Although these faculty did not live in the residential communities, they reported that some of the activities they were involved in, such as sharing meals with students, included their families. Even when families were not directly included in the events with students, deeper life interactions with students would occur through discussions about "life and death, parents, families" (Golde & Pribbenow, 2000, p. 33).

By contrast, these same faculty discussed the tension between spending time in the residential learning community versus spending time with the faculty member's family. One faculty member admitted that the out-of-class interaction with students "comes at a great expense" (Golde & Pribbenow, 2000, p. 33). Another faculty member said that she made time for the students in the residential learning community because she found it rewarding and enriching, which therefore benefited her family life. The tension of faculty members having to choose between spending time at home with their families or spending time out of class with students during the evening can be alleviated when faculty and their families live with students in the residential communities. FIR programs create environments in which student–faculty interaction can occur more frequently and spontaneously (see chapter 9).

Several studies have reported specifically on FIR, with some of the findings related to families-in-residence. Ellet and Schmidt (2011) conducted a study similar to Golde and Pribbenow's (2000), but they examined faculty who lived in the communities in which they were involved. Although their findings do not focus on families-in-residence, they mention that these programs help to create a sense of community and sustained interactions amid time constraints. Sriram et al. (2011) explored what FIR learn and gain from the experience of living with students, such as benefits to their teaching and to their families. FIR perceived the decision to move on campus as a family decision, and they looked forward to having their families interact with students. Faculty anticipated that their families would make significant contributions to creating a sense of community, but they were surprised by the extent to which living in residence benefited their families. One FIR expressed this sentiment as follows:

> I have been surprised by how remarkably well integrated my professional service and familial life have become. At the time we moved to the [residence hall], my son was . . . a mere toddler with rudimentary language skills. My wife and I wondered whether or not we would find it a strain upon him or upon our family unit. Any concerns or doubts that we entertained were utterly dashed by an experience of unparalleled personal opportunities and socially engaging experiences for our whole family . . . Our young son is thriving, our family is thriving. (Sriram et al., 2011, p. 49)

FIR also shared that they learned more about their own families by witnessing family members live and interact with students (Sriram et al., 2011).

In a related study, Davenport and Pasque (2014) interviewed 12 FIR, two live-in partners, and students to better understand the influences of FIR programs. Nine of the FIR had children ranging in age from newborn to 20 years old. They found that the student–faculty interaction stemming from living in residence humanized students and faculty to one another. Students became like "an extended family" (p. 56), describing to faculty a feeling of safety when spending time with FIR and their families. FIR and their families provided "a supportive and familial environment that may serve as a foundation for student development" (p. 57).

Students also described living with faculty and their families as creating an environment that felt like home (Davenport & Pasque, 2014). The interconnection of family into the out-of-class learning environment led students to greater levels of involvement and fulfillment. Students were grateful for the "family-type setting" (Davenport & Pasque, 2014, p. 58) and sense of psychological safety that invited increased engagement. As one student described, "They always had the kids running around the house and just watching them interact with their children, as well, it was just very—I mean you could feel the love in the room" (Davenport & Pasque, 2014, p. 57). Family members were critical to creating this kind of welcoming environment for students.

FIR programs bring new meaning to work–life balance (see chapter 12), as well as the role of faculty on campus (Sriram, 2015). As Sriram (2015) argued, FIR have the potential to shift the campus culture around what it means to be a professor and how faculty can directly influence student success. This positive influence extends to families-in-residence. When Humphrey et al. (2015) conducted a case study of two FIR with families in the residential communities, the faculty described the tensions between an old model of evaluating faculty and a new model of using faculty to promote student success. At many institutions, FIR duties are separate from traditional faculty responsibilities such as teaching, research, and other service requirements. Therefore, faculty must navigate how to accomplish the additional responsibilities while also giving proper attention to classes, publishing, and conducting committee work. Institutions can and should help navigate these tensions through policies and practices. Without more institutional support in the form of release time from other duties, FIR essentially work overtime. And yet, the willingness and motivation of their families to move on campus to help the student experience can be a major factor for faculty agreeing to the role in the first place (Humphrey et al., 2015).

An important and universal goal for FIR programs is to help develop a sense of community for students. Families-in-residence can be key constituents in forming a community because of the natural link family members make to faculty's personal lives. Families-in-residence help to blur the lines between personal and professional in a healthy, appropriate manner. The result can be families-in-residence receiving invitations to some of the most significant and meaningful moments of students' lives, such as weddings, graduations, or culminating academic performances (Humphrey et al., 2015).

Although the literature on families-in-residence is sparse, studies of FIR provide helpful information on how families can positively influence student success and broaden understanding of student learning. The ability of families-in-residence to form a sense of community and help students succeed can be amplified or limited by campus policies and practices. Drawing from my own experience as a FIR, the shared experiences of other FIR on my campus, and what I have learned about FIR programs during campus visits or related conferences, in the remainder of this chapter I discuss practical considerations for maximizing the benefits of these families by engaging families-in-residence.

Move to Practice: Considerations for Engaging Families-In-Residence

Institutions currently engage families-in-residence in a variety of ways. The differences can be attributed to how institutions arrange people, policies, programs, and places. Logistical considerations surrounding FIR programs vary greatly between institutions. These details make a difference. How FIR programs are implemented is just as important as whether or not FIR programs exist on campus. By thinking carefully about the people involved, the policies governing FIR programs, the events associated with these programs, and the facilities available to FIR, campus leaders can make intentional decisions regarding the role of families-in-residence in fostering a sense of community and promoting student success.

People

So much attention goes toward the faculty member in FIR programs that other people involved can be overlooked. The biggest decision campus leaders make for families-in-residence pertains to how families are viewed by the institution. Are families considered full-fledged partners in the FIR program, or are they considered nonessential add-ons that tag along with the FIR? The answer to this question is more complex than it appears. For example, at Rice University, FIR are called College Magisters. The partners of FIR are not only considered College Magisters alongside the faculty member but are also listed on the website with the faculty member and paid a separate stipend from the faculty member. In essence, they are considered part-time employees of the institution. The advantages of such an approach is clarity of the role, honoring the partner-in-residence for the role they play in student learning, and essentially doubling the number of FIR by fully embracing partners.

But there may be disadvantages to such an approach as well. If partners are considered equal to FIR, then they must be interviewed alongside the faculty member. This can create a situation where decision makers desire the faculty member for the role but are hesitant about the partner. Or what if the partner gives their full attention and efforts to the role, but the faculty member does not? Another issue is whether such an approach disadvantages those faculty without partners. Although families-in-residence present a wonderful contribution to the community, faculty without partners or children can be just as effective, and this is something that must be considered in interview processes.

On the other hand, if the partners of FIR are simply considered add-ons, how does that honor the sacrifice they make to move their families onto campus? These partners will certainly have interactions with students apart from the faculty member, and students may prefer the partner as a mentor over the faculty member because of gender or other points of connection. At my institution, the philosophy toward partners-in-residence leans more toward add-on than full-fledged employee. And yet there are many female students who step over me to seek out mentorship from my wife. I am not at all offended when this occurs; instead, it makes me proud of the contribution my spouse makes to the college environment. But the acknowledgment of partners' roles in fostering student success may vary by institution.

Institutions should be intentional regarding the role of families-in-residence—particularly partners—and clarify those roles in position announcements and job descriptions. The role that families will play in interviewing for the position is important decision, and campus leaders should make sure that those faculty without families are not disadvantaged in their application process.

Policies

For campuses initiating a new FIR program, policies governing day-to-day needs and activities for families-in-residence are easily overlooked. These policies matter, however, because of the ways they influence living on campus. The first consideration for campus leaders is to evaluate policies regarding meal plans for FIR and their families. Eating together is one of the best ways for faculty and their families to interact with students, and this activity is encouraged or hindered by the policies governing meals. Are meals in dining halls provided only for the FIR, or are they also provided for partners/families? Do meal allotments increase as the size of the family-in-residence increases? Additional meals come at a cost to institutions, so the level to which they are provided reflects the institution's philosophy of the purpose of families-in-residence.

There are other logistical policies that can make the sacrifice of living on campus more feasible and enjoyable. Such categories include family access to campus internet, permission to use library resources, policies regarding the use of recreation/wellness centers, and access to particular buildings or spaces. These accommodations may require families-in-residence to obtain official university credentials, ID cards, and keys. Parking and the distance of vehicles to the residence can make a substantial difference in the daily lives of families-in-residence as well. These logistical policies can serve as positive benefits to the FIR role or create daily challenges for families navigating life on a college campus.

Compensation for FIR and their families comes in a variety of forms. Most FIR programs provide free housing, but some charge rent because of university and/or state policies. Compensation can also take the form of stipends and course releases. Many institutions consider FIR job duties as a form of unofficial overtime and therefore do not provide any release time to faculty. Other institutions consider the FIR role a form of teaching that justifies course releases. Institutions that provide housing, meal plans, course releases, and a stipend make a substantial investment in FIR programs that require support from both the divisions of academic affairs and student affairs (Healea et al., 2015).

Policies also matter in regard to the training of families-in-residence. As mental health concerns increase for college students, families-in-residence are on the front lines of student care. Institutions need policies that specify the role of families-in-residence in these situations. One approach is to always ask the faculty member and their partners to refer issues of crisis or mental health to a particular staff member, such as a residence hall director. Although this strategy may be appropriate, it risks making students feel uncared for and "handed off" after confiding about a deeply personal matter. Another approach is to train both FIR and their partners in mental health, threat-to-harm, Title IX, and risk management policies and procedures. The advantage of this kind of training is that it equips FIR and partners with the best information on when to try to help students directly and when to delegate to appropriate resources. A possible disadvantage is the potential of a FIR or partner attempting to handle a situation themselves that should be directed to a professional staff member. Policies governing families-in-residence can be created reactively or proactively. *Reactive policies* refers to the creation of rules and norms only after encountering unanticipated situations with families-in-residence. *Proactive policies*, on the other hand, require an espoused philosophy around the role of families-in-residence that serve as the foundation for necessary rules and norms. All constituents involved are better served when institutions first reflect on the role of families-in-residence and then develop policies that reflect those ideals.

Programs

Families-in-residence have the potential to make a great impact on programmatic offerings within a living–learning community. Key programmatic questions to reflect upon include (a) When is it best not to have families present? (b) When is it best to have families present but not central to the program? and (c) When is it best to make families the feature of the programming? Family members may cause awkwardness for some programs or decrease participation from students. If programs have a serious theme around them and invite vulnerability from students, such as topics pertaining to racial or gender equity, it may be best to not have families present. Students may be more likely to share and will not have to worry about the age appropriateness of content if it is decided beforehand that certain events will be family free.

Often, however, families can increase the sense of community and decrease the level of awkwardness at events through their presence. Families can create a homelike environment and invite students to relax and enjoy themselves. Some students may be intimidated by their own peers but have no problem starting a conversation with someone younger than themselves. If events are more casual and social in nature, families often enhance the event. When events involve meals, the presence of families-in-residence can even symbolically enhance the importance of the event in the eyes of students. Students know that having family members participate in an event requires more effort and planning on the part of the FIR. Therefore, it shows students that they are worth the extra work.

In a few cases, families can contribute by being the focus of an event. One example is when a family-in-residence invites students into their home for a meal. The purpose of the event is for the students to spend time with the family-in-residence, and events like these provide opportunities for deeper life interactions. Another example comes from my own experience: Students in my residential college strongly advocated for my wife and me to do a series of events around relationships, dating, marriage, and parenting. We were not eager for our family life to be the event itself, but we reluctantly agreed. To our surprise, students filled our living room each week. We tried to be honest about our journey, struggles, and failures. After those sessions, students expressed deep appreciation and wrote us some of the kindest notes we have received.

Knowing when to have families present at events is not always obvious. Student affairs professionals, such as residence hall directors or program directors, are a valuable resource in making this decision. If FIR establish a collaborative working relationship with student affairs professionals and view them as peers and colleagues, student affairs professionals can provide great insight into how to best utilize families for programs (see chapter 12).

Places

FIR programs are significant investments for colleges, and perhaps the greatest area of financial commitment is the FIR apartment/home. These homes can range from a modified student suite to combining and renovating several student suites to planning the FIR home when designing the residential community. They vary in size from 1,000 square ft to 3,000 square ft. The size and design of these homes send symbolic messages about the purpose of FIR programs and logistically enable (or limit) the level of impact FIR have within a community.

Symbolically, the FIR home communicates who the home is for. If the home has just enough space (or not enough space) to accommodate the FIR and family, students will interpret this to mean that the home is not a space for them. Students will feel like they are intruding and will be reluctant to enter the space often. If the design of the home places most of the space into bedrooms rather than living areas, students will understand that this home is meant only for small student gatherings rather than large ones. Where the home is located within the living–learning community also communicates a symbolic message. If the FIR home is in a central location that is easily accessible to students, students feel invited and welcome. If the home is not on the first floor or tucked away in a corner, it sends a message that this family is not to be bothered other than occasionally. These options have logistical ramifications as well. Quantity and quality of space allows for families-in-residence to invite large groups of students into their homes and encourages families-in-residence to stay for multiple years, allowing for a greater engagement with and impact on students.

My home in Brooks Residential College incorporates many of the features described previously. Because Brooks Residential College was a new residential community, faculty, administrators, students, and architects came together in conversation about how design could positively influence behavior. The result was a three-bedroom, two-story apartment that is approximately 2,000 square feet in size. The second story allows the more personal space, such as bedrooms, laundry, and full bathrooms, to be separate from the space on the first floor that is frequented by students. On the first floor, almost all of the space is devoted to a large living room that connects to an open dining room. The living room comfortably fits 20 students, and the dining room seats 10. This space is a key reason why our "Tuesday Teas" have averaged more than 50 students stepping into our home each week, and we have seen an even higher number for some movie nights and football watch parties. Although we try to be friendly and inviting as a family-in-residence, I cannot overstate how much the design of the facilities contribute to our ability to reach students. Vanderbilt University, Rice University, and Washington University in St. Louis are other places I have had the opportunity to visit where the institution invested heavily in the quality and space of the FIR apartment because of its importance to the success of the program. Such homes are not identical to each other, but they share features that help FIR succeed, such as an inviting space for lots of students and amenities that appeal to families.

Conclusion

In this chapter, I have discussed faculty with families who live in residence on campuses. I offered a broader definition of student learning and advocated for the essential roles that community and interactions play in the research on college student success. Families-in-residence influence the campus environment, and institutions can best capitalize on FIR programs when they are intentional about issues pertaining to the people, policies, programs, and places associated with FIR. Thoughtful reflection and purposeful planning can transform families-in-residence into key stakeholders of college student success. Understanding the important role families-in-residence play requires a paradigm shift of what learning means for college students.

Experiences outside of the classroom should bring faculty, staff, and students together in ways that are not possible or practical within the classroom setting. Rather than a sleep and eat model or a market model, residential communities should implement a learning model that views the out-of-class experience as an essential part of student learning and development. Student learning should be an outcome that is pursued by everyone on campus in every space. FIR and their families connect with students where they reside, enabling more opportunities to help students thrive.

Universities best promote student success when campus leaders view learning as something that occurs through interactions both in and out of the classroom. If interactions that matter most for students occur through academic, social, and deeper life interactions with faculty, staff, and students, and if faculty and staff are best equipped to initiate deeper life interactions with students, then FIR programs are primed to make a significant difference in the lives of students. An important and universal goal for FIR programs is to help develop a sense of community for students. Families-in-residence can be key constituents in forming community because of the natural link they make to faculty members' personal lives. Families-in-residence help to blur the lines between personal and professional in a healthy, appropriate manner. Institutions engage families-in-residence in a variety of ways, and these differences can be conceptualized into the categories of people, policies, programs, and places. By thinking in these categories, campus leaders can make intentional decisions regarding the role of families-in-residence in fostering a sense of community and promoting student success.

In our sixth year as a family-in-residence, we learned that my wife was pregnant with our fourth child. My immediate reaction was that this life moment signaled it was time to transition out of my FIR role. But the more I reflected on it, and the more I spoke with my family, the more I reconsidered that initial reaction. Living in residence with college students has been the most meaningful experience of my career. My family has contributed much to the success of this community, but I also cannot accurately calculate the profound positive impact this community and its students have had on my family. I could not imagine raising three children in this environment, with the many benefits Lily describes in her vignette, but then depriving our fourth child of it. So, to my surprise, we decided to stay in the community with our new addition. We were the first faculty family on our campus to have a baby while in residence. Welcoming our new baby into this community was marvelous. I have never seen a baby so loved and adored by people of no relation. Several students told me that my baby was the first one they ever held.

When students from my residential college take time to write me notes of appreciation, it is clear that they are not just thanking me. They never express appreciation for my work as a FIR without also talking about my family. When students come to my residential college from supportive families, my family reminds them of home. When students come from less-than-ideal circumstances, my family can help to fill some of those gaps and show students a different example of family from what they have known. Families-in-residence will have a positive impact on students with or without broader institutional help. Institutions, however, can fully capitalize on the substantial investment made in FIR programs by better utilizing and supporting the families that often come with the faculty members.

References

Beckowski, C. P., & Gebauer, R. (2018). Cultivating deeper life interactions: Faculty–student relationships in a nonresidential learning community. *Journal of College Student Development, 59*(6), 752–755. https://doi.org/10.1353/csd.2018.0070

Chambliss D. F., & Takacs, C. G. (2014). *How college works*. Harvard University Press.

Davenport, A. M., & Pasque, P. A. (2014). Adding breadth and depth to college and university residential communities: A phenomenological study of faculty-in-residence. *Journal of College & University Student Housing, 40*(2), 46–61. https://www.nxtbook.com/nxtbooks/acuho/journal_vol40no2/index.php#/p/8

Ellet, T., & Schmidt, A. (2011). Faculty perspectives on creating community in residence halls. *Journal of College & University Student Housing, 38*(1), 26–39. https://doi.org/10.1080/1937156X.2013.11949691

Golde, C. M., & Pribbenow, D. A. (2000). Understanding faculty involvement in residential learning communities. *Journal of College Student Development, 41*(1), 27–40. http://chris.golde.org/filecabinet/facultyinvolvement.html

Healea, C. D., Scott, J. H., & Dhilla, S. (2015). The work of faculty-in-residence: An introduction and literature review. *Work, 52*(3), 473–480. https://doi.org/10.3233/WOR-152189

Humphrey, M., Callahan, J., & Harrison, G. (2015). Living with students: Lessons learned while pursuing tenure, administration, and raising a family. *Work, 52*(3), 497–501. https://doi.org/ 10.3233/WOR-152197

Shushok, F., Henry, D. V., Blalock, G., & Sriram, R. (2009). Learning at any time: Supporting student learning whenever it happens. *About Campus, 14*(1), 10–15. https://doi.org/10.1002/abc.278

Shushok, F., Scales, T. L., Sriram, R., & Kidd, V. (2011). A tale of three campuses: Unearthing theories of residential life that shape the student learning experience. *About Campus, 16*(3), 13–21. https://doi.org/10.1002/abc.20063

Sriram, R. (2015). The influences of faculty-in-residence programs on the role of the professoriate: A case study. *Work, 52,* 515–519. https://dx.doi.org/10.3233/WOR-152194

Sriram, R., Haynes, C., Cheatle, J., Marquart, C. P., Murray, J. L., & Weintraub, S. D. (2020). The development and validation of an instrument measuring academic, social, and deeper life interactions. *Journal of College Student Development, 61*(2), 240–245. https://doi.org/10.1353/csd.2020.0020

Sriram, R., Haynes, C., Weintraub, S. D., Cheatle, J., Marquart, C. P., & Murray, J. L. (2020). Student demographics and experiences of deeper life interactions within residential learning communities. *Learning Communities: Research & Practice, 8*(1), 1–17. https://washingtoncenter.evergreen.edu/lcrpjournal/vol8/iss1/8

Sriram, R., & McLevain, M. (2016). Developing an instrument to examine student–faculty interaction in faculty-in-residence programs. *Journal of College Student Development, 57,* 604–609. https://doi.org/10.1353/csd.2016.0065

Sriram, R., Shushok, F., Perkins, J., & Scales, L. (2011). Students as teachers: What faculty learn by living on campus. *Journal of College & University Student Housing, 38*(1), 40–55. http://www.nxtbook.com/nxtbooks/acuho/journal_vol38no1/#/42

Sriram, R., Weintraub, S. D., Murray, J. L., Cheatle, J., Haynes, C., & Marquart, C. P. (2020). The influence of students' academic, social, and deeper life interactions on their psychological sense of community. *Journal of College Student Development, 61*(5), 593–608. https://doi.org/10.1353/csd.2020.0057

Tinto, V. (1975). Dropout from higher education: A theoretical synthesis of recent research. *Review of Educational Research, 45*(1), 89–125. https://doi.org/10.3102/00346543045001089

Tinto, V. (1987). *Leaving college: Rethinking the causes and cures of student attrition.* University of Chicago Press.

VIGNETTE

Life Chronicles From a Faculty-in-Residence

Wendy Cohn

Achieving work–life balance is difficult, but it is even more tenuous as a faculty-in-residence (FIR) because the separation between work and life is blurred. The strategy that worked the best for me was to abandon compartmentalizing my life as having two distinctions: family life and work life. It was through connecting and integrating all the pieces that it became manageable and enjoyable.

The life of a FIR is vastly different than most college faculty are used to leading. I served as the principal for Hereford Residential College at the University of Virginia from 2014 to 2019. My experience as a FIR was simultaneously engaging, rewarding, overwhelming, and energizing.

My approach with my family was to involve them 100%. My children (then between ages 7 and 13) attended stress management seminars, dinners with authors, worked alongside students in our college garden, and generally participated in all residential college activities. We ate meals in the dining hall, got mail from the mailroom, and kicked the soccer ball in the green space. I had other obligations that took me away from them, but by integrating my family into the experience it became shared by our entire family and rewarding for all of us.

I connected my academic work to the residential college as much as possible. As a health sciences researcher, I was able to offer research opportunities to our students by providing basic research assistant training in a one-credit seminar and then using my own contacts to match students with researchers. In most cases, the students were able to earn a small stipend since they came with research experience. At the time, one of my research emphases was understanding cancer disparities across our state. We had just acquired statewide data and, with a top-notch team including experts in epidemiology, breast cancer, and leaders of our cancer center, we developed an academic course for students at Hereford to work alongside us, giving the students an incredible opportunity while connecting both sides of my work life.

Being the principal of Hereford Residential College was a gift. It is important to know that academic productivity will likely be less than usual. Considering where a faculty member is on their tenure clock, or with other responsibilities, is important in determining whether the timing is right. Being realistic about the time it takes to do the job well is important so that it doesn't lead to additional frustrations trying to balance responsibilities. For me, it was worth it in so many ways. Most important, my relationships with the students are deep and rewarding in a way that is not possible in the classroom or in a research relationship. Through the special interactions you have while a FIR you can advise and mentor students in areas that will affect them as future citizens.

12

KEYS TO FACULTY-IN-RESIDENCE SUCCESS

Balancing Career and Life

Kirsten Kennedy

Professor Johnston, a hypothetical faculty member at State University, looks at her calendar and finds she has been double booked three times this week, and the time she set aside to conduct research has slowly been chipped away by administrative meetings. "Holy cow!" she thinks. Before accepting this FIR position and moving into a residential college, Professor Johnston had more autonomy over her time, but everyone wants to meet about something! In addition to monthly departmental meetings, the administration wants opinions on everything, she reflects. The residence life staff want her opinions on programming and staff selection; the admissions staff want her help in recruiting new students to campus; and the housing facilities staff want to know what she needs in her residence. Professor Johnston already feels like she is asked to do more because she is a faculty of color, and she has more service obligations so she can provide diversity to several department and university committees, as well as mentoring students of color. Professor Johnston begins to wonder if she will be able to manage her faculty and residential college responsibilities. Add two children ready to head into their teenage years and a partner who is also a faculty member, and Professor Johnston knows she must find a way to balance these competing responsibilities.

Faculty-in-residence (FIR) like Professor Johnson frequently face competing demands from their faculty career and home life. In this chapter, I detail the work pressures of being a faculty member, the stress associated with life, and the realities of living in a residence hall, as well as provide guidance on how to successfully balance work and life as a FIR. The content comes from my involvement with living–learning communities (LLCs), where I currently cosupervise the faculty principals for faculty-led LLCs, and it integrates both FIR research and my practical experience.

Background

Existing research on balancing work and life as a FIR consists of anecdotes of the FIR experience (Rhoads, 2009; Shushok et al., 2009; Sriram, 2015) and the impact of the faculty role on families (Humphrey et al., 2015; Jacobs & Winslow, 2004). However, no direct guidance exists on balancing the faculty role, the FIR role, and the family role.

Work–Life Balance

Khallash and Kruse (2012) presented the work–life balance definition most salient to postsecondary faculty: "managing *external pressure* from a competitive work environment with leisure and/or family" (p. 682). Faculty work has three major components: research, teaching, and service (Misra et al., 2012; see also chapter 2 and chapter 6); and life has many components too, such as self, family, and community (Friedman, 2019a). Balancing multiple work and home roles is difficult because inevitably work priorities will conflict with life priorities. When no solution exists to address work–life conflicts, stress, anxiety, and frustration result. Feelings of conflict have a negative impact on both faculty's effectiveness at work as well as their quality of life outside of work (Ehrens, 2015). Thus, achieving work–life balance is not only desirable, but crucial to FIR success.

Work and life frequently alternate in taking time and attention. One way to imagine work and life are two equally sized triangles—and some would like to keep those separate and equal—imagining that as a *balanced* life. Better descriptors include prioritizing, integrating, and harmonizing all of life's roles. Imagine the two triangles in Figure 12.1 with their various components. The first triangle represents work's components for the faculty role: research, teaching, and service. The second triangle represents personal life, with self, family, and community. Integration and harmonization can occur where the two triangles overlap, but they also represent where conflict can emerge. Unfortunately, work may view FIR activities as belonging in the personal triangle, while the family may view the FIR responsibilities as being associated with the work triangle. The overlap between work and life necessarily becomes greater as a FIR, as Wendy Cohn describes in her vignette for this chapter, and more attention must be given to reduce the conflict.

Figure 12.1. Work–life balance.

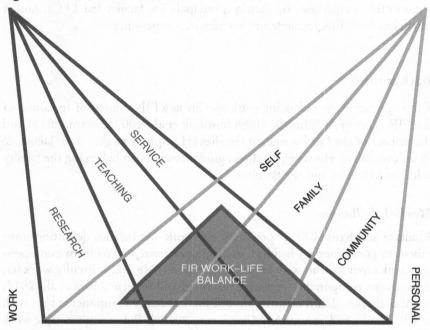

Note. FIR = faculty-in-residence.

When work and life are out of balance, the stress of the conflicts can lead to burnout. Pope-Ruark (2020) vividly described feelings associated with burnout: "I was emotionally and physically exhausted, dreaded every single aspect of my work including my students, and I felt shamefully empty inside about my work" (para. 4). The American Institute of Stress (as cited in Lynch, 2019) defined burnout as "a cumulative process marked by emotional exhaustion and withdrawal associated with increased workload and institutional stress" (p. 46). Add living in a residence hall to the mix, and stress, anxiety, and frustration may increase with a greater probability of FIR burnout. Lack of work–life balance among faculty "has been associated with negative consequences in terms of emotional and physical well-being, retention, advancement, and job satisfaction" (Denson et al., 2018, p. 239). Burnout comes from enduring both work and life stress, which I discuss next.

Work Stress

The life of a faculty member is stressful. Most faculty spend more than 50 hours per week in work functions, with the percentage of time devoted to research, teaching, and service activities depending on institutional type and career stage, something Misra et al. (2012) termed "work–work balance" (p. 313). Failure to balance work–work expectations can be career ending, never mind the impact on one's work–life balance. Owens et al. (2018) identified six variables that "significantly predicted the inability to attain a healthy work–life balance" (p. 61): (a) lack of personal time, (b) self-imposed high expectations, (c) committee work, (d) research/publishing demands, (e) institutional procedures, and (f) colleagues. How faculty manage these variables is informed by the type of institution where they work.

Although faculty spend about the same amount of time in service activities (French et al., 2020), research and teaching demands are dictated by institutional type. Faculty working at doctoral institutions spend more time on research activities, and faculty at associate colleges spend more time on teaching activities (The Carnegie Classification of Institutions of Higher Education, 2018). Faculty allocate their time according to institutional expectations, which, in turn, affect faculty's strategy in balancing work and life. The trade-offs are unique to each faculty member as they evaluate how to fulfill their FIR obligations without negatively affecting their career.

Over time, research expectations across institutional types have grown, which can be explained by a phenomenon termed "upward drift" (Aldersley, 1995, p. 50), or institutions increasing research productivity to move up in institutional type prestige in the Carnegie Classifications. The need to produce more research creates an "academic ratchet" (Massy & Zemsky, 1994, p. 2) where junior faculty requirements for publishing to earn tenure are increased to help the research reputation of the institution. Faculty members who experience the academic ratchet need to increase time allocated to research and publication, which they typically carve out of time previously spent with students (Singell et al., 1996). FIR who are caught in the academic ratchet face increased role conflict.

Beyond institutional type, faculty career stage and appointment type determine how faculty spend their time. Faculty generally fall into two major categories: tenure track (TT) and non-TT (see chapter 6). TT faculty experience stress around promotion points from assistant to associate professor and from associate professor to full professor. Publishing the required amount of research is a metric tenure review committees consider in granting tenure (Finkelstein et al., 2016). As TT faculty are promoted, they report that advancing in rank helped create a perception of greater work–life balance (Denson et al., 2018).

Faculty with marginalized identities such as gender, race, class, and sexual orientation face increased time in service (see chapter 4). Women tend to spend more time teaching and less time on research activities than men (Winslow, 2010). These differences are important because faculty with heavier teaching obligations report more stress (Hart & Cress, 2008). Faculty of color spend 3 more hours a week in service than do their white counterparts (Denson et al., 2018) and report more service commitments, including representation on committees and serving as mentors to underrepresented students (Lee et al., 2016). The increased service load leads to faculty of color feeling exhausted and culturally taxed (Tierney & Bensimon, 1996). Being in control of how one spends their time is important because "Satisfaction with time spent on research had the most consistent, positive relationship with perceived work–life balance for all racial groups" (Denson et al., 2018, p. 238). In addition to stress from work, stress can come from everyday life.

Life Stress

For the purposes of this chapter, life components include the following categories: self, family, and community. *Self* refers to the multiple ways a person might identify—for example, a person who identifies as a woman, an assistant professor of engineering, and a FIR (Caza et al., 2019). Green (2017) discussed the extent to which a person chooses to share identities that are not readily observed, for example, sexuality, political leanings, or religious beliefs. The choice to share or conceal those identities depends on the context—like in an LLC—and requires constant management that may create stress. Furthermore, a person's identities themselves may conflict, creating additional stress.

Family can be thought of in two ways: form and features (Weigel, 2008). *Form* refers to blood relationships that create a structure with roles assigned to those relationships, for example, parent, child, sibling, cousin, grandparent, aunt/uncle, and so on. Although not noted by Weigel (2008), this form could also include families not related by blood, but by family structure, like adopted children and stepparents. *Features* refers to the qualities and attributes associated with family—"love, honesty, trust, encouragement, caring, support, respect, acceptance" (Weigel, 2008, p. 1441)—and people who will support an individual for a lifetime.

Community is a group of people in the same geographic area who share common interests (Jones & Wells, 2007). More specifically, community is "a group of people with diverse characteristics who are linked by social ties, share common perspectives, and engage in joint action in geographical locations of settings" (McQueen et al., 2001, p. 1929), much like those in an LLC. Modern definitions include virtual and online communities. Which communities a person identifies with can be traced to their personal identities, for example, a person identifies as a faculty member and belongs to the

American Association of University Professors. Each of these is an important element to consider in negotiating stress management. Beyond the stress of work and life, there is one more element to consider: living and working in the same location.

Realities of Life in a Residence Hall

Faculty living in a residence hall can expect it to be very different from their permanent residence. Because the faculty residence is integrated into student living quarters, technically faculty are always available to students, with their personal life visible to residents. On the positive side, the increased access can mean that relationships may evolve into discussions that deepen a student's understanding about an academic discipline, world issues, or finding meaning in life. One of the positive aspects of being a FIR is that faculty can

> implement their philosophies of teaching, namely through the students desiring to learn from faculty in new ways, an environment conducive to weakening the divide between academic and social interaction, and the increase of time that allows for constant, informal conversation. (Sriram, 2015, p. 517)

In turn, students may form relationships with FIR family, including children and pets.

FIR and their family may also be exposed to disruptive student behaviors, like late night noise, drinking alcohol, and vandalism, as well as personal problems, like parental divorce; sexual assault and interpersonal violence; significant other breakups; anxiety, depression, and suicidality; and the like. Actual fires, false fire alarms, and fire drills are disruptive to a FIR and their family, as are police and emergency medical technicians who come to the residence hall to address the most serious issues. Discussing these issues with the FIR's family can better prepare them for the unique situations they may experience while living in residence.

Combining Work and Life Into One Space

Recent research provides insight into how a FIR can successfully combine work and life (Ehrens, 2015; Rankin & Yancey Gulley, 2018; Woods-Johnson, 2018). Ehrens (2015) suggested that a supportive institutional environment is helpful in combining roles, but they could be managed in other ways.

The first is to evaluate the extent to which work and life are integrated. Although the work of entry-level residence life professionals is markedly different from faculty work, the commonality of living and working in the same space can be informative. Rankin and Yancey Gulley (2018) offered a 5-point work–life integration scale that ranges from full integrator to integrative segmentor. A *full integrator* would allow staff and/or students into their personal space, have highly informal interpersonal boundaries established with staff and students, and consider work and personal life as one, with less focus on distinct personal time, as Wendy Cohn outlines in her vignette. An *integrative segmentor* would not typically allow staff and/or students to access personal space, sets clear and formal interpersonal boundaries with staff and students, and sets strict time boundaries around work, allowing few exceptions. FIR should consider which part of the continuum suits their circumstances the best.

The second is to develop resiliency skills. Woods-Johnson (2018) studied entry-level, live-in residence life professionals for how they developed their resiliency skills. Woods-Johnson found that the sources of stress stemmed from high organizational demands and high self-expectations. Subjects indicated using "buffers" (p. 82), like engaging with activities and commitments outside of work, helped mitigate stress. Woods-Johnson found two dimensions of resilience: mindsets (beliefs about adversity and beliefs about self) and behaviors (self-aware strategies, self-compassion and empowerment, support seeking, negotiating boundaries, influencing culture, and unproductive behaviors). One of Woods-Johnson's participants stated that he knew he was always going to have stress in his life, so he should just embrace it. Another participant described a continuum of "no stress" to "too much stress," and she found the key was to find the sweet spot where she could be productive but not overwhelmed. Participants identified being organized, communicating effectively, advocating for themselves, and practicing mindfulness as ways to help avoid burnout. Those participating in her study agreed that resilient responses could be learned, and they acknowledged the importance of feedback to learn from their mistakes. These strategies will be helpful to any FIR in managing the stress of living where they work.

Multitasking Responsibilities

To understand their motivation for participation, Kennedy (2005) conducted a study of faculty associated with, but not living in, LLCs. She reported that faculty used multitasking as a way of balancing work and life. In some instances, faculty reported doing two things at once, like grading papers while watching TV with a significant other. Instead of responding to email during typical working hours in the office, some faculty answered email at home after hours. Another faculty member reported that she would schedule an off-campus appointment during the traditional workday and resume academic responsibilities in the evening.

In addition to multitasking at home, some faculty combine their FIR responsibilities with their research agendas. For example, a faculty member in an LLC focused on women in science, technology, engineering, and mathematics produced research on how that community aided in retention of women in male-dominated fields (Kennedy, 2005; Szelényi & Inkelas, 2010). Another faculty member, in sociology, conducted research on drinking patterns of students involved in LLCs (Brower et al., 2003). Producing research related to the LLC is an effective method to multitask provided the research will be positively reviewed by a tenure and promotion committee.

Creating Work–Life Balance for FIR

This section speaks primarily to faculty serving as FIR, although staff and administrators working in FIR programs may find it useful in supporting FIR. The following pages serve as a template you can use to create conditions for success in your FIR role. I will provide a step-by-step process to set yourself up for success in the FIR role. Merging faculty career, FIR, and home responsibilities takes thoughtful reflection and intentional effort.

What Is Your "Why"?

A question worth pondering is why you are interested in the FIR position. Understanding your "why" is a process of examining past behavior patterns to learn what inspires you (Sinek, 2009). Consider why this position is important to you and how it meets your needs, because it will be helpful in identifying competing priorities. Two studies have specifically addressed why faculty participate in LLCs, although these studies are not specific to FIR.

Golde and Pribbenow (2000) investigated why faculty, despite the professional pressures they face, became involved in learning communities at the University of Wisconsin—Madison and learned that faculty "were interested in bringing intellectual life into the residence halls" (p. 36). Their reasons for participation fell into three distinct categories: "(a) a chance to know students better, (b) an opportunity to act in congruence with their beliefs about interdisciplinary and innovative education, and (c) a commitment to the residential learning community idea and purpose" (p. 32).

Faculty in this study found personal satisfaction when they could operationalize their personal values within the LLC environment.

A second qualitative study, conducted by Kennedy (2005), examined why TT faculty participated in LLCs. Faculty in that study said that interacting with students and having a positive impact were the primary reasons they participated in an LLC. More specifically, faculty wanted to help students have an enhanced academic experience, develop friendships, adjust to college, and humanize the stereotypical image of a college professor. Participants had an overwhelming calling to help students grow and develop while at the same enhancing the academic environment. Perhaps one of these studies identified your "why," or maybe you have a "why" that is unique to you. What are your motivations for accepting the FIR role?

Boundary-Setting Conversations

Effectively managing multiple roles starts with boundary setting with personal and professional constituents. Conversations with partners, family, and/or children; your home department; and residence life staff are essential in creating boundaries and expectations.

Partner/Family/Children

A boundary-setting conversation with your partner and/or child(ren) is an important first step. A partner and/or child(ren) who move into a residence hall will experience a transition and a change to their lives, and your conversations with them should focus on how the change will affect everyone (see chapter 11). Friedman (2019b) provided a template for approaching that conversation, which I now describe.

The first step is to set the context for your family members for what living in a residence hall will mean for them. School-age children might have to change schools, and a partner may have an extended or reduced commute to work. The family may need to discuss the pros and cons of (possibly) changing school districts or the impact of staying in the same school, with transportation provided by the family. The biggest change, however, may be that the new responsibilities will take time from the family. In addition, your family may observe inappropriate student behaviors, like overconsumption of alcohol and drug usage, which may involve ambulances, fire trucks, and police cars. They may observe displays of affection between students that make them uncomfortable. On the flip side, they may make long-lasting friendships with students, be closer to campus academic and cultural events, and spend time with in-hall residence life staff. What do you see as the potential rewards and drawbacks of serving in the FIR role for you and your family?

Second, explain why making this change is important to you. Helping your family understand why becoming a FIR is meaningful is crucial. Some faculty want to recreate a small-school experience at a larger institution, some faculty enjoy watching students grow and develop, and others like hearing about former student successes. Some faculty like deepening their relationship with students. Others want to understand students at a deeper level when they live with students in a residence hall as part of their research. Whatever the reason, you should share that with your partner and/or family.

Third, ask your partner and/or child(ren) what they believe the impact on their lives will be. Children might anticipate losing friends by changing schools. A partner might be worried about having a reduced amount of time for activities as a couple. Some partner worries might include logistical items like where to park, how to get card access into the residence hall, whether the meal plan covers the family, access to the campus gym, and other amenities offered to employees. Everyone may be concerned about continuing family dinners. No matter the concern brought forward, it is important that you listen and resist the temptation to become defensive or explain away their concerns.

Fourth, express genuine remorse about the ways that a partner and/or child(ren) may be disappointed because of the change in residence and the change in duties. Helpful language might include, "I'm sorry that my being unavailable is hurtful to you" (Friedman, 2019b, p. 179). The most important part of this conversation is to own the disappointment you created for people significant to you.

Fifth and last, explore possible alternatives on how the negative effects might be minimized. Thoroughly explore your family's suggestions for making up for not being as available. They may suggest that there is special, reserved, untouchable time for the family to be together. Offering to adjust the time of a sacred activity, or periodically making a trip to a special location, are some suggestions. This position might be an opportunity to create new traditions, like eating in the dining hall, going to the campus gym together, taking walks around campus together, going to sporting events, or attending plays/concerts on campus.

Home Department

Accepting a FIR position requires a conversation with your home department. Denson et al. (2018) reported that "faculty perceptions of departmental support specifically for work–life balance were positively and strongly related to faculty work–life balance" (p. 241). Departmental willingness to support your FIR appointment may be contingent on the length of your FIR appointment, so providing that information to your department is vital. If your department is supportive, asking for the FIR experience to count for promotion and tenure is appropriate. You might ask for a letter of support to include in your application to become a FIR, and some institutions require it to be an eligible applicant. Small departments require a certain amount of administrative work that must be covered, so be sensitive to what departmental service activities are sacrificed for becoming a FIR. You could ask for a one-course teaching release to better manage the multiple FIR responsibilities. A teaching release will be highly dependent on the extent of specialization of the course topic and the department's ability (both in human and fiscal resources) to accommodate such a request. At some institutions, the FIR position is financially supported by the provost's office.

Residence Life Staff

In addition to family and the faculty member's home department, FIR will need to develop relationships with residence life staff. You should understand the expectations for the number, frequency, and duration of meetings; for programming; and for being visible to the residents of the LLC. You should also ask for an explanation of the FIR role and purpose in meetings as a way of distinguishing those that require FIR participation and those where it is just nice to have you there. You should ask for introductions to primary contacts for questions and problems, so that you can avoid organization chart roulette to find answers. For students in distress, you need to understand your role (or not) and what your reporting responsibilities are in these situations. If this is a distressed student that you identified and have been directly involved with, you will want to ask what follow-up you can expect. Sometimes the university is not permitted to share the follow-up care, but in some instances it can.

In this section, I have outlined three groups with whom you should have expectation conversations. Are there other people to be considered in these conversations? If so, who?

Thinking About Work Time and Place Boundaries

One of the unique aspects of a FIR position is that the physical location for home and office/classroom is one in the same; thus, observing typical work hours will have little relevance when living in a residence hall. The following are guidelines to help you think about how you might manage the time and place overlap. You should think about what content you are comfortable disclosing to students and what you are comfortable having students share with you.

Time

You should set boundaries about when you meet with students. You might set specific hours where you will meet with students—like office hours, but for your LLC students. Because of the nature of the FIR position these hours will probably not be from 9 to 5, and you will want to vary office hours on the days of the week because students' schedules will vary. You might consider creating similar boundaries around when students can contact you and whether you will provide your cell phone number. You should think about how you can communicate these expectations, perhaps through the resident advisor floor meetings.

Place

You should also decide where you want to meet with students. Options include meeting in your faculty office, in your FIR office (if you have one), in your residence, or in residence hall lobbies and lounges. I discourage you from meeting students in their bedrooms because it could be viewed as inappropriate. Similarly, you should decide if students can contact you in your residence, as opposed to contacting you through email, phone call, or text message. If you are opposed to students knocking on your residence door, you should consider posting instructions on your door directing them to the acceptable ways to contact you. If you are open to having students contact you in your residence, you should post the hours that knocking on the door is appropriate. Furthermore, you should set expectations with your partner and/or children about where they can be physically within the building and whether they need you to accompany them.

Content

Students in LLCs might bring personal issues to you. You will need to learn when it is appropriate to refer students, such as in situations of alcohol/drug abuse, an abusive partner, sexual assault, depression, anxiety, or suicidality. If your institution has a care team for students, make sure you know how to make a referral. Conversely, you will want to internally set boundaries about what you will and will not disclose to residents about you and your family. There are certainly times when it is appropriate for you to reveal personal aspects of your life, but your partner and/or children may not be comfortable with revealing things about them.

How have you thought about work time and place boundaries? Are you inclined to hold rigid boundaries, or are you more likely to integrate those two elements? What would be the benefits and drawbacks of each approach?

Prioritization to Avoid Burnout

People who live and work on campus can feel like they are always working, and the emotional toll can be great. Warning signs of prolonged exposure to stress include feeling hopeless, a sense that enough can never be done, hypervigilance, diminished creativity, inability to embrace complexity, chronic exhaustion, deliberate avoidance, guilt, fear, anger, cynicism, and the inability to empathize (Lipsky & Burk, 2009). If you or those around see these characteristics in your behavior, it might indicate that you are burned out from the conflict created when work and life are out of balance. Lynch (2019) reported that identifying positive characteristics associated with yourself, your personal competencies, and your support mechanisms are ways to help build resilience and combat burnout.

Being a FIR will mean more work is scheduled on your behalf, reducing autonomy in managing time. You can expect administrative meetings from residence life and housing to include meetings with the building's professional, graduate, and/or student staff, FIR staff meetings, and search committee meetings for residence life staff, especially for vacancies in your community. In taking on these new responsibilities you will necessarily have to say "no" to new opportunities, while at the same time withdrawing from some current obligations.

Green (2017) provided a guide to prioritize obligations and manage time. The first step is asking the question "What is important to you?" You might want to consider goals in your faculty role, personal life, and FIR responsibilities. Once you establish your goals, Friedman (2019a) suggests a prioritization exercise to help make decisions about how to spend available time. See Figure 12.2 (adapted from Friedman, 2019a) for a worksheet to assist you with this process.

Determine how important each of the work–life domains is to you and assign a percentage of time to each. For example, overall, work might take 60% of available time, and a personal life might take 40%. Within work,

Figure 12.2. Work–life domains.

Time Allocation

Domain	% Time
Research	%
Teaching	%
Service	%
Personal	%
Family	%
Community	%
TOTAL	100%

Satisfaction With Time Allocation

Domain	Fully									Not at All
Research	10	9	8	7	6	5	4	3	2	1
Teaching	10	9	8	7	6	5	4	3	2	1
Service	10	9	8	7	6	5	4	3	2	1
FIR	10	9	8	7	6	5	4	3	2	1
Personal	10	9	8	7	6	5	4	3	2	1
Family	10	9	8	7	6	5	4	3	2	1
Community	10	9	8	7	6	5	4	3	2	1

research might take 35%, teaching 20%, and service 5%. In life, family might consume 30%, self 5%, and community 5%. Compare how much time is spent in each function with stated goals. Think about how these percentages might change when FIR responsibilities are integrated while also evaluating if the current time allocation is providing overall satisfaction. Friedman (2019a) provided reflective questions to assist in this process: What are the consequences of your current time allocations? What adjustments can you make to align your values with time allocation?

Even after this exercise, you might need to free up time. Green (2017) provided a guide to identify what activities you might discontinue. Keeping both goals and time allocations in mind, consider these questions: What can you stop doing because it is not vital? What must be done, but does not necessarily need to be done by you? What items can be done only by you? What items can be done differently? Answering these questions can provide insight into how some activities can be eliminated to make time for new priorities.

One of the keys to not taking on more than time will allow is learning how to say no to new opportunities, especially when new to the FIR role, because it will reduce conflicts that are detrimental to work–life balance. Green (2017) recommended that when you are presented with an opportunity, first pause before answering. Next, decline the opportunity by eliminating hedge words in favor of clearer language: "I'm already committed," or "Not right now, but consider me in the future." This statement should be followed by an explanation that makes sense to the person offering the opportunity. Examples include, "I have a family obligation that is very special to me" or "This isn't my area of expertise." Using this technique of pausing, saying no, and providing a reason will get easier with practice.

Conclusion

Becoming a FIR can be a rewarding experience. Interacting with students as a FIR in an LLC can produce deep, long-lasting relationships with students that are difficult to achieve in the classroom. Taking on a FIR position increases the faculty's responsibilities, which can create stress in addition to normal work and life stress. Faculty stress comes from the three primary roles involved in being a faculty member: research, teaching, and service. Women and people with marginalized identities may feel the work stress more intensely because there are more demands on their time. Thus, adding the FIR responsibility will change how time is allocated, both in faculty responsibilities and in time spent on self, family, and community. Understanding the motivation for accepting the FIR position will assist in prioritizing the multiple responsibilities of both work and life. Setting expectations with people at work and in life is key to enhancing chances of success in the FIR role. Identifying work and life priorities will help frame the process of creating more time by learning to say no gracefully. No doubt, the initial work in all these areas will pay dividends in successfully balancing work with life.

References

Aldersley, S. F. (1995). Upward drift is alive and well: Research/doctoral model still attractive to institutions. *Change, 27*(5), 50–56. https://doi.org/10.1080/00091383.1995.9936448

Brower, A. M., Golde, C. M., & Allen, C. (2003). Residential learning communities positively affect college binge drinking. *Journal of Student Affairs Research and Practice, 40*(3), 132–152. https://doi.org/10.2202/1949-6605.1260

The Carnegie Classification of Institutions of Higher Education. (2018). *Basic classification description.* https://carnegieclassifications.iu.edu/classification_descriptions/basic.php

Caza, B., Ramarajan, L., Reid, E., & Creary, S. (2019). Make room in your work life for the rest of yourself. In S. D. Friedman, E. G. Saunders, P. Bregman, & D. Dowling (Eds.), *HBR guide to work–life Balance* (pp. 53–62). Harvard Business Review Press.

Denson, N., Szelenyi, K., & Bresonis, K. (2018). Correlates of work–life balance for faculty across racial/ethnic groups. *Research in Higher Education, 52*(2), 226–247. https://doi.org/10.1007/s11162-017-9464-0

Ehrens, H. (2015). *Work and life integration: Faculty balance in the academy* [Unpublished doctoral dissertation]. Seton Hall University.

Finkelstein, M. J., Conley, V. M., & Schuster, J. H. (2016). *The faculty factor: Reassessing the American academy in a turbulent era.* Johns Hopkins University Press.

French, K. A., Allen, T. D., Miller, M. H., Kom, E. S., & Centeno, G. (2020). Faculty time allocation in relation to work–family balance, job satisfaction, commitment, and turnover intentions. *Journal of Vocational Behavior, 120*, Article 103443. https://doi.org/10.1016/j.jvb.2020.103443

Friedman, S. D. (2019a). Assessment: Are you focusing on what's important to you? In S. D. Friedman, E. G. Saunders, P. Bregman, & D. Dowling (Eds.), *HBR guide to work–life balance* (pp. 33–40). Harvard Business Review Press.

Friedman, S. D. (2019b). Keep your home life sane when work gets crazy. In S. D. Friedman, E. G. Saunders, P. Bregman, & D. Dowling (Eds.), *HBR guide to work–life balance* (pp. 177–181). Harvard Business Review Press.

Golde, C. M., & Pribbenow, D. A. (2000). Understanding faculty involvement in residential learning communities. *Journal of College Student Development, 41*(1), 27–40.

Green, D. R. (2017). *Work–life brilliance: Tools to break stress and create the life and health you crave*. Brilliance.

Hart, J. L., & Cress, C. M. (2008). Are women faculty just "worry-warts?" Accounting for gender differences in self-reported stress. *Journal of Human Behavior in the Social Environment, 17*(1/2), 175–193. https://doi.org/10.1080/10911350802171120

Humphrey, M., Callahan, J., & Harrison, G. (2015). Living with students: Lessons learned while pursuing tenure, administration, and raising a family. *Work, 52*(3), 497–501. https://doi.org/10.3233/wor-152197

Jacobs, J. A., & Winslow, S. E. (2004). Overworked faculty: Job stresses and family demands. *The ANNALS of the American Academy of Political and Social Science, 596*(1), 104–129. https://doi.org/10.1177/0002716204268185

Jones, L., & Wells, K. (2007). Strategies for academic and clinician engagement in community participatory partnered research. *JAMA, 297*(4), 407–410. https://doi.org/10.1001/jama.297.4.407

Kennedy, K. (2005). *Understanding tenured/tenure-track faculty motivation to participate in residential learning communities at research-extensive institutions* [Unpublished doctoral dissertation]. University of Missouri.

Khallash, S., & Kruse, M. (2012). The future of work and work–life balance 2025. *Futures, 44*(7), 678–686. https://doi.org/10.1016/j.futures.2012.04.007

Lee, P.-L., Mansfield, K. C., & Welton Anjalé, D. (2016). *Identity intersectionalities, mentoring, and work–life (im)balance: Educators (re)negotiate the personal, professional, and political*. Information Age.

Lipsky, L., & Burk, C. (2009). *Trauma stewardship: An everyday guide to caring for self while caring for others*. Berrett-Koehler.

Lynch, R. J. (2019). An interdisciplinary approach: Using social work praxis to develop trauma resiliency in live-in residential life staff. *Journal of College and University Student Housing, 46*(3), 42–55.

Massy, W. F., & Zemsky, R. (1994). Faculty discretionary time: Departments and the "academic ratchet." *The Journal of Higher Education, 65*(1), 1–22. https://doi.org/10.1080/00221546.1994.11778471

McQueen, K. M., McLellan, E., Metzger, D. S., Kegeles, S., Strauss, R. P., Scotti, R., Blanchard, L., & Trotter, R.T., II (2001). What is community? An evidence-based definition for participatory public health. *American Journal of Public Health, 91*(12), 1929–1938. https://doi.org/10.2105/AJPH.91.12.1929

Misra, J., Lunsuiar, J. H., & Templer, A. (2012). Gender, work time, and care responsibilities among faculty. *Sociological Forum, 27*(2), 300–323.

Owens, J., Kottwitz, C., Tiedt, J., & Ramirez, J. (2018). Strategies to attain faculty work–life balance. *Building Healthy Academic Communities Journal, 2*(2), 58–72. https://doi.org/10.1111/j.1573-7861.2012.01319.x

Pope-Ruark, R. (2020, April 28). Beating pandemic burnout. *Inside Higher Ed.* https://www.insidehighered.com/advice/2020/04/28/advice-faculty-help-them-avoid-burnout-during-pandemic-opinion

Rankin, P. R., & Yancey Gulley, N. (2018). Boundary integration and work/life balance when you live where you work: A study of residence life professionals. *Journal of College and University Student Housing, 44*(2), 64–80.

Rhoads, R. A. (2009). Reflections of a professor on nine years of living in the dorms . . . I mean residence halls! *About Campus, 14*(3), 17–24. https://doi.org/10.1002/abc.291

Shushok, F., Henry, D. V., Blalock, G., & Sriram, R. R. (2009). Learning at any time: Supporting student learning wherever it happens. *About Campus, 14*(1), 10–15. https://doi.org/10.1002/abc.278

Sinek, S. (2009). *Start with why: How great leaders inspire everyone to take action.* Penguin Group.

Singell, L. D., Jr., Lillydahl, J. H., & Singell, L. D., Sr. (1996). Will changing times change the allocation of faculty time? *The Journal of Human Resources, 31*(2), 428–449. https://doi.org/10.2307/146070

Sriram, R. (2015). The influences of faculty-in-residence programs on the role of the professoriate: A case study. *Work, 52*(3), 515–519. https://doi.org/10.3233/wor-152194

Szelényi, K., & Inkelas, K. K. (2010). The role of living–learning programs in women's plans to attend graduate school in STEM fields. *Research in Higher Education, 52*(4), 349–369. https://doi.org/10.1007/s11162-010-9197-9

Tierney, W. G., & Bensimon, E. M. (1996). *Promotion and tenure: Community and socialization in academy.* State University of New York Press.

Weigel, D. J. (2008). The concept of family: An analysis of laypeople's views of family. *Journal of Family Issues, 29*(11), 1426–1447. https://doi.org/10.1177/0192513x08318488

Winslow, S. (2010). Gender inequality and time allocations among academic faculty. *Gender & Society, 24*(6), 769–793. https://doi.org/10.1177/0891243210386728

Woods-Johnson, K. (2018). *Reframing responses to workplace stress: Exploring entry-level residence life professionals' experiences of workplace resilience* [Unpublished doctoral dissertation]. Virginia Polytechnic Institute and State University.

13

FORGING FORWARD

Concluding Thoughts and Practical Tips for Faculty

Jennifer E. Eidum and Lara L. Lomicka

Our goal for *The Faculty Factor: Developing Faculty Engagement With Living–Learning Communities* is to create a resource that provides a space and place for the collective knowledge about faculty work in LLCs—through both academic research and individual experiences. In this book, researchers and practitioners have discussed the importance of faculty members in LLCs. In this conclusion, we, the editors, look toward the future of faculty involvement in LLCs. We explore pathways for both expanding and deepening faculty involvement in LLCs, especially among underrepresented faculty groups and at underrepresented campus types. To support faculty, we underscore the many avenues for faculty support and incentives presented throughout the book to enable administrators, staff, and faculty themselves to advocate for resources they need to thrive while working with students in LLCs.

Importantly, this concluding chapter confronts many of the logistical challenges that face faculty working in LLCs, bringing together actionable solutions that are both structural and practical. Research and stories from the field often paint a rosy picture of faculty experiences in LLCs, but faculty engaging with students outside the classroom face many hurdles in their campus environments with work–life balance, university culture, and the logistics of working and, for FIR, living, in residential spaces. As with so much university work, those working in LLCs never have enough time and often are challenged by a lack of funds; however, they are rarely short on ideas and enthusiasm. We offer suggestions from our experience that help to channel that enthusiasm into meaningful and efficient faculty–student engagement in LLCs.

Expanding Faculty Involvement in LLCs

At the end of chapter 1, Dahl, Youngerman, Stipeck, and Mayhew conclude with a call for "tectonic shifts in how faculty engage with students in meaningful and intentional ways," recognizing the positive impact of faculty involvement in LLCs for new majority students. In pondering the future of faculty involvement with LLCs, we identify three areas for expanding faculty involvement: (a) incorporating equity and inclusion principles into faculty–student engagement practices to create LLC environments that are more welcoming for nontraditional students; (b) adapting faculty recruitment processes to be more inclusive for underrepresented faculty members; and (c) diversifying the types of LLCs campuses offer (and the way faculty engage with them), recognizing that all institutions create LLCs where students and faculty can make meaningful connections.

Faculty–Student Engagement

Faculty play an important role in creating an inclusive environment within LLCs, and faculty–student interactions are critical to student educational success and can "moderate the effects of a negative campus climate, especially for students of color" (Cress, 2008, p. 107). However, faculty should be intentional when designing these engagement opportunities. Cress reminds us that faculty must "reach out to students of color to develop interpersonal relationships in an effort to level the academic playing field" (p. 107). This intentional engagement of underrepresented students—including students of color, first-generation students, LGBTQ students, students with disabilities, veterans, older students, and other campus-specific populations—can be extended to all aspects of LLCs, including selection of student leaders, advising and mentorship, and opportunities for engaged learning.

Creating more equitable and inclusive LLCs requires new ways of engaging with students that do not reify existing power structures. With a rapidly diversifying student population, LLCs have an opportunity to create inclusive spaces, whether they are focused on the general population or identity-specific student groups. In the conclusion to their book, *Living Learning Communities That Work,* Inkelas et al. (2018) offered three recommendations for faculty involved in LLCs to create more inclusive spaces:

1. Faculty and staff should be aware of social dynamics within the LLC and work with student leaders to create a welcoming environment.
2. When working with underserved student populations, faculty should review existing research on the specific student population, maintain positive messaging about student achievement and progress, and advocate

for systemic institutional change (Fink & Hummel, 2015, cited in Inkelas et al., 2018).

3. Faculty and staff leading LLCs should consider equity and inclusion while recruiting students for the LLC; provide support while students are living in the LLC; and work with campus partners to ensure that the LLC—and the students participating in it—relate to broader campus equity initiatives.

In addition to creating inclusive spaces in LLCs, diversity-related programming needs to be intentionally designed so that it can meet the goals of increased understanding and empathy. As Hurtado et al. (2020) found in their research on student engagement in LLCs, simply holding events related to diversity does not increase students' interaction with diverse populations. Instead, they recommend including a "talk back or reflection component to diversity-related events" to maximize the impact (p. 14). Whether incorporated into events or added as a part of surveys after the event, integrating reflection regularly into LLC practice is important for creating inclusive communities.

Inclusive Faculty Recruitment

Inclusive LLC initiatives should be extended to faculty as well as students. It is essential for institutions to hire more faculty that are representative of the student population. Research indicates that faculty from underrepresented groups can serve as important role models and mentors for students, including those who work in LLCs (Cress, 2008; Eidum et al., 2020; chapter 1). Living–learning programs should aim to recruit faculty who reflect their target student populations as well as faculty who are underrepresented at the institution as a whole, which might include faculty of color, faculty who were first-generation college students, LGBTQ faculty, veterans, faculty with disabilities, single parents, and others. However, research and experience both indicate that there are barriers to faculty participation in LLCs, from a lack of knowledge about their existence, hesitance to interact with students, lack of financial resources, and lack of support for promotion and tenure (Kennedy, 2011). In chapter 6, Krieger points out that student affairs professionals and faculty have very different knowledge and training, and in chapter 2, Shushok and Bohannon note that there is often a tension between student affairs and faculty in their professional goals and reward structures. Because of these differences in workplace culture, recruiting and supporting faculty in LLCs requires both flexibility and adaptation to create true partnerships (see chapter 5).

Recruiting underrepresented faculty might mean broadening the selection pool for higher-stakes LLC roles, such as linked-course faculty, LLC advisor, or faculty-in-residence (FIR) to consider untenured, clinical, or even adjunct faculty for these positions. When recruiting and selecting faculty for LLC roles, existing advice suggests that administrators reach out to faculty with college-age children, faculty with teaching awards, and tenured faculty who interact with students (Golde & Pribbenow, 2000); however, we argue that limiting LLC recruitment to these established faculty groups withholds institutional resources and benefits from groups of faculty who can bring energy and mentorship to LLC students. In addition to the groups Golde and Pribbenow (2000) identified, we recommend that living–learning program leaders reach out to faculty from underrepresented groups serving the institution in similar engaged learning roles and ask that they recommend colleagues who might be newer to the institution or who may not have previously considered—or known about—LLC roles. Opening LLC roles to faculty beyond those with tenure can be mutually rewarding for the LLC and the faculty member: The faculty pipeline still has few faculty of color and other underrepresented groups at the professor and associate professor levels (National Center for Education Statistics, 2020), so broadening the recruitment pool may bring energized and experienced mentors into the LLC while at the same time LLCs may be able to offer resources or connections to the faculty member that their home department may not (Inkelas et al., 2018).

Expanding Access to LLCs

As it stands, there are at least 600 LLCs at more than 125 colleges and universities in the United States, ranging from 2-year colleges to research-extensive universities (Inkelas et al., 2008; Kinzie, 2018)—and this number appears to be growing. As we look toward the future of LLCs, we see multiple opportunities for expanding faculty involvement. First, as we described in the introduction, living–learning programs can develop a variety of faculty roles, ranging from one-time participant to multiyear academic leader. This variety enables living–learning programs to create a pipeline of faculty involvement that corresponds to faculty availability and goals throughout their career.

Second, attracting underrepresented faculty members to LLC roles can enable new programs and new LLCs that respond to student needs. For example, with increasing visibility of first-generation college students at campuses nationwide, living–learning programs have partnered with faculty and academic support staff to create LLCs especially for first-generation college students (Lomicka & Eidum, 2019).

Finally, the increasingly global reach of many campuses provides opportunities for redefining LLCs to include global campuses. Typically, study-away (including both domestic and international study) programs are under the purview of study abroad offices; however, strengthening the connection between LLC faculty, living–learning programs, and study abroad faculty might yield important innovations and collaborations that can help students strengthen their intercultural awareness. As we described in the introduction, the opportunity to join study abroad programs can be an exciting benefit for LLC students, but that is just the beginning. Faculty joining university-run study abroad centers might undergo training alongside LLC faculty advisors and residence life staff, as their program goals (to provide a safe and educational living and learning environment) are likely quite similar.

Support and Incentives

Beyond recruiting faculty to work with students in LLCs, it is important to actively support their ideas and efforts and publicly recognize the work they do. In chapter 2, Shushok and Bohannon emphasize that truly inclusive faculty engagement requires a campus culture that rewards that involvement. When developing incentives for faculty working with LLCs, administrators should specifically consider underrepresented faculty needs by asking: What do you need to be able to do this work, and how can we support you in the process? The answers may be surprising.

In addition to creating a campus culture that incentivizes faculty involvement in LLCs, in chapter 3, Lundeen and Penven offer recommendations for stakeholders working with faculty in LLCs. They specifically focus on supporting faculty while doing the work (including onboarding sessions, workshops, and creating a community of practice), articulating clear expectations for faculty roles in the LLC, recognizing individuals' professional and personal motivations in their work, and offering sufficient incentives for participation—especially those incentives that help faculty meet their professional and personal goals.

When faculty participate in LLCs, whether as academic leaders or program participants, it is important to provide mentorship and support for the work they do and the ideas they have. Mentorship and support should be provided from both sides of the university: from fellow faculty or administrators in academic affairs who understand the importance of residential learning initiatives, as well as from residence life and other student affairs leaders who can translate student affairs research and practice to the LLC (see chapter 6). Faculty involved with LLCs should be provided with training in the day-to-day operations of the LLC, workshops on LLC best practices, institution-specific knowledge shared by fellow faculty who have previously served in LLC roles, and one-on-one mentorship (chapter 3). It is important to recognize, however, that faculty typically take on LLC work in addition to their primary teaching and research responsibilities and therefore should not be overloaded with extraneous meetings.

Beyond offering support and mentorship to faculty engaged with LLCs, administrators should help faculty translate their work to external audiences. Administrators should work with their teams to provide language about LLC work for faculty to use in their departmental annual reviews and promotion and tenure documents; moreover, senior leaders should write letters of support for promotion and tenure committees (see chapter 2 and chapter 3). Faculty should be recognized as experts in their academic fields and, once in the LLC role, as insiders to the student experience; therefore, they should have opportunities to share their academic and experiential knowledge with home departments, within the broader living–learning program community, and with the campus community. Both academic affairs and student affairs divisions at the university should consider creating awards for faculty–student engagement; in addition, this work should be promoted via university media channels.

Finally, an important way that institutional leadership can provide support for faculty engaged with LLCs is to connect personally with their work: Faculty should invite departmental chairs, deans, and other academic leaders to relevant programs within their LLC—and those senior leaders should occasionally attend and participate. For example, the FIR and community director of an upper-class community at Elon University organized "house calls," where senior administrators walked through the residence hall to visit students in their space, joining them for conversation and a snack before they moved to the next space. The participation of these senior leaders not only shows support for the faculty and staff doing the LLC programming but also provides genuine opportunities for them to interact with students and get to know students in their own space.

Ultimately, for faculty to be successful in fulfilling their role in the LLC and participating in meaningful student interactions, they need support from both academic affairs and student affairs leadership. We advise LLC leaders to be thoughtful about how they support faculty who are affiliated with LLCs and be creative in providing sufficient incentives—including recognition and rewards that translate to academic audiences—for them to continue participating in LLCs and recruiting their colleagues. LLC leaders should leverage campus initiatives to secure financial resources for LLCs, including faculty, as well as translational support in articulating how LLC work fits into faculty job expectations—and not just service, but also as teaching and research.

Support for Faculty-in-Residence

Although serving as a FIR is one of the most time-intensive options for faculty involvement in LLCs, it can be rewarding work. The live-in role gives faculty a new perspective on the rhythms of campus life, and the partnerships with student affairs colleagues can lead to lifelong relationships with colleagues on "the other side of the house." Moreover, the many, layered, interactions FIR have with students, from teaching residentially linked courses to eating alongside students in the dining hall, can lead to meaningful relationships with students. Finally, bridging the divide between work and home life can be especially rewarding for faculty and for students who can now see their faculty as real people.

As we look toward the future of FIR, we see increased opportunities for faculty from underrepresented backgrounds to serve in these roles. As with general faculty involvement with LLCs, diversifying the FIR candidate pool may require some reimagining of the role. When recruiting colleagues for FIR roles, hiring teams should consider the many policies, practices, and campus interactions that may unexpectedly limit the candidate pool. Sample questions might include the following:

- What are the expectations for after-hours (evening, weekend) meetings and programming? What is flexible and what is not?
- How kid friendly is your campus and the residence life team?
- Within existing live-in partner policies for students and staff, how are single parents, same-sex relationships, dependents (young and old) defined and supported?
- What is the relationship between campus police and colleagues of color? LGBTQ colleagues?

Many of the same practices that create inclusive communities for students can be extended to the broader culture of living–learning programs and the surrounding campus community. For faculty to consider living in residence, they need to be assured that they are supported not only professionally but also personally.

A significant part of welcoming faculty into FIR roles is also welcoming their family: This may include partners, children, elders, and/or pets. FIR families can contribute significantly to the impact FIRs can have in their communities: Partners often have knowledge and experiences to contribute to the community, while children can play an important role in helping students feel at home. Making sure the families of FIR feel included in the LLC family can hinge on small details like WiFi logins and parking enforcement. Although these families may be brought to campus because of the faculty member, they should not be treated only as an extension of the FIR. As Sriram discusses in chapter 11, there are several different ways to incorporate spouses and families into the FIR role (e.g., including partners in the interview process; giving titles to FIR partners; and encouraging families to attend—and potentially lead—LLC programs). The role family members play in the LLC will depend on the family members themselves and the campus they are living at; however, we encourage living–learning program leaders to engage with families thoughtfully, as their happiness living on campus will significantly affect the FIR's ability to balance work and family needs.

Practical Tips for Faculty Engagement

There are many aspects of effective faculty engagement in LLCs, from designing curricula to developing authentic faculty–student interactions that are described in depth in this book. As two FIR with many years of experience working and researching in LLCs, in this final section we have created the following guide filled with recommendations for increasing faculty confidence when interacting with students in residential spaces.

Faculty Roles

When faculty engage in LLCs, there is no one-size-fits-all faculty role. In fact, each faculty member can and should find their own way of engaging authentically with students. In the introductory chapter to the book, we described nine roles for faculty in LLCs and three general categories of faculty-led programming: academic, social, and experiential. As this book has shown, however, many faculty are drawn to these positions because of the connection between the professional and the personal (see chapter 3 for more discussion of faculty engagement). This connection is especially true for FIR because they live where they work. To account for both the professional and personal experiences faculty can offer students in LLCs, we encourage faculty to look beyond academic expertise and traditional academic roles.

Once a faculty member becomes involved in residential communities, no matter the context or motivations, we can use these concepts to brainstorm possible locations of faculty–student engagement. In fact, we encourage faculty to think about their possible participation on a matrix: formal

TABLE 13.1
Faculty–Student Engagement Matrix

	Formal Engagement	*Informal Engagement*
Professional Engagement	Teaching a class; serving as an academic advisor	Joining student-led discussion on an academic topic; organizing a museum visit led by a professional colleague
Personal Engagement	Leading a hobby workshop unconnected with your faculty expertise (e.g., photography, sewing, or financial planning)	Inviting students to your home for a meal with your family; planning a social trip to a nearby city

versus informal engagement, and professional versus personal engagement (see Table 13.1).

Of course, many activities do not fall perfectly into one category: For example, in chapter 11, Sriram describes a relationship series he offers for Baylor students where he and his wife candidly discuss dating, marriage, and parenting. Their program blurs the boundaries of formal and informal, professional and personal—but perhaps this is the sweet spot for students to find meaning and to enjoy deeper interaction with faculty and their families.

To help faculty to creatively brainstorm pathways for engagement beyond traditional roles, here are some questions to consider:

- In what ways am I engaging academically with the LLC? Are there opportunities to share my academic knowledge beyond the classroom?
- What kinds of academic and nonacademic expertise do I have to share with LLC students? How might I share that expertise in fun or interesting ways?
- What hobbies or interests could I share with LLC students (whether related thematically to the LLC or not)?
- What aspects of my identity or personal life/family am I willing to share with students?
- What are my personal boundaries?

These questions may lead to new ideas for faculty–student engagement or LLC programming, ultimately generating meaningful academic, social, and experiential programming for LLC students.

Student Roles

Engaging students is the goal of faculty involvement in LLCs; however, the ability for faculty to connect with students can vary wildly depending on

LLC size and structure. LLCs range greatly in size, from just one floor of students to over a thousand (see Inkelas et al., 2008, or chapter 10, this volume, for more information about LLC size.). In a smaller LLC, it can be very easy to get to know every student in your community, especially if you also teach them in class, serve as their academic advisor, or have a formal mentoring relationship. In contrast, in an LLC of several hundred students (or more), it can be difficult to be in the same room with all the students, learn their names, or learn anything meaningful about their lives. Therefore, as Jessup-Anger and Benjamin point out in chapter 9, working with student leaders is essential for getting to know students in a meaningful way and for designing programs that are effective for the broader community.

Student leaders in LLCs might include resident assistants, who live among students, are employed by residence life, work to create community, respond to interpersonal challenges among students, and respond to student health and safety issues. In LLCs there are often other student leader roles: these might include elected residence hall association representatives or other forms of student government leaders, peer mentors, or student leadership roles related to the theme of the LLC. Faculty working with LLCs should work alongside these student leaders to meet their goals for the LLC— whether designing the LLC curriculum or planning a social event in the common room, it is important to include student leaders meaningfully in the process.

In the online supplement for this book we have included some concrete suggestions for advertising events, breaking the ice, and meaningful interaction with examples. Please refer to the supplement for more information on how to get started "doing the work." Although the type of engagement may differ widely from one faculty member to another, or from one campus to another, it is critical that faculty be visible, present, and intentionally engaged with a community. Aspiring to offer a visual presence, your human side, and opportunities to engage—all while setting clear boundaries— creates varied opportunities for both faculty and students to make meaningful connections.

Conclusion

LLCs are critical to shaping the academic culture of a university: Their relevance became all the more clear during the COVID-19 pandemic, which affected universities worldwide. As we have been writing this book, we have also been grappling with the core meaning of LLCs as our campuses have faced online learning, residence hall closures, suspension of campus activities, and other decisions that have often changed from week to week. It is clear that for campuses with student residence halls (the majority of campuses), LLCs offer an added value during crises, such as a global pandemic. Not only are they income-generating homes for students, but they give students a reason to be in community: There is thoughtful programming, community events, and often a theme that brings students together. Dedicated faculty and staff provide resources and mentorship that students who have faced—over a year, in many cases—of online learning sorely need. Although COVID-19 has reinforced the value of LLCs for resident student populations, it has also asked faculty to engage in new ways: Traditional programs have moved online or outdoors, dinners together have become grab-and-go events. Casual conversations in the hallway have turned into walk-and-talks around campus. We hope that the emphasis on community and the pedagogical innovations that have emerged from this global crisis will continue to inform faculty–student engagement in the future.

As we look at the future of LLCs, we see there are not only opportunities for more inclusive student and faculty engagement but also new research horizons. Some of these future opportunities may include:

- faculty representation in LLCs: What contributions can underrepresented faculty make for LLC students?
- faculty recruitment/selection: What kinds of faculty are drawn to this work? How can faculty be prepared for this work?
- multi-institutional research on FIR experiences: How can multi-institutional projects be encouraged and supported?
- support for faculty involvement with LLCs at community colleges, historically Black colleges and universities, and Hispanic-serving institutions through funding and research: how can higher education organizations invest in programs at these campuses?

By bringing together this edited collection that focuses on faculty involvement in LLCs, we can provide a foundation for continued research on models of faculty engagement in LLCs, a new focus on LLC partnerships, and of course, a deeper understanding of FIR.

References

Cress, C. M. (2008). Creating inclusive learning communities: The role of student–faculty relationships in mitigating negative campus climate. *Learning Inquiry*, *2*(2), 95–111. http://dx.doi.org/10.1007/s11519-008-0028-2

Eidum, J., Lomicka, L., Chiang, W., Endick, G., & Stratton, J. (2020). Thriving in residential learning communities. *Learning Communities Research and Practice*, *8*(1), Article 7, 1–32. https://files.eric.ed.gov/fulltext/EJ1251578.pdf

Golde, C. M., & Pribbenow, D. A. (2000). Understanding faculty involvement in residential learning communities. *Journal of College Student Development, 41*(1), 27–40.

Hurtado, S. S., Gonyea, R. M., Graham, P. A., & Fosnacht, K. (2020). The relationship between residential learning communities and student engagement. *Learning Communities Research and Practice, 8*(1), Article 5, 1–18. https://files.eric.ed.gov/fulltext/EJ1251590.pdf

Inkelas, K. K., Jessup-Anger, J. E., Benjamin, M., & Wawrzynski, M. R. (2018). *Living–learning communities that work: A research-based model for design, delivery, and assessment.* Stylus.

Inkelas, K. K., Soldner, M., Longerbeam, S. D., & Leonard, J. B. (2008). Differences in student outcomes by types of living–learning programs: The development of an empirical typology. *Research in Higher Education, 49*(6), 495–512. https://doi.org/10.1007/s11162-008-9087-6

Kennedy, K. (2011). Understanding faculty's motivation to interact with students outside of class. *Journal of College and University Student Housing, 38*(1), 10–25. https://www.nxtbook.com/nxtbooks/acuho/journal_vol38no1/index.php?startid=10#/p/10

Kinzie, J. (2018). Foreword. In K. Inkelas, J. Jessup-Anger, M. Benjamin, & M. Wawrzynski (Eds.), *Living-learning communities that work: A research-based model for design, delivery, and assessment.* Stylus.

Lomicka, L., & Eidum, J. E. (2019, November–December). Pathways to thriving: First-generation students and living and learning communities. *Talking Stick Magazine.* http://read.nxtbook.com/acuhoi/talking_stick/november_december_2019/pathways_to_thriving.html

National Center for Education Statistics. (2020). *Characteristics of postsecondary faculty.* https://nces.ed.gov/programs/coe/indicator_csc.asp

EDITORS AND CONTRIBUTORS

Editors

Lara L. Lomicka is the past faculty principal of Preston Residential College and a professor of French and applied linguistics at the University of South Carolina in Columbia, South Carolina.

Jennifer E. Eidum is the past faculty director of the Global Neighborhood and an assistant professor of English at Elon University, Elon, North Carolina.

Contributors

Timothy D. Baird is the faculty principal of the Creativity and Innovation Living–Learning Community and an associate professor of geography at Virginia Tech, Blacksburg.

Mimi Benjamin is a professor of student affairs in higher education at Indiana University of Pennsylvania, Indiana, Pennsylvania.

C. L. Bohannon is the associate dean for justice, equity, diversity, and inclusion; associate professor of landscape architecture in the School of Architecture at the University of Virginia; and former faculty principal of the Leadership and Social Change Residential College at Virginia Tech.

Connie Ledoux Book is the president of Elon University, Elon, North Carolina.

Darleny Cepin is the director of student life of Mathey College at Princeton University, Princeton, New Jersey.

Wendy F. Cohn is an associate professor of biomedical informatics at the University of Virginia, Charlottesville.

Laura S. Dahl is an assistant professor of education at North Dakota State University, Fargo.

Leia Duncan is the program director of the Baylor & Beyond Living–Learning Community at Baylor University, Waco, Texas.

Ryan W. Erck is the program director of the LEAD Living–Learning Community at Baylor University, Waco, Texas.

Terri Garrett is the associate director of academic initiatives at Baylor University, Waco, Texas.

Dustin K. Grabsch is the assistant provost for undergraduate education and academic success at Southern Methodist University, Dallas, Texas.

Ellen Gundlach is the senior managing director of professional, continuing, and online education in the College of Agriculture and Veterinary Medicine at Purdue University, West Lafayette, Indiana.

Jody E. Jessup-Anger is a professor of higher education at Marquette University, Milwaukee, Wisconsin.

Caleb J. Keith is the director of institutional improvement at Indiana University Purdue University–Indianapolis, Indianapolis, Indiana.

Kirsten Kennedy is the associate vice president of student housing and sustainability at the University of South Carolina, Columbia.

Tim Knight is the director of the Environment, Technology, and Economy Program for College Park Scholars LLC at the University of Maryland, College Park.

Carl Krieger is the director of residential education for student life at Purdue University, West Lafayette, Indiana.

Karen Kurotsuchi Inkelas is the principal of Hereford Residential College and an associate professor of higher education at the University of Virginia, Charlottesville.

Kevin M. Leander is a professor of literacy, language, and culture in the Peabody College of Education at Vanderbilt University, Nashville, Tennessee.

Shannon B. Lundeen was the director of Academic-Residential Partnerships and an associate professor of philosophy at Elon University, Elon, North Carolina. She now works as Director of Programs at HERS (Higher Education Resource Services).

Jonathan W. Manz is the director of Academic Success at Warner Pacific University, Portland, Oregon.

Matthew J. Mayhew is the William Ray and Marie Adamson Flesher Professor of Higher Education at The Ohio State University, Columbus.

James C. Penven is the director of Living-Learning Programs at Virginia Tech, Blacksburg.

Jennifer B. Post is the director of Residence Life at Southern Methodist University, Dallas, Texas.

Nishi Rajakaruna is the faculty-in-residence of the yakʔitʸutʸu residential community and a professor of plant biology at California Polytechnic State University in San Luis Obispo.

Melissa M. Shew is a visiting associate professor of philosophy at Marquette University, Milwaukee, Wisconsin.

Frank Shushok, Jr., is the former vice president for student affairs and an associate professor in the College of Agriculture and Life Sciences Department of Agricultural Leadership and Community Education at Virginia Tech, Blacksburg. He is now president of Roanoke College, Salem, Virginia.

Lily Sriram is the child-in-residence of Brooks Residential College at Baylor University in Waco, Texas.

Rishi Sriram is the faculty steward of Brooks Residential College and an associate professor of higher education at Baylor University, Waco, Texas.

Jeffrey P. Stein is the vice president for Strategic Initiatives and Partnerships and an assistant professor of English at Elon University, Elon, North Carolina.

Christopher J. Stipeck is the director of residential staff and programs at New York University, New York, New York.

Jill Stratton is the assistant provost for residential education and the associate dean for residential colleges at Vanderbilt University, Nashville, Tennessee.

Mark Daniel Ward is the director of The Data Mine and professor of statistics and (by courtesy) agricultural and biological engineering, computer science, mathematics, and public health at Purdue University, West Lafayette, Indiana.

Ethan Youngerman is the Faculty Fellow in Residence in University Hall and a senior lecturer for the expository writing program at New York University, New York, New York.

CENTER FOR
Engaged
Learning

The Center for Engaged Learning at Elon University (www .CenterForEngagedLearning.org) brings together international leaders in higher education to develop and to synthesize rigorous research on central questions about student learning. Researchers have identified "high-impact" educational practices—undergraduate research, internships, service-learning, writing-intensive courses, study abroad, living-learning communities, and so on. While we know *what* these practices are, we could know much more about three essential issues:

1. *how* to do these practices well and in diverse contexts,
2. how to *scale* these practices equitably to all students, and
3. how students *integrate* their learning across multiple high impact experiences.

The Center for Engaged Learning fosters investigations of these and related questions, principally by hosting multi-institutional research and practice-based initiatives, conferences, and seminars. To date, the Center's events have focused on topics like civic engagement, mentoring undergraduate research, global learning, residential learning, capstone experiences, and preparing students for writing beyond the university.

The Center also develops open-access resources on engaged learning practices and research for faculty and educational developers. Visit www .CenterForEngagedLearning.org to access supplemental resources for books in this series, as well as weekly blog posts, hundreds of videos, and introductory resource pages on specific engaged learning topics and on strategies for pursuing scholarship of teaching and learning.

Jessie L. Moore
Director
jmoore28@elon.edu

Peter Felten
Executive Director
pfelten@elon.edu

Stylus

22883 Quicksilver Drive
Sterling, VA 20166-2019   Subscribe to our email alerts: www.Styluspub.com

Cultivating Capstones

Designing High-Quality Culminating Experiences for Student Learning

Edited by Caroline J. Ketcham, Anthony G. Weaver, and Jessie L. Moore

Part of The Engaged Learning and Teaching Series

Capstones have been a part of higher education curriculum for over 2 centuries, with the goal of integrating student learning to cap off their undergraduate experience. In practice, capstones are most often delivered as a course or include a significant project that addresses a problem or contributes new knowledge. This edited collection draws on multiyear, multi-institutional, and mixed-methods studies to inform the development of best practices for cultivating capstones at a variety of higher education institutions.

The book is divided into three parts: Part One offers typographies of capstones, illustrating the diversity of experiences included in this high-impact practice while also identifying essential characteristics that contribute to high-quality culminating experiences for students. Part Two shares specific culminating experiences with examples from multiple institutions and strategies for adapting them for readers' own campus contexts. Part Three offers research-informed strategies for professional development to support implementation of high-quality student learning experiences across a variety of campus contexts.

Cultivating Capstones is an essential resource for faculty who teach or direct disciplinary or interdisciplinary capstone experiences, as well as for faculty developers and administrators seeking ways to offer high-quality, high-impact learning experiences for diverse student populations.